Savannah Martin has always been a good girl, doing what was expected and fully expecting life to fall into place in its turn. But when her perfect husband turns out to be a lying, cheating slimeball - and bad in bed to boot - Savannah kicks the jerk to the curb and embarks on life on her own terms. With a new apartment, a new career, and a brand new outlook on life, she's all set to take the world by storm.

If only the world would stop throwing her curveballs...

Savannah Martin's real estate career has been an uphill battle. As far as Savannah is concerned, her personal zenith was getting Aislynn Turner and Kylie Mitchell into their dream home, a Victorian cottage in the hip and happening historic district of East Nashville, last January.

That was six months ago, and now the dream has turned sour. Someone is sending Aislynn and Kylie threatening letters, warning them to get out while they can. Aislynn is terrified and Kylie is ready to cut her losses.

But finding a poison pen is only the beginning. When Kylie is attacked and the previous owner of the house is killed, the hunt is on for a murderer, and Savannah is determined to get to the bottom of what's going on before Aislynn and Kylie have to give up their dream home, and maybe each other, in the process.

D1027414

.y

OTHER BOOKS IN THIS SERIES

Adverse Possession

Jenna Bennett

ADVERSE POSSESSION

Savannah Martin Mystery #11

Interior design and formatting: B. Gallagher
Cover Design: Dar Albert, Wicked Smart Designs

Magpie Ink

One

"I'm sorry, Savannah," Kylie said. "Aislynn didn't even want me to contact you, she's so embarrassed. But you were so nice when we bought the place…"

"It's OK." I swallowed the lump in my throat. It was the *'didn't even want me to contact you'* that had caused it. "I understand. People sometimes sell their houses." Even houses they had just bought. Even houses they loved. And they didn't always—didn't usually—hire me to do it. Even if I had helped them buy the house in the first place. "It's just… you've only owned it five or six months. And you seemed so excited when you bought it…"

"We love the house," Kylie said. "It isn't the house."

I wrinkled my forehead and then immediately smoothed it out again. "The location?"

The house they'd bought back in December, a lovely Victorian cottage, sat in the middle of historic East Nashville. It was a very nice neighborhood, full of old, renovated houses, hip people, popular restaurants, and health food stores catering to dogs and people. It was hard to imagine that they weren't enjoying it, especially considering how excited they'd been just last winter.

"We love the location," Kylie said. "We couldn't ask for a better place to live."

"Then…" I glanced over my shoulder and lowered my voice, "the price?"

I was sitting in my office, a converted coat closet off the lobby at LB&A, a real estate company in the heart of historic East Nashville. The only person in sight was Brittany, the receptionist, and she had her nose buried in the most recent issue of

Cosmopolitan. She couldn't care less what I was saying. But it's unladylike to inquire about someone's finances, or lack thereof, so I kept my voice low anyway.

Kylie sounded amused. "It isn't the price."

I hadn't thought so. Renovated Victorians in East Nashville come at a premium, but Kylie worked in banking and made good money. Unless she'd suddenly lost her job, she shouldn't have a problem paying the mortgage.

"I don't understand," I said. "If you like the house and the location, and the money isn't an issue…"

Kylie sighed. "It's the letters," she told me.

Letters? "Isn't the postman delivering your mail?" That was a simple problem to fix. All I'd have to do was talk to the post office that serviced their address, and straighten things out.

"He is. That's the problem."

So they were getting mail they didn't want. "You can opt out of getting junk mail, you know."

"It isn't junk mail," Kylie said. "Or it is, sort of. I think we should just ignore it. But Aislynn is afraid. And I don't want Aislynn to be afraid."

I didn't want Aislynn to be afraid, either. She was a sweet young woman, a waitress I had met last November, while trying to figure out what had happened to my late sister-in-law. Aislynn had fed Sheila her last meal, unbeknownst to either of them. Aislynn and her girlfriend Kylie had wanted to buy a house, and after the thing with Sheila was all over, had asked me to help them. They had invited me over to the house a couple of weeks after moving in, to eat dinner and see the place, and they had seemed thrilled to be where they were. It was disconcerting to learn, just a few months later, that something was wrong enough that they wanted to sell.

"What is she afraid of?"

"It'll be easier if I show you," Kylie said. "Are you free for dinner tonight?"

For a change, I was. "Rafe is taking some of the rookies out for surveillance and shadowing."

My husband works for the TBI—the Tennessee Bureau of Investigation—training new recruits in undercover maneuvers, and once a month or so, they go out to sneak around after each other and the occasional unsuspecting civilian. It's part of the training—how to follow someone, how to pick up on someone following you—but mostly I think they're just out there having fun.

Anyway, Rafe wouldn't be home until nine or ten tonight.

"We got the wedding invitation," Kylie said. "Sorry we couldn't make it."

"It's OK. I know it was last minute." Rafe and I had intended to get married at the courthouse the first weekend in June, with just a handful of people in attendance. Instead, we'd ended up tying the knot a week later, at my childhood home in Sweetwater, Tennessee—the Martin Mansion—with almost everyone we knew in attendance, including half of our old hometown. But it had been short notice, so there were a few people who received Mother's nicely calligraphied invitation who had been unable to make it.

"Can you stop by the house around five-thirty tonight?" Kylie asked. "I should be home by then. Aislynn is doing the cooking."

I told her that would be fine, and I'd see them both. Then I hung up, and leaned back in my chair to gnaw the lipstick off my bottom lip.

I'd had my real estate license for a little over a year. In that time, I had sold a few houses to a few people. Not as many as I should have. I kept getting sidetracked by dead bodies, and by people gunning for Rafe. But Aislynn and Kylie were one of my few success-stories, and I wanted them to be happy. If there was anything at all I could do to help figure out whatever was wrong, I'd do it.

I stayed in the office until five twenty-five, when Brittany and everyone else had left, and then I got in the Volvo, the only relic from my disastrous first marriage to Bradley Ferguson, and drove over to Aislynn and Kylie's house.

It's just few minutes, along tree-lined streets with picket fences and renovated cottages, low-slung bungalows, and prissy Victorians. It wasn't long before I pulled up at the curb outside the house and cut the engine.

Aislynn met me at the door. Kylie had just gotten home and was upstairs changing out of her business suit and into something more comfortable. "She'll be right down," Aislynn told me. "Can I get you something to drink?"

"Sweet tea?"

"Green OK?"

Not exactly what I had in mind—Southern sweet tea isn't green; it's brown—but then she added, "Better for the baby."

I nodded. I was going on five months pregnant, and my diet revolved around what was best for the baby. I had cut out coffee and Diet Coke, and wine of course... Instead, I was drinking more milk and juice, and packing on the pounds. I wasn't surprised that Aislynn had taken one look at me and diagnosed my condition.

The green tea wasn't really a surprise, either. The café where Aislynn worked, Sara Beth's in Brentwood, was a healthy sort of place, with lots of different lettuces on the menu, and quinoa salads with tofu and the like.

So I followed her out into the kitchen, and received a tall glass of green tea over ice. While Aislynn turned to the stove to stir a pot of something that smelled like it might turn out to taste good, if spicy, I took an experimental sip.

Not bad, although it wasn't proper Southern iced tea. Still, if it was better for the baby...

I hiked my butt up on a chair at the island and put the glass in front of me. "Kylie said you're having a problem with the mail. What's going on?"

"Someone's sending us letters," Aislynn said, as she scooped rice onto three plates she had lined up on the counter. Upstairs, I could hear footsteps as Kylie came down the hallway toward the staircase.

"What kind of letters?"

"Creepy ones," Aislynn said, putting the pot of rice back on the stove and picking up a plate. She ladled some sort of yellowish stew over the rice and put the plate back down. Then she repeated the process with the second plate, and the third.

She put one in front of me. "Let's go to the dining room."

"Sure." I slid off the chair and took the plate in one hand and the glass of tea in the other. Aislynn led the way with her own and Kylie's food, and then she went back to the kitchen to fetch their drinks and eventually, a basket of something I discovered was naan.

Meanwhile, Kylie came down the stairs and into the dining room.

Once upon a time, someone had cut the brake cables on her car, a darker blue Volvo than mine, thinking she was me. Poor Kylie ended up in the hospital.

There's a resemblance. Not so much that anyone who knows either of us would be fooled, but enough that I had been able to tell the nurses at the hospital that she was my sister. Aislynn is a few years younger, and sports Goth-girl makeup and dreadlocks halfway down her back, but Kylie is my age or a little older, and has shoulder-length blond hair a few shades lighter and a few inches shorter than mine, and neither tattoos nor piercings. Or if she has them, they're in a place you can't see unless you know her really, really well.

She gave me a tired smile. "Savannah. Thanks for coming."

"I'm always happy to see you," I said, since it was the truth.

She gestured to the stomach. "That's new."

"It's actually about five months old, but it's only in the past few weeks I've started to look pregnant."

She nodded, as she pulled out the chair across the table. "Aislynn and I have talked about having a baby. Although so far all we've managed to do is argue about who gets to be the carrier."

"You could always adopt and avoid the problem."

She smiled. "I guess. Assuming we're both capable of carrying a child, it would be nice to create our own, though."

I guess it would. Rafe and I had certainly enjoyed the process.

Not that Kylie and Aislynn would have the opportunity to create a baby in the same way that Rafe and I had. Their process would be a lot more clinical. But I understood the desire to carry the baby of the man—or in this case woman—you love. So I just smiled and told her I understood completely. And then I added, just as Aislynn came through the door from the kitchen carrying the basket of naan, "Aislynn told me you've been getting weird and creepy letters."

Kylie nodded. "Why don't we tell you about it while we eat? I'm starving. And then, when you're done, you can take a look. It's quite a collection."

"That'll be great." These days, I was always happy to prioritize food. Being pregnant was making me eat like a horse. And while I worried about the weight I was gaining and the need to lose it again once the baby was born, it was also quite freeing to eat what I wanted when I wanted to. For the first time in my life, I wasn't worried that my stomach was too big. The bigger it got, the more excited everyone was.

The food was some sort of Indian stew; tasty, but spicy. I knew I'd pay for it later, so I did my best to cut the spice with the naan, iced tea, and rice. I'd just take a few extra Tums before bed. The conversation was too fascinating to leave for another glass of water.

"The first letter came in early April," Aislynn said between bites of stew. While Kylie and I were taking frequent sips of liquid, she was shoveling in spicy chicken and chickpeas like her life depended on it. I have no idea how she managed to keep that girlish figure the way she ate. High metabolism, I guess. And the spice didn't seem to bother her at all. "We figured it was a late April Fool's joke, and we almost didn't keep it. But it was just so weird that it didn't seem right to throw it away. So we stuck it in a drawer and forgot about it."

"For a couple of weeks," Kylie picked up the story. "Until another letter came. And then another."

"How many in all?"

They looked at one another. "Five or six?" Aislynn said.

Kylie nodded. "Less frequent at first. Three or four weeks between. Then two weeks. Then one week. Last week we got two."

So whoever was sending the letters, was escalating. A fancy term I had picked up from Rafe, relating to certain types of criminals. Serial killers, serial rapists, and the like. And, I guess, poison pens.

Assuming the letters were poisonous, and it sounded like they were. "What do the letters say?"

"You can read them when we've finished eating," Kylie said. "They're not really appropriate for the table."

"Threatening?"

They glanced at one another. "Not so much directly threatening," Kylie said, "as implied."

"They're scary," Aislynn added, with a little quiver in her voice.

I took a bite of stew and chewed. And chased the burning sensation in my mouth with a sip of tea before I picked up the conversation. "Do you have any idea who's sending them?"

They exchanged another glance, and looked away.

"No," Kylie said.

"Not really," Aislynn added.

"Not even a wild guess?"

Aislynn shook her head. Kylie shrugged. Neither of them looked at me for more than a second. It sounded to me like they were both a lot less sure than they were trying to make it seem.

As soon as we'd finished eating, Kylie pushed her chair back. "Come on, Savannah. I'll show you what we've got."

I rose, too. Aislynn remained seated. "I'll stay here," she said. "The letters give me the creeps. I don't want to see them again."

Kylie nodded. "We'll take care of it."

"Thank you."

"You don't have to thank me," Kylie told her. "I wish they didn't bother you. But since they do, I'm not going to make you look at them. Savannah and I'll take care of it."

"I'll clean up." Aislynn pushed back from the table. "And get dessert." She smiled at me, although I could still see shadows in her eyes. "Kheer."

Rice pudding. Lots of dairy for the baby. *Yum.* "Sounds great."

"You'll need it," Aislynn said, "after what you're about to read."

She didn't wait for me to answer, just stacked the three plates one on top of the other and headed for the kitchen. Kylie waved me in the other direction, toward what had been the priest's parlor when the house was built—the room with the door to the outside, at the front of the house next to the foyer—and which was now used as an office.

"Nice," I told her, looking around at the pale blue walls, the dark furniture, and the upholstered wingback chairs in front of the desk.

"Thanks." Kylie was in the process of opening the desk drawer. "We love it here. It makes me sick that this is happening."

She straightened, with a stack of envelopes in her hand. "Have a seat."

She waved me into the desk chair and put the envelopes on the desk in front of me.

I reached for the top one. "Are they in order?"

"Not sure." She took a seat in one of the wingbacks. "Check the date stamps."

The letters had been sent through the mail, and been delivered by the mailman. I wasn't sure whether that was good or bad. If they'd been hand delivered, we could have set up a camera, or at least a stakeout, to see who dropped them off. But if the mailman was the guilty party—by default—there was no way to know who the sender was.

"On the other hand," Kylie said when I pointed this out, "it has to be a crime to use the US postal service to make threats."

You'd think. "I'll ask Rafe. Or Tamara Grimaldi."

Rafe, as I mentioned, works for the TBI. Tamara Grimaldi is a friend of ours, a homicide detective with the Metro Nashville PD. Poison pen letters wasn't in either of their jurisdictions— Grimaldi's job was murder and Rafe's organized crime, pretty much—but I'm sure they both knew the law on something like this.

"I guess there's no chance we'll find fingerprints on any of these," I said.

Kylie shook her head. "Between the mailman, and Aislynn and me, and everyone else who's handled them..."

"Who else have you shown the letters to?"

While I asked, I grabbed the first envelope by the sides and wiggled it until the first letter sailed out and onto the surface of the desk. Then I used a letter opener and a Bic pen to unfold it.

"Just a couple of friends," Kylie said vaguely.

That probably hadn't been a good idea, and the police would have chastised her about it. Since I wasn't the police, I didn't say anything, just focused on the letter.

It was written on your basic piece of copy-paper, the kind you find in printers and fax machines all over the country.

Untraceable, pretty much. Anyone can buy a ream of copy paper almost anywhere. The grocery store, the drugstore, the Dollar store, Office Depot, and any number of online stores, delivered straight to your door. The LB&A office was full of them. And there was an open ream sitting on a table in the corner of Kylie's home office, next to a combination printer/scanner.

The words were written with black marker, all in capital letters: spiky and oversized, stark against the bright white paper.

I AM WATCHING YOU.

I glanced up. "This is the first one? The one that came in early April?"

Kylie nodded. "We thought it was a belated April Fool's joke."

I might have thought the same thing. The words were almost a cliché, and not so much sinister as roll-your-eyes exasperating.

Until the second letter said the exact same thing. The envelope was still addressed to Aislynn, and the letter—still on the same basic copy-paper, still written with the same, or a similar, marker in the same spiky block letters—said,

I AM WATCHING YOU.

"It's a bit more creepy the second time."

Kylie nodded. "Wait until you see the next one."

I opened the envelope carefully and shook the letter out.

YOU SHOULD GET OUT WHILE YOU CAN.

I arched my brows, but didn't comment. I had once walked into my apartment to find my bed sheets and nightgown slashed to ribbons and the word *trollop* written on the wall in red lipstick;

now *that's* something that'll scare you. So far, this was still just on the edge between a joke and just a bit troubling.

IF YOU WON'T LISTEN, the anonymous letter writer wrote, *YOU HAVE NO ONE TO BLAME BUT YOURSELF.*

"Blame?" I said.

Kylie nodded. She was biting her lip. I could hear clicking and clanging from the kitchen, where Aislynn was cleaning up.

"Blame for what?"

She shrugged.

LEAVE, the next letter said, *BEFORE IT'S TOO LATE.*

The last letter was the most directly threatening.

THIS IS YOUR LAST CHANCE. IF YOU IGNORE MY WARNING, SOMEONE WILL DIE.

"That's a bit disturbing." And a bit melodramatic, but I didn't say that. I just leaned back on the chair, away from the letters laid out in two neat rows on the desktop.

Kylie nodded. "I'm worried, Savannah. Not so much about this," she gestured to the letters, "although I guess there are plenty of wackos in the world, and you never know what someone might do."

No, you don't. The world is full of sick people, and sick people do sick things. This might be nothing, just somebody's sick joke spurred by April Fool's Day and taken to greater lengths in the months since. On the other hand, it might be something real and dangerous. Ignoring it didn't seem like a good idea.

"But I'm more worried about Aislynn," Kylie said. "She's

totally wigged out. Jumps at the least little thing. Sleeps with the light on. I'm afraid she's going to leave."

I tilted my head to look at her. "Do you think that's what the letter writer wants?"

"I don't know what he wants!"

Her voice was shrill enough to break glass, and I glanced at the snow globe paper weight on the corner of the desk to make sure it was holding up under the strain. Anyone who's ever broken one knows the mess that results when the water and all that glitter goes everywhere.

Kylie took a breath, and when she spoke again, her voice was calmer. "I don't know whether this is someone's idea of a joke, or whether this person, whoever it is, will actually hurt Aislynn."

"Or you."

She shrugged, as if that possibility didn't matter. Her voice was low and intense. "I want her to be safe, and I want her with me. And if I have to sell the house and move somewhere else for that to happen, then that's what I'll do!"

Two

"Give me a little time to look into it," I said. "I'll talk to Detective Grimaldi and Rafe. Between them, I'm sure they'll have some ideas about what's going on and whether it's something you need to worry about."

We had moved back into the dining room for kheer, and were sitting around the table spooning it up.

"I don't know, Savannah," Kylie said. "Maybe we just need to do what this nutcase wants, and put the house on the market."

Aislynn nodded, spoon in her mouth.

"But that's the problem," I pointed out. "You don't know what the nutcase wants." They didn't even know that the letter-writer was a nutcase. The whole thing could be a joke. Or it could be someone totally sane, who wanted to separate the two of them for one reason or another. It wasn't necessarily that he or she wanted them to move out of the house. To me, it sounded more like he or she wanted Aislynn gone.

"The letters started after we moved in," Kylie said. "If we leave, they'll stop."

I dipped my spoon back into the rice pudding, but left it there. "You don't know that. They didn't start for several months after you moved in. Chances are, it wasn't you moving in here that set someone off. Whatever gave this person the idea to do this probably happened just before the first letter came. Can you think of anything that happened in late March or early April? Anything out of the ordinary?"

Neither of them said anything, so I started throwing out ideas. "Did someone new move in nearby? Did you argue with one of the neighbors? Block someone's driveway? Let your dog poop on someone's grass?"

Aislynn's lips twitched. "We don't have a dog."

"Maybe you should get one," I said. "It might make you feel safer."

Nobody responded to that. Nor to the other questions.

"No arguments? Nobody new in the neighborhood?"

"Nobody we've talked to," Kylie said. "Although there are always houses changing hands around here. You know how it is."

I did. Historic East Nashville is a hot neighborhood, with rapidly increasing property values. There are always people wanting to move in, and people wanting to cash out.

"The people two doors down are moving," Aislynn said. "We have new neighbors on the next block in either direction, and new people on the next street over."

I'd have to find out who they were. Not too difficult, with access to the Multiple Listings Service and the Courthouse records, to learn which houses had changed hands in the past few months, and which were about to.

"Anything else? You guys go out occasionally, I'm sure. Any weird conversations with store clerks or bartenders? Parking disputes? Argument over the check?"

They shook their heads.

"How about at work? Any weird co-workers? Or could a customer have followed either of you home and discovered where you live?"

"Kylie doesn't have customers," Aislynn said. "I do, but I wouldn't know if anyone followed me."

"But you don't remember anyone acting weird? Staring at you? Trying to pick you up and getting upset when you said no?"

She shook her head.

"How about you?" I turned to Kylie. She was watching Aislynn and looking worried, and it took her a second to meet my eyes.

"I can't think of anyone."

They both said the words, but I didn't think either of them meant them. It was like earlier. They both had ideas, but it was obvious that they were both reluctant to talk in front of the other. I'd just have to talk to them separately sometime.

"I'll talk to Rafe when he comes home tonight," I said, going back to spooning up the kheer. "If he thinks it's a good idea, I'll call Detective Grimaldi in the morning. How long do you want to wait before you decide whether or not to put the house on the market?"

They glanced at one another.

"Twenty-four hours?" Aislynn suggested.

Cripes. Nothing like a little pressure to make a girl do her best.

"How about we make it through the weekend instead?" That'd give me a few days, at least.

"I don't know..." Aislynn said, glancing at the dusk gathering outside the windows.

"I'd like to know something sooner than that," Kylie told me. "How about you come over Saturday morning and tell us what you've found out? And then we'll see whether it's worth continuing. Nine o'clock?"

She sounded determined, so I told her I'd be here. And since there didn't seem to be a whole lot more to say just then, I asked whether they wanted my help in cleaning up after dinner. When they said they didn't, I excused myself and headed home, to wait for Rafe and ponder what I'd learned.

By the time he walked in, I was already in bed. It takes a lot of effort to create a baby from scratch, and I was tired almost all the time. It was rare that I managed to stay up past ten o'clock anymore.

I was still awake, though, if barely, and only because I had both the light and the TV on. If I fell asleep before he came home,

I wouldn't be able to talk to Rafe about Aislynn and Kylie's predicament, and since I'd probably sleep through the alarm in the morning, and he'd leave without waking me, I wouldn't be able to talk to him then, either.

No, it had to be now. Hence the glaring light and reruns of *Full House*.

I heard the rumble of the engine first, and the crunch of gravel as he guided the Harley-Davidson up the circular driveway. Then the engine shut off, and there were muffled footsteps on the porch. The front door opened and closed, and I heard the snick of the deadbolt and the rattle of the security chain as he pulled it across the door. Then came his steps on the stairs. By the time he appeared in the doorway, I was sitting bolt upright in bed, waiting.

We had been married less than three weeks. Since we'd been living in sin for six months prior to that, I hadn't expected the marriage certificate and the ring on my finger to make much difference. We'd already made the commitment to one another, after all. I loved him. He loved me. We were having a baby together.

But being married was different. I can't explain it, but somehow the knowledge that he was mine, that we were stuck together for better or worse until one of us died of old age (or something else) made all the difference.

And unlike my brief but unhappy marriage to Bradley Ferguson, being married to Rafe for life didn't sound like a death sentence.

He stopped in the doorway, with the light from the hall behind him giving him a halo, and as usual, my breath went away at the sight. It had always been that way, and I hoped it always would be.

It isn't just because he's gorgeous, although he is. Tall, dark, muscular. Handsome, with dark eyes, dusky skin, and a great smile. One he was flashing at me right now. "Darlin'."

"I wanted to talk to you," I said, answering the unspoken question I knew he was asking. "I knew if I fell asleep, you'd leave before me in the morning, and I wouldn't get to."

The smile dropped off as he took in the papers strewn across the comforter. I had made Kylie give me copies of each of the letters. I wanted to have them to show him and Grimaldi in the morning, but I didn't want to handle the originals any more than necessary. I was pretty sure we wouldn't be able to get fingerprints or DNA off them, not after so many people had handled them, but better safe than sorry.

"What's going on?"

"Kylie called me," I said. "Just before I left the office. She invited me to dinner to talk about selling the house."

He tilted his head and left the doorway, after flicking off the hallway light and removing that undeserved halo. "Didn't they just buy their house?"

I said they had. "Beginning of the year. We were going around looking at properties while you were hanging out with Carmen and trying to nail Hector last year."

Carmen Arroyo was an employee of Hector Gonzales's, and Hector had been running the biggest SATG—South American Theft Gang—in the Southeast until Rafe stopped him. It had taken ten years to do it, and things came to a head just before Christmas. Aislynn and Kylie had closed on the house in late January, if memory served. Things take a little longer over the holidays.

Anyway, Carmen and Hector were both in prison now. Hector somewhere in Georgia—he'd been operating his criminal empire out of Atlanta—and Carmen in Southern Belle Hell north of Nashville, since her crimes had been committed here.

"What's going on?" The bed moved when Rafe sat down on his side of the mattress and reached for one of the letters.

I snatched it out of his reach. "This one came first."

I handed him *I AM WATCHING YOU*. And watched him as he

looked at it.

Not that there was much to see. His face was impassive, except for, perhaps, an almost imperceptible tightening of his lips.

"It came in early April," I said. "They figured it was an April Fool's joke." I gave him the rest of the letters. "Until the next one came. And the one after that."

He flipped through them. I watched. Until he dropped them all to his lap and looked at me. "What's this gotta do with you?"

"The letters started coming a couple months after they moved into the new house. They think if they sell, the letters will stop."

Rafe nodded. "Makes sense."

"I don't want them to sell."

He quirked a brow.

"They're one of my success stories," I said. "One of my *few* success stories. I want them to be happy in the house they bought."

"You could have another success story if you sold the house again."

I could. Maybe. However... "What if the next person who moves in starts getting letters, too? That would be horrible. And is this a material fact? Something I'll have to disclose? *The sellers are moving because someone is sending them creepy, anonymous letters.* That'll really help the resale value!"

"I dunno about material facts and what you gotta disclose," Rafe told me. "But if the new buyer starts getting anonymous letters, too, at least you'll know your friends are safe."

"I'll still feel bad!"

He shrugged. "Somebody else's problem."

"Unless I get both the buyer *and* the seller. Then it'll be my problem."

"What are the chances?" Rafe wanted to know.

Slim to none, if you want to know. It happens. One realtor

often has both the seller and buyer under contract, and gets twice the commission, or gets to build goodwill with the seller by taking a percentage—higher than the single broker commission, but lower than the double—instead of the full, negotiated fee. It just doesn't happen to me. I have problems enough snagging one party to the transaction, let alone both.

"I told them I'd ask you about it. And Grimaldi."

He didn't respond immediately, and I added, "They don't really want to sell. Or at least Kylie doesn't. Aislynn is so scared that I think she'd be happy to move out tomorrow if she could. Kylie is afraid she will."

Rafe nodded.

"I don't want to be responsible for them breaking up."

"Unless you're the one sending the letters," Rafe pointed out, "you ain't gonna be responsible."

"You know what I mean. I told them I'd look into it. Just for a day or so. We're getting together on Saturday morning so I can tell them what I've found out. I need you to tell me what to do."

"Stay out of it," Rafe said.

I rolled my eyes. "I can't do that. I just explained why."

He didn't answer, and I continued, "You don't think there's anything to worry about, do you? I mean, I know there's a little escalation on the messages and the timing..."

His eyebrow rose again.

"You told me what escalation means," I told him. "Last month, when we were dealing with Hernandez. The letters are coming faster now, so whoever is sending them is escalating."

He nodded.

"But they're still just letters. And could just be a joke."

"But if he don't get the reaction he wants," Rafe said, "eventually he'll stop writing letters and do something else instead."

"Not to me, though. I'm not involved in this." It wasn't my house. And nobody was sending me letters.

"Until you get yourself involved."

Sure. But... "How would he know that? Or she? It's not like I'm going to be living there with them. And anyway, they just got a letter. There probably won't be another in the next thirty-six hours." And by then I'd have done my initial investigating and would be reporting to Aislynn and Kylie over breakfast on Saturday.

"I don't like it," Rafe said.

I blinked. "Do you think this person is dangerous? It might just be a joke."

He ran a hand over the top of his head. It's his version of shoving his fingers through his hair. "It could be a joke. But it don't feel like it."

I glanced at the letters in his lap. "How can you tell?"

He shook his head. "Dunno. Just a feeling."

We sat in silence for a moment, him on the edge of the bed and me under the blankets.

"All the more reason to find out who it is," I said. "Before he can hurt anyone. Or she."

He shook his head. "How'd I know you were gonna say that?"

"You didn't." I smiled. "I'll talk to Grimaldi in the morning, and dump the problem on her. There's probably someone down there who specializes in this kind of thing, don't you think?"

He nodded. "Tammy'll find you somebody."

"And maybe I'll just have a talk with Tim, and see if his clients know about any letters that might have come before they sold the house."

Timothy Briggs is by way of being my boss, or at least my broker at LB&A. The B is his. The L is Lamont, Walker Lamont, who was the broker before Tim—currently serving twenty-five to life in Riverbend Penitentiary for multiple counts of murder and attempted murder. The A stands for Associates. That's me and everyone else.

Anyway, Tim had had the listing side of what was now Aislynn and Kylie's house back in December. The sellers had been his clients. If they had been the recipients of creepy, anonymous letters, he would have known. Or so I assumed.

And while I was at it, I could ask him whether creepy, anonymous letters were a material fact that needed to be disclosed to potential buyers. That would give me a nice segue into the conversation. And would also give me a nice cause for blackmail if he said they were, but then it turned out he'd known about them but hadn't informed me or Aislynn or Kylie.

Tim had tried to fire me not too long ago. He said my getting involved in crimes gave LB&A a bad rep. And that was in spite of my meddling having saved his sorry butt on at least on occasion. With a little help from Rafe.

Anyway, Rafe had sweet-talked him into taking me back, but having blackmail material is never a bad idea.

"You wouldn't mind if I talked to Tim," I asked, "would you?"

His lips quirked. "No, darlin'. Unless you think he's got plans to kill you so he can have me all to himself."

I tilted my head to look at him. It was no secret that Tim had had a—pardon the pun—man-sized crush on Rafe since the first time he saw him.

Yes, Tim is gay. Rafe, however, is not, even if he had occasionally amused himself by making Tim hot and bothered. He's an equal opportunity flirt.

"Are you trying to tell me something?" I wanted to know. "Like, if I weren't here, you'd consider Tim?"

He put his head back and laughed. "No, darlin'. But he might not know that."

"I'm sure he does," I said. "And anyway, if he wanted to kill me to get to you, he wouldn't have waited until we were married."

"No chance he's the one writing the letters?"

It sounded like a joke, but something told me he might be serious.

"I can't think of one," I said, after considering it. "Why would he?"

Rafe shrugged. "Maybe just 'cause he's a malicious little gnat who likes to create trouble."

He was. Tim definitely had the personality for something like this.

I thought for another few seconds before shaking my head. "I really can't think of a reason why he would. There's nothing in it for him. If Aislynn and Kylie wanted to sell the house again, they wouldn't come to him. They'd come to me. Like they did."

"But you work for him."

"That doesn't make it his money," I said. "But if I ask him about it, and then my car suddenly develops brake line trouble, I'll know who's to blame."

"Let's hope it don't come to that," Rafe said and put the stack of letters on the bedside table. On his side. He reached a hand over his head and yanked his shirt up, in that manner that efficient men have of getting undressed. "You tired?"

"Yes," I said, my eyes on his chest, "but if you're getting naked, I'm sure I could keep my eyes open for a bit longer."

He grinned. "I need a shower."

"If you get in the shower, I'll probably be asleep by the time you come out. Much better if we get the sex out of the way first."

"You sure you wanna say it like that?"

"Just come here," I said, and reached for him.

He came.

Three

By the time he got out of the shower, I was dead to the world, and when I woke up in the morning, he was gone. I rolled out of bed—literally; it had gotten to the point where I had to turn on my side to get up—and padded into the bathroom to take my own shower. By the time I had dried my hair and put on makeup, and was standing in front of the open closet contemplating my rapidly dwindling wardrobe, it was almost nine o'clock.

The more pregnant I became, the less any of my old clothes fit. Obvious, right? But it meant that I would have to go clothes shopping soon.

Albeit not today. I had too many other things to do.

I pulled out an eggplant-colored wrap dress I'd bought for my high school reunion a couple of months ago, and wrapped it around myself. I have a black wrap dress, too, one that Rafe is particularly fond of, but it was July and almost a hundred degrees in the shade; I wasn't about to wear black unless I was going to a funeral.

I got to the office by nine-thirty. Tim's baby blue Jaguar—the same color as his eyes—was parked in the lot.

I slotted the Volvo next to it and entered through the back door. Tim's office was the first door on the left.

I heard him before I saw him. When he was in his early twenties, before coming back to Nashville and making a go of real estate, Tim spent some time in the Big Apple trying to get on Broadway. He has the voice for it: a big, brassy tenor. He has the looks, too: curly, golden hair, bright, blue eyes, and a handsome, if pouty, face. And I'm sure he can move well, as the cliché goes. I don't know why things didn't work out for a show biz career.

Maybe he just didn't have the chutzpah. Maybe he didn't have the talent. Or maybe he got sidetracked somehow. I've never asked and he's never told.

Anyway, he was singing. I stopped in the open doorway and knocked. Tim stopped singing and turned to face me. "Oh," he said after a second. "It's you."

"Nice to see you, too." I didn't bother to sound as if I meant it.

Tim and I have had an awkward relationship for as long as we've worked together. He doesn't really like me, and the feeling is mutual. He likes to tweak me—that malicious quality Rafe mentioned—and he isn't above making people squirm, me included. He isn't above backhanded machinations, either. Last August, when our colleague Brenda Puckett was murdered, it was Tim who leaked the information about her illegal shenanigans to a reporter at the *Nashville Voice*. The leak resulted in a front page spread that proclaimed that Brenda Puckett had kicked the bucket, and it caused our then-broker, Walker Lamont, to have conniptions, since the aforementioned shenanigans implicated LB&A—or Walker Lamont Realty, as it was called back then—in the misdeeds, as well. I'm surprised Walker didn't kill Tim, too. He certainly killed—or tried to kill—enough other people.

But no, Walker named Tim broker in his absence. And now I was saddled with him.

Between you and me, I'd rather have Walker back. I'd always gotten along well with him, at least up until the point when he tried to kill me. Twice.

Tim pulled out the executive leather chair from behind the desk and planted his butt in it. "How's married life?"

"Fine," I said, perching on the edge of one of the uncomfortable seats in front of the desk.

"Rafael still looking good?"

"He looks the same way he looked the last time you saw

him." Which was a month or two ago, when he leaned on, or charmed, Tim into hiring me back after firing me.

And my statement wasn't entirely true, actually. Rafe had picked up some cuts and bruises since then. But since most of them were in places Tim would never get to see anyway, I saw no reason to mention that.

"Well, then he's looking remarkably fine," Tim said, smacking his lips. "You're a lucky girl, Savannah."

Yes, I was. Although it was a little disconcerting to hear my male boss say so, in such very sincere tones.

I put it out of my head, or tried to. "I need some advice."

"Oh, dear." Tim clicked his tongue and leaned back in his chair, baby-blues gleaming. "Did he shave his legs and wear a thong to the beach? I hate to be the one to tell you, Savannah, but he's turned gay."

"Don't be ridiculous," I said. "He isn't gay. And he didn't... actually, he did wear a Speedo. But not a thong. And not to the beach. Just in the privacy of our room. But he didn't shave anything first. And besides..."

Tim wasn't listening. He had snatched up a folder from the desk and was leaning back in his chair, eyes closed, fanning himself with it. I rolled my eyes and sat back to wait for him to finish having the vapors.

"Speedo?" he said faintly after a minute.

I nodded. "Metallic gold. Tiny."

The folder went into action again, so vigorously that Tim's curls bounced in the breeze. Another minute passed while he recovered.

"About the question," I said.

He cracked an eye to look at me. "Question?"

"The one I wanted to ask you. The advice."

He sat up and put the folder down. "Are you sure he isn't gay?"

"Positive," I said.

Tim sighed. "It was nice while it lasted."

"It didn't happen," I said. "Or only in your mind. About my question."

"Yes, yes. Ask me your question. Even though I'm sure it won't be as intriguing as the possibility that Rafael might swing my way."

Since there was no possibility at all that Rafe would swing Tim's way, the reality of the anonymous letters were far more intriguing, at least as far as I was concerned. "It's about disclosure. Material facts and things like that."

Tim nodded.

"Say you had a client who wanted to sell his house. And say it was because he had been getting anonymous letters."

Tim looked interested. I watched him closely, to see if it was more than just normal interest—like maybe he'd had a client of his own with this problem—but if he had, I couldn't tell.

"Has anything like that ever happened to you?"

Tim shook his head. "If it has, nobody's told me about it. Which client is this?"

I hesitated. I had gotten Kylie's and Aislynn's permission to talk to Rafe and the police, but I hadn't gotten their permission to talk to Tim. And between you and me, he's a horrible gossip. Besides, he had represented the former owners. What if he told them what was going on, and warned them not to talk to me?

"Nobody you know." I reached up to twist the end of a strand of hair around my finger, and had to force myself to stop. People who know me—like my brother—know it's my tell for lying. "Nobody from around here. Someone in Sweetwater."

My hometown, where people know me, and can tell when I'm lying. Tim didn't seem able to.

"That's awkward," he remarked. "For something like that to happen in a small town where everyone knows everyone else."

I nodded, relieved that he seemed to believe the lie. "Which is why I don't want to have to disclose it unless I have to."

"It isn't a material fact," Tim said and put his fingertips together, preparatory to lecturing. "In the state of Tennessee, we are not required to disclose murders and suicides taking place on the property, or individuals with AIDS or other communicable diseases living in the property. We are not required to disclose if the house has been used for cooking meth. We are not required to disclose if the previous owner was a convicted felon. We are not required to disclose anything that doesn't—and I quote—have an effect on the physical structure of the property."

"So I don't have to disclose the letters."

Tim shook his head. "Although..."

My heart sank. "Although what?" It wasn't like I wanted Aislynn and Kylie to decide to sell the place, but if they did, I didn't want to have to stigmatize the property.

"If it comes out later, things could get ugly."

Yes, they could. Just as a for-instance: if Tim's clients had been receiving letters and that's why they'd decided to move, and Aislynn and Kylie had bought the house in good faith and had, so to speak, inherited Tim's clients' anonymous correspondent, they wouldn't be happy about the non-disclosure. Even if Tim hadn't been required, by law, to disclose anything, Aislynn and Kylie would still be upset, and with good reason. There are legal issues, and then there are ethical ones, and they don't always coincide. It might not have been a legal requirement, but if the previous owners had known about the letters, it would have been nice of them to share.

Hypothetically, of course.

"I'll keep that in mind," I said, getting to my feet before he could ask me anything else. I had what I needed—or at least I had some of it. "What are you up to today?"

The look he gave me was a little strange, but he answered easily enough. "Paperwork. And I have a listing appointment at eleven."

"Good for you." I sidled toward the door. "A house in the

neighborhood?"

Tim shook his head. "Brentwood. I'll be leaving in less than an hour."

Excellent. "Good luck," I said, since listing appointments can go either way. Sometimes the potential client loves you and wants you to take on the job of selling their house, and sometimes they don't like you, and you don't get the listing.

"I'm not worried," Tim answered.

I spent the hour before he left huddled in my office. I did a CMA—comparative market analysis—for Aislynn and Kylie's house, just in case I couldn't find out anything about their anonymous letter writer, and they decided to put the house on the market and asked me how much it was worth. And since I was looking at houses for sale and recently sold in the neighborhood, I made note of which houses had changed hands in the last six months, as well. There weren't a whole lot. As the girls had mentioned, they had new neighbors a block away on either side, and someone new on the next street over. I'd have to drive by and take a look, I guess. Not that I expected to be able to tell from the outside of the houses whether anonymous letter writers were likely to live inside, but it was something to do. And maybe I would come across someone cackling maniacally while he or she was penning another anonymous tome.

I spent some time on the internet researching anonymous letters in general—a couple in New Jersey had been getting some extremely creepy ones recently, a lawsuit was pending, and Hollywood was sniffing around the movie rights—and after that I called Tamara Grimaldi to ask her opinion on the subject.

The phone rang a couple of times, and then she picked up. "Ms. Martin."

Detective Grimaldi was maid of honor at my wedding, and is sort of dating my brother Dix—'sort of' because Dix lost his wife last November and isn't really ready to move on to a new relationship yet. Although something's going on. They could just be good friends, but I suspect it's a little more than that.

Anyway, she should probably be calling me Savannah by now, but calling me by my last name seemed to be a hard habit to break. It wasn't even my last name anymore.

And I had no room to talk, since I had the worst time trying to get used to calling her Tamara.

"Detective," I said instead.

"Everything all right?"

"Fine," I said. "I have a question. Do you know anything about poison pen letters?"

There was a pause. "Not much," the detective said. "Pretty much just what I've read in Agatha Christie."

"You're the police. Don't you deal with stuff like that all the time?"

"First," Grimaldi told me, "people don't really write letters at all anymore. They call or text or email."

"Sure," I answered, "but those are traceable. You know who's contacting you. It isn't possible to contact someone anonymously."

"Of course it is. Spoofing can make someone's phone number look like it comes from the White House or your own home."

Fine. "You said 'first.' What's second?"

"What?... Oh. People don't write letters anymore. And when they do, those letters rarely end in murder. I work homicide."

She had a point. "So no experience with anonymous letters?"

"Not since I was a kid and we sent them to other kids we didn't like," Grimaldi said. "Are you getting anonymous letters?"

I told her I wasn't.

"Mr. Collier?"

She's worked with Rafe before. She calls him by his last name, too.

"No," I said. "Rafe isn't getting threatening letters."

That would be a much bigger deal than this was. And no offense at all to Aislynn and Kylie, but with all the—pardon me—crap in his past, someone sending Rafe anonymous letters would be an oversized, red flag that something was wrong. "A couple of clients of mine have been getting them."

I laid out the situation, starting with the first letter just after April 1st, and ending with the phone call and visit yesterday. "They're giving me the day today to see what I can find out. We're meeting again tomorrow morning to talk about putting the house on the market. I don't really want to do that."

"You probably won't have to," Grimaldi said. "Poison pens aren't usually violent. They avoid conflict. That's why they send anonymous letters, instead of confronting whoever they have the beef with."

That made sense.

"In the few instances where poison pen letters have ended in murder, it has usually been the letter writer who ended up dead. And it's usually in cases where he or she claims to know the recipient's secrets. Some people have secrets they're willing to kill for."

It would have to be a pretty damn—excuse me: darn—big secret to cause me to kill someone over it, but diff'rent strokes, I guess.

"So you don't think Kylie and Aislynn have to worry?"

Grimaldi hesitated a moment. "I wouldn't think so. But there are always exceptions to every rule. And I'd hate to be wrong."

I'd hate for her to be wrong, too.

"The letters were sent through the mail," I said, "and handled by a lot of people. I don't suppose there's any point in looking for fingerprints?"

"Probably not," Grimaldi answered. "Every criminal with a TV knows to wear gloves these days."

"Any other suggestions? I have less than twenty-four hours. Can you think of anything I can do?"

"Talk to the previous owners," Grimaldi said, "and make sure they didn't get letters, and that's why they sold."

"Already doing that."

"Also, make sure that they don't regret selling and aren't sending letters to your clients to get the house back."

I hadn't considered that possibility. Now I did. "You think they'd do that?"

"I have no idea," Grimaldi said. "I don't know them. But people do strange things for all sorts of reasons. Anything's possible."

"You don't think this is a bad idea, do you? For me to talk to them?"

Grimaldi hesitated. "You do have a habit of getting yourself in trouble," she said, which was totally unfair, if you ask me. I rarely get myself in trouble. When I get in trouble, it's usually someone else's fault. And contrary to what Rafe claims, dead bodies do not follow me around.

"Maybe I'll just go talk to Aislynn and Kylie first. I think there were things they didn't tell me yesterday. Maybe they'll tell me if I get them each alone and ask."

"You think they know who's sending the letters?" Grimaldi asked, interested. And added, before I could answer, "Is it one of them?"

Something else I hadn't thought about. "Why would they?"

"The house is too expensive," Grimaldi suggested, "and they want a way out, without admitting it? Or there's something going on in their relationship, and one of them is trying to scare the other away instead of just talking it out?"

I blinked. "I can't imagine Kylie doing that. She seemed very concerned about Aislynn last night. She's willing to sell the house to keep Aislynn happy."

"So maybe it's Aislynn who's doing it," Grimaldi said. "She wants to leave, but she doesn't dare come out and say so. So she's writing the letters to give herself an excuse."

That made a weird and creepy sort of sense. Aislynn was young, and perhaps a bit immature. As Rafe and Grimaldi had both mentioned, anonymous letters are sort of a high school thing to do. And it was easier to imagine Aislynn making herself look like the victim than to imagine Kylie wanting to scare Aislynn, anyway.

"I'll go talk to them both," I said. "Separately. If neither of them confesses—" and what were the chances that either of them would? "—I'll decide whether to talk to the previous owners."

"Stay out of trouble," Grimaldi told me. "Keep me up to date, and let me know if there's anything I can do to help."

I said I would, and we hung up. Me to wait for Tim to vacate the office so I could raid his filing cabinet, and Grimaldi, I guess, to deal with another dead body. Unlike me, they really do follow her around.

It wasn't long after that, that Tim left. I gave him ten minutes just to make sure he wouldn't come back for something he'd forgotten, and then I headed through the lobby. If Brittany asked, I was going to tell her that I was going to the bathroom, but she didn't even look up from the fashion magazine spread open on her desk.

The other offices in the back of the building were occupied by other realtors, and I heard phone calls and the sounds of activity when I walked past. Papers shuffling and pens scratching, fingers tapping on computer keys. Some doors were open, some closed; some offices were dark, others brightly lit.

Tim had turned his ceiling light off but left his door open. I went inside and debated for a second on whether I should close it behind me or leave it. I had no business being here, so it was tempting to close it so no one would see me. But leaving it open would make what I was doing look more innocent, like I had every right to be doing it.

I left the door open and made my way across the floor and around the desk to Tim's multi-drawer filing cabinet.

I can count the real estate transactions I have done on one hand and maybe a few fingers of the other.

Maybe.

Tim had drawers full of folders, separated out by year and month. I went to the drawer for January and opened it. Folders were neatly hung, one after the other, in alphabetical order by last name.

Bummer. I had hoped they'd be filed by street number and address, since I knew what the address was. The late Brenda Puckett, back when I had been snooping through her drawers, had used that method. But not Tim. He filed by last name. Last name of *his* clients, not mine. And since they'd been his clients and not mine, I had no idea what their names were. I'd known it in January, I guess, but a lot of things had happened since then, and that wasn't one of the pieces of information I had retained.

There was nothing for it but to open every file in the drawer and check the address. And I was just getting started on that when the door to the hallway opened wide—wider—with a squeak.

I spun on my heel.

"What are you doing?" Heidi Hoppenfeldt asked suspiciously, hands on her ample hips.

Heidi is by way of being Tim's assistant, gofer, and general dogsbody. She was Brenda Puckett's protégée before Brenda died, and when Walker was sent up the river and Tim ended up in charge, he took over not just the brokerage and Walker's office, but Heidi, too.

She's about my age, a couple of years shy of thirty, with fluffy brown hair and a round face. These days, we're pretty close to the same size. The difference is that Heidi isn't pregnant. She just likes to eat. There were orange crumbs on the front of her green dress. Cheetos, or maybe nacho chips; something she must have been snacking on, on her drive to work.

I swallowed my heart back down into my chest and turned

back to the filing cabinet. It's easier to lie when you're not facing the person you're lying to, I've found. "Looking for something."

"Those are Tim's files," Heidi said.

"It was my transaction, too."

"Then you should have a copy of the file," Heidi said, her voice getting louder as she came toward me.

"I can't find it," I told her, without looking up. "That's why I need a copy of Tim's."

"Have you asked him?"

"He isn't here," I said, stuffing one manila folder back into the drawer and pulling out the next.

Heidi slapped her hand on it before I could open it up.

"Hey!" I protested. "Knock it off. It isn't like it's anything secret. It's a closed transaction. Over and done with. They aren't even Tim's clients anymore."

"Until they want to move again," Heidi said, "and then Tim would want them to call him. He wouldn't like it if you started farming to his clients."

Farming, in case you're unfamiliar with the term, is the marketing act of sending postcards and letters to everyone in an area in an effort to pick up new business. I had no plans of farming to Tim's clients, and told Heidi so.

"All I want is a copy of the paperwork for the transaction we did together in December and January. He had the listing, I had the buyers." Just to mess with her mind a little, I added, "And I'd better not find out that Tim has been soliciting my clients."

Heidi looked mulish.

"If you just want to find that folder for me," I said, "I'll stop looking through the files right now. Make me a copy of the paperwork, and I'll walk away from Tim's filing cabinet right this minute."

Heidi thought about it for a second. "What's the name?" she asked.

"If I knew that, I wouldn't be standing here looking at every folder."

I told her the address instead, and stepped away from the drawer so she could start digging. A few seconds later she pulled a folder out and handed it to me. "Make your own copy."

"What do you want me to do with the original when I'm done?"

"Give it to me," Heidi said, "and I'll put it back."

Fine. She waited for me to walk out the door into the hallway, and then she closed Tim's door ostentatiously behind us both. I rolled my eyes and headed for the copier while Heidi disappeared into the much smaller office next to Tim's that was her domain.

Copying everything didn't take long. I fed the originals through the machine, it spat them out on the other side, and while I waited for the print job to be done, I took the originals back to Heidi. "Here you go. Thanks."

She was sitting behind her desk, and there was orange dust on her chin. I heard the telltale crinkle of a chip bag from under the desk. She didn't answer, either because her mouth was full or because she didn't feel she had to. I put the folder on the desk and retreated to the copier.

Back in my own office, I put the copies on the desk and started looking at them.

I did have my own copies of a lot of the paperwork, and I knew exactly where it was: in the bottom drawer of my desk. Unlike Tim, I have neither space nor need of a filing cabinet.

But Tim's file included things mine didn't. Most importantly, information about the sellers—Virgil Wright and Stacy Kelleher.

The first thing I did was check the online property records, to see where Virgil and Stacy lived now.

It didn't take long, mostly because there wasn't much to find. Neither of them showed up as owning property in the Nashville area, so they didn't seem to have bought another house in the time since they'd sold the one Aislynn and Kylie now lived in.

Someone named Stacy Kelleher rented an apartment in Brentwood, but there was no Virgil Wright listed there, so it might be someone else. It isn't a particularly unusual name. Or they could have left town and moved to another city or state, and I wouldn't know.

So I flipped through the paperwork until I got to the client information sheet, where both names were listed with phone numbers and other pertinent information. I picked up the phone and dialed Virgil's number. A couple of rings passed, and then a canned voice came on. "You've reached the voicemail for Virgil Wright. I can't pick up right now, but leave a message after the tone, and I'll get back to you."

I hung up without leaving a message. I still wasn't sure I should be doing this, and if there was no chance I'd get to talk to him anyway, I didn't want to tip my hand.

At first I thought the same thing would happen when I dialed Stacy's number. It rang, and rang again. I was preparing myself for another voicemail, and another disconnect, when a male voice answered. "Hello?"

"Oh," I said, rattled. "Hello. Um... I'm looking for Stacy?"

There was a moment's pause. "Who's this?" the voice said suspiciously.

"Oh. Um... My name is Savannah. I'm calling from LB&A. Lamont, Briggs and Associates. Real estate company."

I waited for some sort of acknowledgement—something like, "we're not interested in selling our home," since that's what usually happens when you cold call people to talk about houses—but it didn't happen.

"Stacy sold her house in East Nashville in January," I said eventually, when the silence had dragged on for long enough, "and I had a couple of follow-up questions about the transaction. Whether there were any problems. Her level of satisfaction with her agent." Whether she'd been receiving creepy anonymous letters. "That kind of thing."

There was another pause. "We were satisfied with our agent," the guy said.

"Oh." This must be Virgil. "Thank you."

"Don't mention it," Virgil said, and hung up. I arched my brows and did the same.

Four

Kylie worked in one of the high rise buildings in downtown. I caught her just as she was crossing the lobby to head out to lunch with a coworker. "Kylie!"

She glanced at me, and for a second I was afraid she would pretend she didn't know me. It looked like she was thinking about it. Then she said a few words to her associate, and changed direction to intercept me, while the other woman continued on out the door, after a curious glance in my direction.

"Savannah," Kylie said. She sounded about halfway between surprised to see me and annoyed that I was there. "What are you doing here?"

"I had a couple of questions," I said, "that I couldn't ask yesterday, with Aislynn there. I thought maybe you had time to grab lunch so we could talk."

She hesitated, and glanced over her shoulder, to where her friend had walked out.

"My treat," I added. Not because she couldn't afford to pay for her own lunch—and mine—a lot better than I could, but because it was all I could think to say. When she still looked unwilling, I got desperate. "Or I could just walk there with you and let you have lunch with your friend. This won't take long."

She looked relieved. That didn't feel good, but at the moment I'd take what I could get.

"I spoke to Rafe last night," I told her as I fell into step beside her and we passed through the doors to the outside. A wall of humid heat hit us as we left the air-conditioned lobby for the sweaty outside. "He said I should talk to Detective Grimaldi, so I did."

Kylie gave me a sideways glance. "What did the detective

say?"

A lot of things, most of which I didn't want to share with her. "That I should talk to the previous owners and see if maybe they're regretting selling the place and want it back."

Kylie nodded.

"I plan to do that this afternoon. But first I have a question for you."

She looked wary.

"Last night, you said you didn't have any idea who might be behind this. But you didn't look like you were telling the truth. I thought maybe you didn't want to talk about it in front of Aislynn. So I thought I'd get you alone and ask."

We traveled a couple of yards along the sidewalk while she thought about it. It was close to a hundred degrees, and the blacktop felt squishy under my feet. The occasional blast of cold air from inside a door that opened and closed felt good. I had pinned my hair up this morning, but the wisps at the back of my neck were wet. And my stomach was getting big enough to be unwieldy. Although I could console myself with the knowledge that by the time I got *really* pregnant, at least the weather would be cooler.

Kylie sighed. "I was wondering about Aislynn's parents," she said.

That was not what I'd expected at all. "Her parents?"

Kylie nodded. "They weren't happy when she 'turned gay.'" Her tone of voice made quotation marks around the words. "I think they blame me. They wanted her to marry and give them grandbabies."

"She could still marry and give them grandbabies."

Gay marriage was legal in Tennessee now. And they'd already talked about having children.

"It wouldn't be the same," Kylie said. And I guess for parents who wanted a traditional relationship for their daughter, with a strapping husband and a white picket fence and 2.5 kids, it wouldn't. Rafe hadn't been my mother's first choice for me, either, so I could relate.

"Do you think they'd go as far as to scare her like this, though? She's their daughter. Surely they care enough not to do that."

Mother may not have been happy about my choice, but other than voicing her opinion, loudly and clearly, she hadn't actually done anything to interfere. I wouldn't have tolerated it if she had.

"They don't care enough to be happy that she's happy," Kylie said, stopping in front of the entrance to a café. "Or that she *was* happy, anyway. She isn't so happy now."

No, she wasn't. "I don't suppose I can come right out and ask them."

Kylie shook her head. "Don't do that."

"Will you at least tell me who they are and where I can find them? Are they local?"

"Aislynn's from Bowling Green," Kylie said.

"Kentucky?"

She nodded. "The family name is Turner. They live somewhere on Green Street. I can't remember the number."

"That's all right. I'll look it up." And call them, or else make the trip up there. Bowling Green is less than an hour away.

"Anything else you need to know?" Kylie asked, with a glance at the café door.

I shook my head. "Thank you for the time. Have a good lunch."

She nodded. I had turned away when she stopped me. "Savannah?"

I turned back, thinking that maybe she'd changed her mind and was going to ask me to join her and her friend after all.

She didn't. "Did the detective you talked to say anything else? Anything I should know?"

I hesitated, while I tried to figure out whether it was

suspicious that she didn't want to have lunch with me. We were three women around the same age. It wouldn't have been strange to invite me to tag along.

"She said she doesn't have much experience with poison pen letters," I said eventually. "People don't write letters anymore. They spoof their phone number and make prank calls instead. But she said that anonymous letters don't usually escalate into violence. That people who write letters, do it because they're afraid of confrontation."

Kylie nodded, looking relieved.

"I don't think you have to worry about anything happening to Aislynn. Or to you. The most someone is trying to do, is probably scare you."

She smiled. "Thank you, Savannah."

"You're welcome," I said. "I'll see you tomorrow morning."

She ducked into the café. I turned back in the direction we'd come, back to the parking lot and my Volvo. If I wasn't having lunch with Kylie, I might as well drive to Brentwood, to Sara Beth's, and talk to Aislynn over a salad.

By the time I had driven there and found a parking space in the crowded strip mall lot, it was the end of the lunch hour. I only had to wait a couple of minutes for a small, round, marble-topped table over in a corner. "Is Aislynn working?" I asked the beefy young woman who brought me the menu and asked if she could get me a drink.

She looked mutinous.

"I'll have sweet tea," I added, so she wouldn't think I wanted Aislynn to be my waitress instead of her.

"She's in the back." The waitress nodded to a curtain behind the counter as she walked away.

"Can I talk to her a minute?" I asked when she came back with the tea, just as if she'd never left. "I'd like the pear and berry salad, please." Mixed greens, chopped pears and dried cranberries, walnuts, feta and balsamic vinaigrette. Lots of nutrition for the baby.

"I'll go get her." She took the menu back and headed for the kitchen to put in my order. Now that she was assured of a tip, I guess she was more willing to let me speak to Aislynn.

It was a couple of minutes before Aislynn came out. I busied myself sipping tea and looking around at the young hipsters and middle-aged business people shoveling in field greens and quinoa.

I've spent a lot of my life eating lettuce and watching my weight. A Southern Belle is supposed to eat like a bird and have a wasp waist. We wouldn't want a potential suitor to think I'd be expensive to keep, or for that matter that I don't care about looking my best for him. But between Rafe and the baby I'm slowly getting over that. Rafe has always taken great pleasure in enticing me to do things I know I shouldn't do. Eating hamburgers and French fries was on that list, and so was getting involved with him in the first place. And lately it's been nice to eat what I want—even if that's been Mocha Double Chunk ice cream at eleven o'clock at night—and not have to worry about gaining pounds. I'm supposed to gain pounds at this point.

"Savannah?"

Aislynn had a tiny wrinkle between her brows, and like Kylie, didn't seem that happy to see me.

"Hi." I put on a bright smile. "How are you?"

"Fine?" Aislynn said, and made it sound questionable.

I lowered my voice. "I just wanted to update you on what's happened since last night."

She paled. "What's happened? Another letter?"

"No, no. Nothing like that. Nothing's happened at all. Just that I've spoken to Rafe and to Detective Grimaldi. I wanted to tell you what they said."

Aislynn looked relieved. And a little skeptical when I told her that Grimaldi had said that anonymous letter writers don't usually resort to violence. "But that's usually," she told me. "That doesn't mean it couldn't happen."

"No," I admitted. "Just that it isn't likely."

"But likely doesn't mean that it couldn't."

No, it didn't. "Detective Grimaldi said you probably don't have to move, though."

"Probably," Aislynn said.

"Right." I gave up. "I'm still working on it. I wanted to ask you a question."

She immediately sank her teeth into her bottom lip. Somehow, in spite of the piercings decorating her ears, her nose, and her mouth, and the Cleopatra-kohl outlining her eyes, she looked like a nervous little girl afraid to get caught in a lie.

"Yesterday, when I asked whether you had any idea who might be behind this, I got the impression you were thinking of someone."

She didn't answer, and after a second I prompted, "Maybe someone you didn't want to mention in front of Kylie?"

"Oh," Aislynn said.

"I thought maybe, if I came and asked you on your own, you'd share what you were thinking."

"It's probably nothing," Aislynn said.

The whole thing might be nothing. But since she hadn't seemed open to that idea, I didn't bring it up again. Just nodded encouragement.

"It could just be that I'm jealous."

I arched my brows.

Aislynn sighed. "There's this woman? Kylie was involved with her. You know, before me?"

She had this habit of ending every other sentence on a high note, as if she was always unsure and asking for reassurance. I nodded before I could help myself.

"They work together?" Aislynn said, and of course my mind went immediately to the woman Kylie had seemed so eager to have lunch with today. The woman she hadn't seemed at all eager to introduce me to.

"Her name is Lauren."

That didn't help me at all, but I nodded.

"She's older than me. And really smart. And she really liked Kylie. And Kylie liked her. Until she met me?"

I nodded.

"So I'm wondering if maybe...?" She trailed off.

"Lauren is trying to get rid of you so she can have Kylie back?" Would a thirty-something, smart woman with a good job in a bank stoop to something like that?

"No," Aislynn said, looking shocked.

"No?"

"I was thinking more like... you know..."

"No," I said. "I don't know." I had given it my best shot, and if that wasn't what she was thinking, I didn't know what she was getting at.

Aislynn squirmed. "I was thinking maybe Kylie was trying to get rid of me? So she could go back to Lauren?"

It took me a second to find my voice. And rather than telling her that Kylie wouldn't do that—my first instinct, as it had been when Tamara Grimaldi suggested the same thing—I said carefully, "Would she do that?"

Because if Aislynn thought so, and Aislynn knew her a lot better than I did, maybe I was wrong.

"I don't know?" Aislynn said. "I don't want to think so. But it makes sense, you know?"

It did, in a twisted way. It was the obvious conclusion, the one Grimaldi had jumped to, as well. Someone was trying to scare Aislynn into leaving, and who better than Kylie?

Always assuming Kylie wanted to get rid of Aislynn, of course. That hadn't been the impression I'd gotten, but the Kylie from last night had been different from the Kylie I'd met this morning. I probably couldn't rule it out.

"Are you and Kylie having problems?" I probed gently.

Aislynn wiggled. "Not to say problems..."

"Friction? Disagreements?"

She sighed. "She gets upset because this scares me. She thinks I should just snap out of it, that it isn't anything to worry about."

"It probably isn't." Hopefully wasn't. "She seemed nice about it last night."

"That's because you were there," Aislynn said. "When it's just the two of us, she's a lot less patient."

"Are you sure she isn't just upset about the situation? And upset that it's upsetting you?"

Aislynn shrugged. "It started before that. She wants to have a baby. I don't think I'm ready. You know?"

She was only around twenty-five, so I could understand that. Kylie, on the other hand, was around thirty, and was probably hearing her biological clock ticking louder and louder.

"We haven't even been together a year. We aren't married. She wants to do that, too."

"And you don't?"

"It's complicated," Aislynn said.

"Relationships usually are," I agreed.

"I just don't know if I'm ready to get married. I mean, I love Kylie. But I'm afraid she's going to get tired of me. That she's already tired of me. I'm younger than she is. And I do stupid things, like get afraid of being home alone." She sniffed. I couldn't tell whether it was an annoyed sniff, or a wet and soggy one. "I bet Lauren wouldn't be worried about the letters."

Maybe not. Then again, if it were me receiving them, I'd probably be a little worried, too.

"Never mind about Lauren," I said firmly. "If Kylie wants to marry you, and have children with you, she can't still be hung up on Lauren."

Aislynn sniffed. It was definitely a wet, soggy sniff. "Unless it's all just a ruse. She wants to get rid of me, but she won't come out and say so. So she's trying to scare me away instead."

Twisted. But possible. "I'll find out," I said. "I'm going to talk to the previous owners, just to make sure they haven't changed their minds about selling and want their house back. And I'll look into Lauren. What can you tell me about her?"

Not much, as it turned out. Aislynn didn't know her last name, just that her first name was Lauren and she worked with Kylie. They'd been involved, but not really seriously, before Aislynn entered the picture.

"They came here for lunch," Aislynn said. "Kylie used to live down the street, remember?"

I nodded. When I met them, they had lived in Kylie's townhouse in a development in Brentioch—the Brentwood/Antioch area, down Old Hickory Boulevard from Sara Beth's.

"I waited on them. Kylie came back the next day, alone, and asked me out."

"That's nice," I said. It was certainly a very much more ordinary courtship than Rafe and I had had.

Aislynn shrugged skinny shoulders inside the cropped T-shirt. "She said it hadn't been serious with Lauren, although it looked serious to me."

All the more reason to make sure Lauren wasn't targeting Aislynn to get Kylie back. "But that's all you know about her?"

"I only met her once after that," Aislynn said. "At the company Christmas party six months ago. She told me Kylie deserved better than a half-baked girl who didn't even know how to dress properly." She flushed.

"Sour grapes," I told her.

Aislynn shrugged. "That's all I know about her. And you can't ask Kylie. I don't want her to know I'm jealous."

I promised I wouldn't. I had no idea how to find out anything about Lauren without asking Kylie, but I'd do my best.

"You haven't heard anything from the previous owners since you moved in, have you? No offers to buy back the house or anything?"

Aislynn shook her head. "Nothing like that."

"Get any mail for them?"

"They must have mail forwarding," Aislynn said. "No."

"Anything else you can think of?"

She glanced over her shoulder. "No." She took a step to the side as the waitress from earlier deposited the salad in front of me. "I'll let you eat in peace."

"Just one thing."

She stopped, arrested halfway between stationary and moving.

"You're from Kentucky, right?"

She nodded. "Bowling Green."

"How long have you been in Nashville?"

"Just since last summer," Aislynn said. "I graduated in May and moved in June."

"Can you think of anyone from there who could be doing this?" *Like your parents...?* "Someone you knew when you were growing up, or someone you went to college with? Have you seen anyone from up there recently?"

Aislynn shook her head. "Nobody." She took a step back. "Enjoy your food."

She vanished. One second she was there, the next she was halfway across the floor. I watched, my mouth open, as she disappeared back through the curtain behind the counter.

That was the last I saw of her. She was either avoiding me, or there was something interesting going on behind the curtain. I ate my salad, settled my check with the other waitress, and got up. And then I moseyed over to the counter. And since nobody was watching, I ducked behind it and lifted the curtain.

Aislynn peered up at me, eyes huge. She was sitting on an overturned bucket, with a cardboard container of French fries in her hand. Her cheeks were puffed out like a chipmunk's, and her eyes were wide with guilt.

I smiled sweetly. "I just wanted to say goodbye. I'll see you in the morning."

Aislynn chewed. And chewed again. "OK," she mumbled, around the fries. I withdrew, and went back outside to the Volvo.

I figured Rafe was in the middle of a class, so I didn't call him. I did text him an update, though. *In Brentwood. Been to see Kylie and Aislynn. Going to see former owner of their house.*

I added the address I'd found for Stacy Kelleher. Just in case I never came back, I wanted someone to know where I'd gone.

I'll text you when I'm done, I added. That way, if he didn't hear from me within an hour or so, he'd know to come rushing to the rescue.

That done, I put the address into the GPS and the car in gear and followed the instructions to Stacy Kelleher's apartment.

It wasn't a long drive. Down the road past the fancy McMansion developments, then a left on Edmondson Pike, and into an apartment complex there, not too far past where Aislynn and Kylie had crashed Kylie's Volvo into a brick wall last year. The wall had been built up again now, but I gave a little shudder as I drove past.

The apartment complex wasn't gated. I'd been worried that I'd have to try to talk Stacy into letting me in via intercom, but as it turned out, I could just drive into the complex and make my way to the B-building with nobody accosting me.

Each building was two stories, with a central hallway in the hollowed-out middle, and apartments on both floors. I parked the Volvo one space over from a black Jeep Wrangler, and got out.

Everything was quiet. Maybe too quiet, as they say in the movies. The parking lot was mostly empty, and I didn't see anyone. My impression was that this was a working class development, a little tired and probably full of young professionals, and they were all at work on a Friday just after lunch.

The Kelleher apartment was on the second floor. I trudged up the stairs, dragging my feet. I tire more easily these days, and not only was I carrying a few pounds of baby (and a few extra pounds on top of that), my stomach was full of food, too.

There were four apartments on each floor. Two on each side of the stairs, one on the front of the building, and one on the back. Stacy Kelleher's place faced the front. I staggered over to the door and looked for a bell. When I didn't see one, I lifted my hand and applied my knuckles instead.

I'll readily admit I didn't expect anything to happen. It was likely that nobody was home. Stacy probably had a job, and Virgil—if he was here—probably did, too.

I must admit the juxtaposition between this quite humble apartment complex and the Victorian cottage in East Nashville struck me. I had refreshed my memory vis-à-vis the closing statement earlier this morning. Virgil and Stacy had walked from the closing table with almost a hundred thousand dollars in profit. They'd bought their house during the market downturn in 2008 and -09, and had gotten a good deal back then, and they had sold it again at the height of the new market. They should have been able to afford something better than a rental apartment on the outskirts of town.

The door opening took me by surprise, since I hadn't expected it to happen. "Oh."

A guy stood in the open doorway. My age, give or take a year, with glossy, brown hair—wet from a shower—and with a towel slung around his hips. The swath of white terrycloth was the only thing he was wearing.

Virgil Wright, I presumed.

I took a step back. "I'm sorry."

"It's no problem, doll." He glanced over my shoulder, maybe to see if I was alone.

I did the same. There was no one else around.

I cleared my throat. This was a little weird, to be honest. I mean, it was hot. July in Nashville always is. And he would have looked much the same if he'd been wearing a pair of shorts. But who opens the door to a stranger of the opposite sex, dressed in just a towel?

It was either someone who was supremely confident in his own skin, or someone who wanted to shock or intimidate, I guess.

Between you and me, I'll say I wasn't impressed, though. And I certainly wasn't intimidated.

Not that he was bad-looking. Just shy of six feet and leanly muscled, with defined abs and pecs. It's just that I share my bed with Rafe, who looks way better naked than merely 'not bad.' My husband has the kind of physique that can turn a woman dry-mouthed and make her forget her name. There was none of that here.

"I'm looking for Stacy Kelleher," I said.

The guy nodded.

"Is she here?"

He grimaced. "I'm Stacy."

"You're Stacy?"

He looked offended.

"I'm sorry," I added. "I expected a girl."

He muttered something. I didn't ask him to repeat it.

"I'm Savannah Martin," I told him. "From LB&A? The real estate company you and Virgil used to sell your house in January?"

He looked wary. "Yeah?"

"We spoke on the phone earlier this morning?" And dammit—darn it—now I was starting to sound like Aislynn.

"Oh," Stacy said. "That was you."

"I just had a couple questions. If you don't mind."

Stacy looked like he minded, but like he didn't want to say

so. And I'll admit the fact that he was male had thrown me a little. Yes, Stacy can be a male name. Look at Stacy Keach. When I had read the names of the sellers of Aislynn and Kylie's house this morning, I had expected a traditional male/female couple, though.

Although maybe I shouldn't have. A lot of Tim's clients are gay. He spends four figures a month advertising in *Out & About*, Nashville's gay lifestyle magazine.

I pulled myself together. "So your realtor was Timothy Briggs."

Stacy nodded.

"Were you happy with the job Tim did?"

Stacy shrugged. "He did fine, I guess."

"No problems with the transaction? Or with the closing? Or the process?"

Stacy shook his head.

"Can I ask why you decided to move?"

Stacy's face closed. "Personal reasons," he said.

"It's such a pretty house. I'm surprised you chose to leave it." Especially to live here.

I didn't say that, but he must have read my mind, because he looked around with a sneer. "It wasn't my choice."

"I'm sorry," I said, trying to remember whether I'd seen anything in the file that pointed to a looming foreclosure. Had Stacy and Virgil been behind on the payments? Had the bank been trying to take their house back?

Stacy put his hands on his hips. "Not that it's any of your business, but my boyfriend left me, OK?"

Oops.

"I couldn't afford to keep the house on my own, and he didn't want it—he was going to move in with his new boyfriend—so we put it on the market and split the profit."

"I'm sorry," I said.

Stacy shrugged. "Any other questions?"

Um... "Where did Virgil move to?"

He didn't look like he wanted to answer, but then he did anyway. "Same neighborhood. House on Warner Avenue. It belongs to a guy named Kenny."

"Do you have a last name for Kenny?"

He shook his head.

"I don't suppose you ever got any weird mail while you were living in the house?"

He blinked. He had hazel eyes surrounded by long lashes, and when I asked, they widened in something that was either confusion or innocence. "What do you mean, weird?"

"Anything out of the ordinary."

"No," Stacy said. "So is that what you're here about? Weird letters?"

I hesitated. I didn't want to admit there were letters, but at the same time, if he had information, I didn't want to risk not hearing it.

He cocked his head. "I remember you. You were the buyers' agent when we sold the house. Tim said—" He stopped.

"Tim said what?"

Stacy smirked. "That you were new and didn't know what you were doing."

Of course he had.

"Your clients overpaid, you know. For the house. We would have taken less. Virgil would have taken almost any offer that came in, he was so eager to cut the last tie he had to me."

"I'm sorry to hear that," I said, not entirely sure whether I was responding to his comment about Virgil, or the fact that Aislynn and Kylie had ended up paying more than they needed to. "But my clients were happy with their purchase. And the price." They'd offered what they wanted to offer, and enough to preempt any other offer coming in. And they'd been thrilled with the house, at least until the letters started coming.

"So what kind of letters are we talking about?" Stacy asked.

But at that point I'd had enough. He probably didn't know anything about any letters. Most likely, he was just like Tim: an inveterate gossip looking for dirt.

"Nothing that need concern you. I should go. Thank you for your time."

I took a step back. He took a step forward and lifted his hand. "Wait a minute."

And that's all he said. Instead of grabbing me, he stopped, with his mouth open, to look over my shoulder. I turned, just as the scuff of a foot alerted me that someone was there.

Five

I'm sure that slight noise was deliberate. When Rafe wants to be quiet, he can move as silently as the wind. In this case, he must have moved as quickly as the wind, too, to get here from Inglewood so fast.

I had my mouth open to ask how he'd managed that feat, but he gave me a look, and I shut my mouth again. "Ready?" he asked.

I nodded.

"Excuse us." It wasn't a request. More like a statement of fact. Stacy didn't say anything, but he did close his mouth. There were spots of color on his cheeks.

Rafe stepped aside to let me go down the stairs first. I stopped once I hit level ground to turn to him. "What are you doing here?"

"Making sure you're OK."

Of course. "How did you get here so fast?" It couldn't have been more than fifteen or twenty minutes at the most since I'd texted him. It shouldn't have been possible to get here from the TBI building in Inglewood so fast.

"I didn't," he told me. "We were on a field trip."

"We?"

He gestured across the parking lot, to where a white SUV with the TBI logo on the side was parked. The engine was running, probably to keep the interior cold, and I could see a nose pressed against the passenger side window.

I gave the car a wave and turned back to Rafe. "Field trip?"

He grinned. "To Sally's place."

Sally. I had met her for the first time almost a year ago, when Tamara Grimaldi had suggested I arm myself in case Rafe was as bad as he looked on paper. This was before she realized that he was on the TBI's payroll, and had been for ten years, and that he'd never hurt me.

Sally owns a little yellow cottage in the heart of the antique district on Eight Avenue, where she sells—not seashells at the sea shore, but self defense spray and knives, surveillance equipment, GPS trackers, and the like. I had a miniature knife and a mini-canister of Mace, both disguised as tubes of lipstick, in a compartment in my purse, that I'd bought from Sally. They had actually saved my hide on a few occasions, too.

I couldn't hold back a grin as I shot another glance at the SUV. "How did the boys handle that?"

Sally is nothing if not an original. In her forties, with upper arms that rival Rafe's, and with hair that's shaved into a rooster-red mohawk on top of her head. I could just imagine how Rafe's boys—the three rookies he's training—had reacted to the introduction.

"José was uncomfortable. Clayton was nervous. And Jamal acted like she was his long lost auntie."

About as I had expected. José seemed uncomfortable around a lot of us. Clayton was a skinny twenty-year-old who was probably afraid Sally would break him in two—I'm sure she could have, if she'd wanted to—and Jamal had never met a lamp-post he couldn't have a friendly conversation with. The kid was a natural con-man. It would probably serve him well in his profession.

"So that's how you got here so fast." The antique district was on the south side of town, much closer to Brentwood than the TBI building on the north-east.

Rafe nodded. "And now that I've broken up your conversation with the almost naked guy, I gotta go back to work."

"Sure."

"We'll just follow you outta here to make sure you get on the road safe."

"Dang it," I said, "and here I was just waiting for you to leave again so I could go back upstairs to the almost naked guy."

He arched a brow. "That'd better be a joke."

"Of course. He's gay. And anyway, I've got you."

"Damn straight," Rafe said and took my arm. "And if I didn't have a car full of kids, I'd remind you. C'mon."

I came, and let him put me into the Volvo and close the door. Then he sauntered over to the SUV and got in. When I pulled out of the apartment complex, the SUV was right behind me.

I lost it once we got to the interstate. Rafe drives like he always needs to be somewhere ten minutes ago. As soon as we moved off the exit and merged with traffic, he shot past me and disappeared up Interstate 65 toward town. I made no attempt to keep up. He could probably get away with it, in his official vehicle. I couldn't, in mine.

By the time I reached East Nashville, the SUV was nowhere to be seen. It had been nowhere to be seen a lot longer than that. I exited the interstate at Shelby Avenue and headed away from downtown into the historic district. A few minutes later I was on my way back down Aislynn and Kylie's street, scoping out the new neighbors.

A green Craftsman bungalow one block away had changed hands recently. I rolled past slowly, peering into the yard. A brightly colored big wheel sat on the grass, next to a pink miniature bicycle with training wheels and pink-and-white streamers hanging from the handlebars. A family with young kids, obviously. And while you shouldn't judge a book by its cover—or people by the outside of their house or the contents of their yard—they didn't seem like the kind of people who would send two gay girls a block away anonymous letters.

The other new neighbors, a block in the other direction, had bought a new construction infill: a pale blue two-story with an attached garage. No bikes or trikes here, but there was a rainbow flag hanging limply from a pole, and a porch swing filled with matching pillows. A fat, striped cat was lying in a patch of sunlight on a windowsill upstairs.

I reached the next block just in time to see a figure slip around the corner of Aislynn and Kylie's house and disappear into the backyard.

I slammed on the brakes and skidded to a stop at the curb on the other side of the street. And that description makes it sound louder and more violent than it actually was. I was going less than fifteen miles an hour, so it was really more like rolling gently to a stop at the curb and cutting the engine. Then I was out of the car and hustling across the street.

I really do know better than to follow nefarious characters around. But it was just past two in the afternoon, and broad daylight. The sun was having a grand old time up in the cloudless sky. There were a couple kids playing in a yard up the street, their shrill screams and laughter echoing as they ran back and forth through a sprinkler, and a woman was jogging down the other sidewalk, ponytail bouncing. Why anyone would choose to go for a run during the hottest part of a ninety-degree day is beyond me, but there she was. A dog in a yard ran up to the fence and yipped as she passed.

Aislynn and Kylie's yard had been nicely landscaped, with green bushes and flowers in beds and containers on the porch, and with the stereotypical white picket fence enclosing the front yard, giving way to an eight-foot privacy fence enclosing the back, extending left and right of the garage. That's where the stranger had gone: through the gate and into the privacy-fenced back yard. He could be doing anything at all back there, with nobody being the wiser.

I made my way through the front over to the gate in the privacy fence. It was unlocked—of course; the stranger had just gone through—and yielded to my touch. I was worried it would squeak and announce my presence, but it swung in without a sound. I slipped through and closed the gate gently behind me before looking around.

The backyard was nice, too. There was a wooden deck off the house, with a roof over part of it, with little twinkling Christmas light strung back and forth. They weren't twinkling right now, of course, but I could imagine they would twinkle at night, when it wasn't uncomfortably hot and Aislynn and Kylie were entertaining.

The privacy fence enclosed the entire backyard. There was a gate in the back wall; I assumed they used it to take out the trash. Everything within the yard was open and easy to see. There was a little pond with rippling water in the middle of the grass, with flashes of orange moving through the water. Koi.

Besides that, the yard was empty. Whoever the guy had been—if it had been a guy, and not just a butch girl in jeans and a plaid shirt—he wasn't here.

Maybe it'd just been a neighbor cutting through the middle of the block instead of going around?

Although there had to be easier ways to get across to the next street than to choose a yard with an eight-foot privacy fence. There were properties all up and down the block with no enclosed backyards. Wouldn't it have been easier to cut through one of them?

The conspicuous benefit of a fenced yard was that nobody would see him or what he was doing. But that assumed he was doing something he shouldn't be.

I skirted the koi pond and walked across the grass to the back gate and unlatched it. Like the gate beside the house, it was unlocked. I peered up and down the alley and into the yards on the other side, but saw no sign of the blue and green plaid.

The man in plaid—sounded like the title of an Agatha Christie mystery!—had either hustled away from the alley after coming through the gate (possible), or he hadn't left the yard at all. I turned around to look at the back of the house.

There was the deck, as I mentioned. A set of double doors led into the family room next to the kitchen. I had noticed it when I was inside yesterday. That part of the house was an addition; they didn't build family rooms with kitchens and double doors to the backyard back in 1902.

I made my way back across the grass and up the couple of steps to the deck. My heels thumped against the plank floors, keeping time with the hard thump of my heart.

My palm was sweaty when I reached out and wrapped it around the doorknob and twisted.

The door was locked.

I bent and peered at the lock. It didn't look forced. There were no scratches or anything, and the keyhole looked normal.

I leaned closer and cupped my hands around my eyes to peer in, but there was nothing to see. No movement. No lights—and why would there be, in the middle of a sunny afternoon? No sign of anyone being inside.

I put my hands on my hips and my back to the door to survey the backyard. I could call Aislynn or Kylie to tell them what had happened, but the man in plaid was probably just a neighbor who had cut through the yard because he knew Aislynn and Kylie were at work and the house was empty, and he had made it out of sight before I opened the gate to the alley. Telling them would just make them worry. If they came home and discovered that someone had been inside, there'd be time enough to tell them about the man I'd seen then.

I trudged back to my car and drove off. And although I took a circuitous route back to the office—circling a couple of blocks and keeping my eyes peeled—I saw no sign of the man in plaid.

Back at the office, I booted up the laptop and spent some time in the online courthouse records looking up homeowners on Warner Avenue, where Stacy said his boyfriend had moved in with someone new. There's no way to look up homeowners by first name—just last name or address—so I had to click on each record for each property on Warner and see who owned it. It was tedious and took a long time—Warner is a long street with many houses—but eventually I had what I wanted. A man named Kenneth Grimes owned the property at number 1806. He was the only Ken, Kenneth, or Kenny I could find, so unless Virgil's Kenny was a renter, this was likely to be him.

The tax assessor's image—of the house, not the owner— showed a symmetrical 1920s Craftsman Cottage with stacked stone pillars holding up the front porch and a wide, three-window dormer on the second floor. The tax assessor said it was worth two hundred eighty thousand dollars, which probably meant I could get at least a hundred grand more on the open market. Probably more.

Not that I thought Kenny wanted to sell. He'd paid less than two hundred thousand six years ago. He couldn't hope to get anything similar these days. Not at that price.

But I had his address. I shut off the computer and headed over there.

Warner Avenue was named after the Warners, a family who came to Nashville from Chattanooga just after the beginning of the Civil War—or the War Against Northern Aggression, as we call it in these parts.

James Warner, the father, was one of the founders of the Tennessee Coal, Iron, and Railroad Company, and his sons Percy and Edwin both went on to become civic leaders and benefactors. Percy served on the Nashville Park Board, and both he and Edwin have parks named after them. Percy Warner Park and Edwin Warner Park in South Nashville.

They lived in the Renraw Mansion in East Nashville for a while—Renraw is Warner spelled backwards—and got a street in the neighborhood named after them. Streets in other parts of town, too, for that matter. Warner—like Robertson, Donelson, and Sevier—is one of those names you see again and again in Nashville, in street names and park names and neighborhood names.

Warner Avenue looked just like Aislynn and Kylie's street. Lined with Victorian cottages, Craftsman bungalows, and the occasional new-construction infill made to look old. There were kids playing in picket-fenced yards, dogs barking from behind privacy fences, and a lawnmower humming. Somewhere a band must be rehearsing—there are a lot of musicians in East Nashville—because when I had parked the car and gotten out, I could hear the sound of muffled percussion.

Kenny Grimes's house looked like it had in the website picture, except for the color. Sometime between the time when the picture was taken and now, he had repainted it pumpkin with dark blue trim, instead of sage green with saffron. There was no fence around the front, just a green lawn leading up to two flowerbeds flanking the front steps. They were filled with plants in three precise tiers: small, spiky, pale green clusters in the front, medium-sized round bushes in the middle, and pointy, dark evergreens in the back. It was lovely, and must have taken a lot more thought that I had ever put into the landscaping around my house. My big concession to yard work is sitting on the porch with a glass of sweet tea while Rafe mows the lawn. Shirtless.

The front door was a fifteen-light: three rows of windows horizontally, five vertically. It allowed me to peer into the front room while I waited for my knock to be answered. I saw hardwood floors, a big stone fireplace flanked by two ornate brass sconces—surely original to the house—and a matching brass chandelier suspended from the ceiling. I liked Kenny Grimes already.

But he didn't answer my knock on the door. I knocked again, and waited, looking around.

There was a porch swing suspended from the ceiling at one end of the porch, and a seating arrangement with two Cracker

Barrel rocking chairs on the other. Both were piled high with colorful pillows. The welcome mat was your standard brown bristly construction, but it had *Hello Darling* painted on it. And a brass mailbox was hanging beside the door. With no fence at the street, I guess the mailman had to come up onto the porch to deliver the mail.

I know it's highly illegal to mess with other people's mail. I wasn't really messing with it, though. I was just going to take a quick look. Just in case Kenny and Virgil—mostly Virgil—was also receiving letters addressed in a spiky, anonymous hand.

In spite of telling myself I wasn't doing anything wrong, my heart still beat a little harder as I lifted the lid of the mailbox and stuck my hand inside.

There was a handful of mail in the box. I blushed guiltily as I pulled it out for a closer look.

Bill, bill, what looked like a greeting card—roughly square envelope instead of rectangular; Colorado postmark—another bill, a circular from Office Depot... nothing hand-lettered except the card from Colorado, and the handwriting was neat and rounded.

It was all in Kenny's name except for the circular. Maybe Virgil did the shopping.

That could be significant. Office Depot sells things like plain copy paper and plain envelopes and magic markers. The stuff that was used to create the anonymous letters.

Then again, if Virgil was sitting pretty here, with Kenny, in a house that was just as nice as the one he'd given up, why would he bother? It wasn't like Aislynn and Kylie had cheated him out of anything.

I dropped the mail back into the box and dusted my hands, as if I could rub off the feeling of having broken the law. There was still no answer from within the house. I gave the door one last knock, waited, and was on my way toward the porch steps when I heard the lock tumble.

I swung around on my heel, just as the door opened.

The man on the doorstep looked horrible. He was almost as tall as Rafe—several inches over six feet—but with very little of Rafe's bulk. He was lanky, with reddish-blond hair that stood straight up, and bloodshot eyes. Freckles stood out sharply against pale skin. And while he was probably naturally pale—most redheads are—this wasn't a normal pallor. He looked sick. Or hung over.

"Virgil?" I said tentatively.

He closed his eyes for a second, as if my voice had hurt his head. I was leaning toward hung over, although that was a sad thing to contemplate at three in the afternoon.

"I'm Kenny."

His voice was rusty, like he hadn't used it much lately, or like he smoked a pack a day. He didn't smell so good, either, now that I had moved closer. Someone looked like they hadn't had a shower in a day or two, and it wasn't me. The reason the red hair stuck up was probably because it was dirty.

"I'm Savannah Martin," I said, making sure my voice was low and soothing. "I work for LB&A. Lamont, Briggs and Associates. Real estate. Virgil used one of our agents to sell his house last January."

Kenny nodded.

"I was hoping to be able to ask him a couple of questions about it."

"Can't," Kenny said.

"He isn't here?"

Kenny shook his head. And it must have hurt, because he closed his eyes again, and this time I swear I saw moisture at the corners of his eyes.

"I'm sorry," I said, while I thought to myself that maybe he shouldn't have drunk so much last night. "Maybe I should leave and come back another time. When do you expect him back?"

Kenny opened his eyes. They were a vivid turquoise blue,

made brighter by the fact that they were swimming with tears.

That, and the fact that they were severely bloodshot.

"I don't," he said.

And without giving me the chance to say anything else, he closed the door in my face.

Oops.

I stared at it, open-mouthed, for a second before I turned and scurried down the stairs and through the yard as fast as I could. Embarrassed, yes, but I also felt bad on his behalf. Virgil must have left him, and now Kenny was drowning his sorrows in alcohol.

Really, I reflected as I unkeyed the door and slipped behind the wheel of the Volvo, *Virgil didn't have much staying power, did he?* It was only six months since he'd left Stacy. And how he'd left Kenny, too?

Hit-and-run Virgil Wright. One of those guys who left a trail of broken hearts in his wake, it seemed.

Unfortunately, now I didn't know where to find him, so I couldn't ask him about the letters.

And after my encounter with Kenny, I could tell that *he* wasn't in any kind of mood to tell me anything.

And I only had eighteen more hours to figure out what was going on before I had to face Aislynn and Kylie over breakfast.

I sat in the car and made a mental list of what I had found out and what I still needed to do.

I had spoken to Kylie, who suspected Aislynn's parents of being behind the letters. But they lived in Kentucky, and the letters had been posted right here in East Nashville, at the post office four blocks from Aislynn and Kylie's house. Unless Aislynn's mother or father commuted to Nashville every week or two, chances were they weren't behind any of this. Entirely apart from the fact that I had a hard time believing that anyone's parents would be so callous.

Aislynn suspected Kylie, or Kylie's ex-girlfriend Lauren. I knew nothing about Lauren, but I'd have to find out. And I had no idea how. Kylie had done a good job of keeping us apart at lunch, and it wasn't like I could tell her what Aislynn thought, was it?

Stacy had been forced to leave the house against his will when he and Virgil broke up. He might feel resentful of the women who were now living in his old home. But it wasn't like he'd get the house back if he scared Aislynn away. The house was beyond his means; he'd said so. So even if it went back on the market, he wouldn't be able to buy it.

And Virgil was in the wind. I had no idea where to find him.

Although I did have his phone number. It had been a few hours since I'd tried to call. Maybe this time he'd answer.

I pulled out my phone and dialed. The phone rang a couple of times. Then a male voice said, "Yes?"

It sounded familiar. Probably because I'd heard it on the recording earlier.

"Hi," I said, endeavoring to sound friendly. "This is Savannah Martin, and—"

The voice interrupted me. "I already told you," it said. "He's gone. And if you don't stop harassing me and get the hell away from my house, I'm calling the police."

The next thing I heard was the click as the call was disconnected.

Six

Huh.

So Virgil was gone but Kenny still had his phone.

Shit. I mean... shoot. I had obviously misinterpreted something. Something vital.

When Kenny said that Virgil was gone, and wasn't coming back, he didn't mean that Virgil had left him.

He meant that Virgil was dead.

I drove back to the office in something close to shock—not only had I not known, and not expected it, I had unwittingly broken all rules of proper conduct by intruding on Virgil's nearest and dearest in their time of grief, not to mention that I had chalked that grief up to Kenny being hung over.

Not a stellar afternoon on my part.

But at least I could break the news to Tim. Depending on when it had happened, he might already know, but maybe he didn't. I hadn't heard any talk about it, and considering that Virgil had been one of our clients, someone ought to have mentioned it.

Tim's car was back in the lot, and he was in his office. I knocked on the open door and waited for him to acknowledge me.

"Oh," he said. "It's you again."

I stepped through the doorway. "Do you have a minute?"

He had been in the process of writing, and now he put the pen down. "Is this about your anonymous letters again?"

Yes and no. "It's about one of your clients."

"*My* clients?"

I nodded. "Remember that transaction we did together over Christmas? The Victorian house?"

"Virgil and Stacy's place," Tim said. "Are those two girls the ones getting the letters?"

There didn't seem to be any sense in lying about it anymore. "Yes. But that's not what I wanted to talk to you about."

Tim's brows drew together.

"I went to talk to Virgil and Stacy," I said. "To see if they'd ever gotten any weird letters. If maybe that was the reason they'd decided to sell."

Tim sounded offended. "They'd have told me if they did!"

Maybe, maybe not. Besides, I couldn't trust that Tim would have told me. Client-realtor privilege, and all that. Confidentiality.

"Did you know that they aren't together anymore?"

"Sure," Tim said readily. "That's why they were selling the house. Virgil was moving in with his new boyfriend, and Stacy couldn't afford to keep the place by himself."

Right. "Well, I tried to track them both down today. And I'm sorry to have to be the one to tell you this, but..."

"Oh, my Lord Jesus!" Tim exclaimed, turning pale. He slapped a hand to his chest, right on top of the baby blue silk shirt. "He's dead!"

I nodded. "I'm sorry to be the bearer of bad news..."

Tim was palpitating. Visibly. "I feel so guilty. It's just a couple days since I saw him. If I'd had any idea..."

"I'm sure there was nothing you could have done," I said, although I had no idea.

"How did it happen?"

"I'm not sure. I thought maybe you...?"

Tim shook his head. "I had no idea. He didn't seem like anything was wrong. Certainly not like he was thinking of..." He swallowed.

I wasn't sure if Virgil had taken his own life or not. I had hoped maybe Tim knew something, but it seemed not.

"I feel like I should have realized something was wrong," he whimpered. "Nothing seemed off the other night. He seemed happy. He flirted with me! But he was so distraught back then. Losing not just his boyfriend, but his home..."

"Wasn't it his decision?" If Virgil was moving in with Kenny, surely it was Virgil who had wanted the breakup to happen?

"Of course not," Tim said. "It was Virgil's decision."

"That's what I meant."

We stared at one another for a second, across the desk.

"Isn't it Stacy who's dead?" Tim asked.

I shook my head.

"Virgil's dead?!"

I nodded.

"Oh, my God!" Tim slumped.

"So let me get this straight. You thought it was Stacy who was dead? That he'd killed himself because Virgil dumped him?"

Tim nodded, fanning himself with his hand.

"He was that distraught?"

"Back when it happened, he was pretty upset. He was crazy about Virgil. And yeah, maybe he liked Virgil's money, too. And the house. But he was devastated when Virgil kicked him to the curb."

"It's no fun to find out that your significant other is cheating," I said, since I'd been in just that position with my first husband. Bradley had married his paralegal, Shelby, less than two weeks after our divorce was final.

"No kidding," Tim told me. "I figured if one of them had died, it would have been Stacy. Virgil had no reason to end it all. He was happy. New boyfriend. New house. Plenty of money."

While Stacy lived in a crappy rental in South Nashville and poured drinks for a living. Tim must have spent the night at South Street Bar recently, and seen him there.

"I'm not sure anyone ended anything," I told Tim. "I have no idea what happened. Kenny—the new boyfriend—wasn't forthcoming. He said he'd call the cops if I didn't leave him alone. But for all I know it was a traffic accident. Or an aneurism. Or a heart attack."

"He was my age!" Tim said.

So maybe not a heart attack. Although I guess it could happen to a man in his mid-thirties. I'm sure it has sometime, somewhere.

"I really don't know," I said. "And I didn't know Virgil," or Kenny, "so I'm sure he won't tell me anything."

"Maybe he'll tell me," Tim said, and started flipping through his Rolodex. I sank onto one of the chairs in front of the desk. He hadn't invited me to stick around, but if he found out something, I'd like to know about it. I mean, that's partly why I'd told him, so he could try to figure out what had happened.

I guess it was sort of crazy to wonder if Virgil had been driven to suicide by anonymous letters, but under the circumstances, it might not be as crazy as otherwise. And if there was a connection to Aislynn and Kylie, I wanted to know about it.

So I sat and waited while Tim found the number and dialed. And then I waited for the phone to be answered. And after that I waited for Tim to introduce himself. And that was all it took for the person on the other end of the line to start yapping. I couldn't make out the words, but the thrust of the monologue was pretty obvious, especially when Tim glanced at me with a grimace. "Yes. I'm sorry about that."

Kenny—I assumed it was Kenny—talked some more.

"I'm sorry," Tim said again. "I just wanted to verify something she told me..."

Kenny kept talking.

"About Virgil," Tim said loudly. "What happened to Virgil?"

Kenny talked. And this time Tim didn't try to interrupt him, just listened. I shifted on my chair, annoyed that I couldn't hear anything. Kenny's voice was a whining drone, but I couldn't make out the words he said.

"When?" Tim asked.

Kenny talked for another minute.

"When?" Tim said again.

Kenny answered.

"Is there anything I can do?"

Kenny must have said no, or maybe he told Tim that the best thing he could do was not call back, because Tim's lips tightened and his eyes turned hard. "Thank you for your time," he said, and stabbed the disconnect button with his finger. I just won't repeat the word he directed at the phone after turning it off.

"I'm sure he's distraught," I said apologetically, as if it were my fault. In a sense, maybe it was. I had contacted Kenny first, and now Tim was bearing the brunt of the temper I had stirred up.

Tim scowled at me.

"What did he say?" I added.

Tim looked like he wasn't sure he wanted to share it with me—I mentioned we don't always get along—but in the end, he did. "Virgil died two days ago. Hit over the head with something while he was out jogging in Shelby Park. The police think it's random violence."

So not only was Kenny devastated, it was fresh devastation. Two days ago. Wow.

And then my mind started ticking.

"Why would anyone mug a jogger? It's not like he'd be carrying any money." Or even be wearing a fancy Rolex. I've heard of people getting killed for their sneakers, but that was a while ago, and surely didn't apply to grown men out for a run in a city park.

"Hate crime," Tim said.

"How would anyone know he was gay?" It isn't like you can

tell by the way someone jogs. "Did he look gay?"

"Not particularly," Tim said. "Stacy was definitely the twinkie in that relationship."

Thanks to a visit to a gay leather-bar once—don't ask—I knew what that meant: a young, pretty gay guy. Nice to look at, but no substance.

"Or maybe he saw something he shouldn't have seen," Tim added. "Like a drug deal gone wrong."

Quite possible. All sorts of shady dealings go on in the parks.

"But he didn't kill himself."

"No," Tim said, and sounded disappointed.

So there was probably no connection whatsoever to my—or to Aislynn and Kylie's—threatening letters.

"The funeral's tomorrow," Tim added.

"Someone should go."

He looked at me, and I added, "He was a client. Of the brokerage. If you don't have time, I can do it."

Tim shrugged. "Knock yourself out."

"You don't want to?"

"I've got better things to do on a Saturday," Tim said. "I don't even know Kenny. And it's not like Virgil cares."

Maybe not. But— "What about Stacy?"

"Ooooh," Tim said, his eyes lighting with maliciousness. "Now that might be fun. Stacy and Kenny facing off over the body."

I winced. That wasn't what I had meant, and secondly, the picture his words had painted was quite vivid and uncomfortable. But now that he had put the image in my mind, I could sort of see the appeal of it. However— "I'm sure it won't be an open casket."

"I don't care," Tim said. "I might have to make time for this after all."

And so might I. I hadn't known any of the parties involved, but aside from the sheer ghoulish appeal of seeing Stacy and

Kenny squaring off over their dead lover, I was curious. The letters to Aislynn and Kylie had threatened physical harm. And now the previous owner of the house where the letters were sent had been killed. Violently.

I got to my feet. "Thanks for finding out what happened. Maybe I'll see you at the funeral."

Tim nodded. And although he didn't say anything else, I could feel his speculative gaze on my back as I made my way to the door and out.

I left the office after that. I wanted to get away from Tim, and I didn't really want to make the next phone call from a place where he could overhear me. So I got into the car, turned the AC on, and told myself I was waiting for the interior to cool down before I drove away, and in the interrim, I might as well call Tamara Grimaldi and ask her what, if anything, she knew about Virgil Wright's death.

It took a couple of rings before she picked up. Then—"Ms... Savannah."

"Detective," I said.

"Everything OK?"

"Fine." I told her what had transpired so far today, since the last time I talked to her. My talks with Kylie and Aislynn, my visit to Stacy's apartment. For good measure, I threw in Rafe's appearance, too. She didn't say anything about it, but I'm pretty sure she was amused. I figured she would be; that's why I'd mentioned it.

"I wanted to know if you could tell me anything about what happened to Virgil," I added. "If he was mugged—or beaten up, or hit over the head—in the park, that'd be suspicious circumstances, right? And you'd be involved?"

"Not personally," Grimaldi said, and I could hear the sound of a keyboard from the other end of the line, "but I can check and see who caught the case and maybe have a word with him or her. And maybe mention the letters."

"Do you think there's a connection?"

"Not likely," Grimaldi said, "but you never know. That's why you called me, right?"

She didn't wait for me to answer, just added, "Here we go. Detective Mendoza got that one."

The name sounded familiar, but it took me a second to place it. "That really good-looking guy my mother suggested I marry when Rafe didn't show up at the courthouse? We met him at the Germantown Café for lunch?"

Grimaldi's voice was dry. "That's him."

"Sorry. But he *is* good-looking."

"Believe me," Grimaldi said, "I know it."

Uh-oh. "You don't have a thing for him, do you?" That wouldn't make my brother happy. "Or a past with him, or anything like that?"

"He's married," Grimaldi said, which didn't answer either question.

"He's going through a divorce." At least that's what he'd said on that memorable occasion when my mother had asked him whether he wanted to marry me: that he'd better wait until his divorce was final. "He probably cheated on his wife, didn't he?"

"Undoubtedly," Grimaldi said. "Women commit crimes just so they can get arrested by Jaime Mendoza."

I wasn't surprised. I'd only met him that one time, but it was no problem bringing the image to the forefront. He'd looked like an old matinee idol. Drop dead gorgeous. One of the best-looking men I'd ever seen. A bit too clean-cut for my taste—I wouldn't have considered marrying him even if I hadn't still been convinced that Rafe would turn up—but unquestionably handsome. "Is he any good?"

Grimaldi's tone was frosty. "Excuse me?"

I rolled my eyes. "Not in bed." *Sheesh.* "As a detective. Is he any good?"

"Yes," Grimaldi said. "He's very good."

"So if there's something fishy about Virgil's death, he'd know?"

"If there's something fishy about Mr. Wright's death," Grimaldi said, "I'm sure he'll figure it out. He isn't someone who takes the easy way out."

Good to know. "Can you ask him about it?"

"I was just about to do that," Grimaldi said. "Do you want to hang on, or do you want me to call you back?"

"I'm on my way home from the office. Why don't I just drive," without holding the phone to my ear, "and you can call me when you find out something."

Grimaldi said she would, and we hung up. I put the car in gear and rolled out of the parking lot toward the house on Potsdam.

It wasn't even five minutes before the phone rang. Not unexpectedly, it was Grimaldi calling back.

"Good news?" I wanted to know.

"Depends on what you consider good news. And I can't give you any confidential details."

Of course not.

"And all I have are the basics from the file. I tried to call Jaime, but he didn't answer. So these are just the basics."

"OK," I said.

"The murder happened Wednesday night, sometime between seven-thirty and eight. Mr. Wright was seen entering the park a couple of minutes after seven-thirty. He'd jogged from his home on Warner Avenue. His car was still parked there, and one of the neighbors saw him leave."

So far, so good.

"He took the route around the baseball diamonds," Grimaldi said. "That doesn't mean anything to me, but it might to you."

It did. I lived in East Nashville, and was familiar with the park. However, I had thought the detective was, as well. "You were there in February, weren't you? When what's-his-name was killed? The guy in the sheet?"

"Only in the area where the body was found," Grimaldi said, "and that was nowhere near the baseball diamonds."

"Where was this body found? Virgil's?"

Grimaldi must have consulted her notes, because it took her a second to answer. "He went around the lake, past the duck habitat and the public restrooms, and then he chose a smaller path that ran through the woods back in the direction he'd come."

"That's interesting." The smaller paths weren't anywhere near as comfortable to run on as the paved roads. And by then— close to eight o'clock—the path through the woods must have been getting dark. The roads had lights, but the paths didn't. "I wonder why."

"It might just have been what he did," Grimaldi said. "Or maybe he saw someone he knew. Or had an assignation with someone."

Maybe. "So that's where he was killed? On the path?"

Grimaldi said it was. "When he didn't come home by nine, the boyfriend went looking for him."

"And found him?"

"No," Grimaldi said. "The boyfriend was in his car. He couldn't drive the path. So Mr. Wright wasn't discovered until the next morning, by a man walking a dog."

Poor Kenny. No wonder he was distraught.

On the bright side, he hadn't been the one to find his dead lover. But on the other hand, he must be thinking that if he'd only found Virgil the night it happened instead of the next morning, maybe there would have been a way to save him.

I tried to shake it off. "Does Detective Mendoza have any suspects?"

"That's something I can't tell you," Grimaldi said.

"Why? Because you don't know?"

"That. And also because it's none of your business."

There wasn't much I could say to that. She was right. Still, I wasn't ready to give up. "Tim said it might have been a hate crime."

"It's possible," Grimaldi said.

"Is Detective Mendoza investigating it as a hate crime?"

"I just told you," Grimaldi said, "I don't know what Jaime's doing. But I'm sure he's looking into all the possibilities."

He probably was. "I just want to know if there's a connection, you know? I mean, it's suspicious, isn't it? Aislynn and Kylie get threatening anonymous letters, and the guy who lived in their house before them ends up dead."

"Do you think Aislynn and Kylie killed him?" Grimaldi wanted to know.

"No!" *God, no.* Of course not. "Why would they?"

"Maybe he wrote the letters," Grimaldi said.

"Why would he do that?"

I think Grimaldi shrugged. I got the impression she shrugged. "Why would anyone?"

I had no idea. It seemed singularly pointless. Unless the point was getting between Aislynn and Kylie to break them up. But Virgil would have had no reason to do that. "Does Detective Mendoza know about the letters?"

"Not yet," Grimaldi said. "Until you called, I had no idea there was a connection between his DB and your anonymous letters."

They weren't *my* anonymous letters, even if I had sort of claimed them. "Will you tell him?"

"Of course," Grimaldi said. "It probably won't be connected—I don't see how it could be—but as you said, it's an interesting coincidence."

"He'll probably want to talk to Aislynn and Kylie, won't he?"

"I'm sure he will," Grimaldi said. "Is that a problem?"

Not for me. And likely not for them, either. Even though

Mendoza would be totally wasted on both of them.

"Not at all," I said. "I don't suppose there's any chance he'll want to talk to me?"

Grimaldi was smiling. I could hear it. "What do you think Mr. Collier would say to that?"

"I don't think he'd say anything. He isn't the jealous type." Nor did he have any reason to be. Detective Mendoza was good-looking, but he had nothing on Rafe. "Will you let me know what he says?"

"I'll tell you everything I can," Grimaldi said, and since that was the best I could expect, I had to be satisfied with it.

I pulled up in front of the house on Potsdam a couple of minutes later, and lingered in the circular driveway to admire the view.

Not the house, although it's a very nice, three-story red-brick Victorian with white gingerbread trim on the porch and a circular tower on one corner. You don't see a lot of those around, especially not in this neighborhood. Most of the big, fancy, brick mansions are on the other side of Main Street, in the Edgefield neighborhood. This one was surrounded by rinky-dink 1940s cracker-jack boxes and the occasional new construction infill, where some intrepid builder with more hope than sense had bought a vacant lot and ventured into the 'hood. The area was, as we say in the real estate business, 'transitional,' which is another way of saying that it has a long way to go, but that a few brave souls have moved in and started renovating.

Rafe was one of the first. The house was his grandmother's, and he'd moved in with her last August, and started fixing the place up. No one had done any work to it for at least thirty years before that, so it had been in desperate need of some TLC.

Mrs. Jenkins was in a home now, sad to say. She had dementia, and we couldn't trust her not to wander off and get lost, so Rafe had found her a lovely facility that she enjoyed, and we went and visited her on the weekends. Half the time she knew us, and half the time she didn't, but she was happy to get visitors either way.

The house looked a lot better now than the first time I'd seen it, all decrepit and overgrown. But that was not the reason I slowed the car to a crawl to admire the scenery.

No, my husband was mowing the lawn. Stripped to the waist, with a pair of worn jeans hanging low on his hips, with his upper body glistening with perspiration and muscles bunching under smooth skin, he was pushing an ancient lawn mower back and forth across the front yard.

My tongue got stuck to the roof of my mouth.

After a second, he shot me a glance over his shoulder. I eased my foot off the brake and crept forward. He went back to mowing. Down to the edge of the driveway and back. But when I stopped the car at the bottom of the steps, behind the Harley-Davidson parked there, but didn't cut the engine—why lose the air conditioning?—he dropped the handle of the mower and put his hands on his hips.

I powered down the window. "What?"

"What're you doing?"

"Admiring the view," I said.

He grinned. "Gimme ten minutes. I'll meet you upstairs."

"I think I'll just stay here and watch until you're done," I said.

The grin widened. "Or maybe I'll just finish later. When it cools down."

"Maybe you should do that." I rolled up the window and turned the car off. By the time I'd opened the door and swung my legs out, he was standing next to me. A minute later we were inside the house, with the door locked, the lawn mower abandoned on the lawn, and my clothes strewn from the front door all the way up the stairs to the master bedroom. Rafe's jeans and boots were in a tangle at the foot of the bed, and we were in a tangle on top of the covers.

And that's when the doorbell rang.

We both froze.

"Expecting someone?" Rafe asked, his voice a bit breathless.

I shook my head. "Ignore it." I was breathless, too.

And we tried, we really did. But when the doorbell rang again a minute later, Rafe muttered a curse and rolled off me. "Hold that thought."

No problem. "Put something on before you go downstairs."

"I ain't going downstairs."

He stalked over to the window, which happens to be above the front porch, and yanked the sash up. And stuck his head and upper body through the opening. "Hey!"

I tried to suppress a smile, although I didn't try all that hard, since he had his back to me and couldn't see what I was doing. But the sight of him—upper body outside the window, and his naked butt and muscular legs inside the bedroom with me—was funny.

A few moments passed, while—I assume—the person downstairs tried to figure out where the voice had come from, and then backed up off the porch to see him. I heard a voice—male—say something, and then a snarl from Rafe.

The voice said something else. It sounded soothing.

"Grrr," Rafe said, and pulled his head and torso into the room. He slammed the window shut so hard I was afraid it would break, and turned to me. "We gotta go downstairs."

"We?"

"The cops are here." He yanked his jeans on and tucked himself away, wincing, before pulling up the zipper.

Cops? "Tamara Grimaldi?"

He shook his head as he stalked toward the door. "Put some clothes on. He wants you, too."

He disappeared into the hallway.

"Pick up my clothes on your way down!" I called after him as I scrambled out of bed.

Seven

By the time I made it downstairs two minutes later, my scattered clothes were gone from the stairs and the hall floor. I had no idea what Rafe had done with them. Shoved them in the coat closet, maybe?

At the moment, I didn't care. They were out of sight, and that was all that mattered. There were voices coming from the kitchen, so I headed in that direction. And almost walked into the door jamb when I saw Detective Jaime Mendoza sitting across from Rafe at the kitchen table.

Talk about sensory overload.

My mother had been extremely taken with Detective Mendoza the one and only time she saw him. Taken enough to blurt out the suggestion that maybe, since Rafe was gone, Mendoza would like to marry me in his place.

Not only is he exceptionally handsome, but he's well-groomed and well-dressed, too. All characteristics my mother appreciates. A man in an expensive business suit will always appear more suitable to my mother than a man in faded jeans and no shirt. No matter how good the man in the jeans and nothing else looks.

And unlike Rafe, Mendoza doesn't have that between-the-eyes sex-appeal that can knock a girl flat. To my mother, that's not an admirable quality either, although I've always appreciated it. Or at least I've appreciated it since I got over my upbringing and my need to shut him down.

But I digress. There they were, two of the best-looking men I have ever seen, sitting across from one another at my kitchen table. The testosterone was steaming up the windows.

Rafe turned a jaundiced eye in my direction, and I shook it

off. "Here. I brought you a shirt." I had thought he might want something to cover up the cross-stitch of fresh scars across his chest and stomach. The cuts had all healed by now, a month after the abduction, but they were still pink and sort of obvious.

He took the shirt I handed him and prepared to pull it over his head.

"I heard about that," Mendoza said, with a nod toward the damage. "Very impressive, what you did."

Rafe arched a brow, but didn't respond. It had been impressive, though. Most people with the damage he'd taken, who were pinned to a table with a knife through the forearm, would have been content to stay there. Or wouldn't have had the fortitude to even try to escape. The fact that he had, that he'd gone through all that to get back to me, had played a big part in winning my mother over.

Not that she was won, entirely, but at least she had stopped opposing our marriage long enough for us to tie the knot. Although any day now, she'd probably be back to disapproving again.

Mendoza didn't seem bothered that Rafe didn't answer. He just turned to me. "Mrs. Collier."

Grimaldi must have updated him on the fact that the marriage had taken place after all. When he met me, I'd still been Ms. Martin.

"Detective Mendoza," I responded. "Good to see you again. How's the divorce coming?"

He grinned, and showed dimples. "Very well, thank you." He was ridiculously good-looking, and Rafe's eyes narrowed.

"What can we do for you?" I asked, to forestall any comments.

Not that I couldn't guess. Grimaldi must have told him about Aislynn and Kylie's connection to Virgil Wright, and now Mendoza wanted to talk to me.

I walked around to Rafe's side of the table while Mendoza

explained that he'd heard about the anonymous letters, and he wanted some more information. Rafe made to get up so I could sit, but I put my hand on his shoulder and kept him there. "I don't know that there's a lot I can tell you, Detective, other than what Grimaldi already did. Aislynn and Kylie bought the house in January. I was their real estate agent. They called me yesterday and asked me to come over so we could talk about putting the house back on the market. They told me they'd been getting anonymous letters, and they thought, if they sold the house and moved out, the letters would stop."

Mendoza nodded. He had removed a small notepad and pen from the pocket of his very elegant jacket, and was taking notes. "Did they know the previous owners before buying the house?"

"I don't think so," I said. "I was the one who brought the house to their attention. The listing agent was someone in my brokerage. Tim Briggs."

Mendoza wrote it down. Rafe made a little noise. It might have a been a strangled laugh, perhaps at the idea of Tim and Mendoza coming face to face. I had to admit it had appeal. Tim would take one look at Mendoza and fall into instant lust. As unrequited as what he'd always felt for Rafe. I wondered how Mendoza would handle it. Rafe had been amused, but Mendoza's Latin heritage might make him too macho to laugh at something like that.

"Did you talk about the possibility that Mr. Wright might be responsible for the letters?"

We hadn't. "Do you think he was?"

"I'm just exploring the possible connections," Mendoza said mildly.

"He wouldn't have had any reason to. Would he? He and his partner made lots of money when they sold the place. Virgil moved into another house in the same neighborhood. He wasn't suffering. And if he'd accidentally left something in the house, he could have just knocked on the door and explained, and asked for it back. Aislynn and Kylie aren't unreasonable."

Mendoza didn't reply. "I'll be speaking to them next," he said instead. "To see what, if anything, they know."

I nodded. If it had been Grimaldi, I would have asked to come along. But I didn't think Mendoza would agree to let me, nor did I imagine he needed my help. Grimaldi didn't need my help, either, but she was a bit more... let's say abrasive, than Mendoza. And also a bit more inclined to like me. Mendoza was slick and friendly, but thoroughly professional.

"You also spoke to Mr. Kelleher today."

It wasn't a question. I nodded anyway.

"Tell me about that."

I did. There wasn't much to tell, really. I covered it all in less than a minute, and then Rafe muttered something.

Mendoza glanced at him. "Excuse me?"

"He opened the door wearing a towel and nothing else," I said. "Rafe objected."

"So he was there, too?" He eyed my husband.

"Just for a minute," I said. "To make sure I was OK. He was in the neighborhood." Or approximately three neighborhoods away, but who's counting? Same side of town, anyway.

"Impressions?" Mendoza asked him.

Rafe shrugged. "Didn't see him long enough to know if he's the type to send prank letters."

"How about whether he's the type to hire someone to bash his ex over the head with a rock?"

Rafe's brows lifted. Both of them. "Scuse me?"

"I didn't have a chance to tell you," I said apologetically. "I came home and we got... busy."

Mendoza's lips quirked, but he didn't say anything. Rafe just looked at me. "Darlin'..."

"I'm sorry! I tracked down Stacy, and then I tracked down Virgil, and Kenny told me that Virgil was dead, so Tim called him and got the details, and then I called Grimaldi, and she said that Virgil had been killed in Shelby Park two days ago."

I turned back to Mendoza. "He didn't strike me as a murderer. Then again, I've met a few others who didn't, either."

I've met more than my fair share, as a matter of fact, and with very few exceptions, none of them have struck me as being murderers. It almost always comes as a shock to realize who the guilty party is.

Mendoza looked at Rafe. Rafe shrugged. "No way to tell one way or the other. The place wasn't much. If he thought he got the short end of the deal, he mighta wanted to do something about it."

Mendoza nodded. "Anything else you can tell me?"

Rafe and I glanced at each other. "I think that's everything," I said. Rafe nodded.

Mendoza pushed back from the table. "Then I'll leave you alone. To get back to what you were doing."

I blushed, of course. Rafe just looked at me and sighed. "I'll walk you out," he told Mendoza, and the two of them headed out of the kitchen and down the hallway. "So how long have you been working with Tammy?" I heard him ask, but by the time Mendoza answered, they were too far away for me to hear the answer. Then there was the sound of the door, and Rafe's footsteps coming back, his bare feet almost silent against the wood floors.

"You're terrible," I told him when he came through the door.

"Why's that?"

"You know Grimaldi doesn't like it when you call her Tammy. Now you've probably got him doing it, too."

Rafe shrugged. "How come you never mentioned the guy before?"

"Why would I?"

"It sounded like you'd met him." He imitated my voice, high-pitched and squeaky, with an exaggeratedly refined accent, "'Nice to see you again, Detective.'"

"Good grief," I said, "if I didn't know better, I'd think you were jealous."

Rafe didn't say anything to that, just arched a brow at me.

"Oh, for goodness sake! The day you and I were supposed to get married, my mother and Dix and Catherine," my sister, "drove up from Sweetwater for the ceremony. When you didn't show up, we couldn't just send them on their way again. So we went to the Germantown Café for lunch."

"We?" Rafe said.

"Mother, Dix, Catherine, Grimaldi, and I. We invited Wendell, too, but he wanted to start looking for you."

Rafe nodded.

"And Detective Mendoza was there having lunch with his divorce attorney. Who happened to be Diana Morton, of Ferncliff and Morton, where Bradley used to work."

Rafe's lip curled when I mentioned Bradley.

"He stopped by the table to say hello to Grimaldi on his way out. And was introduced to the rest of us."

"I bet your mother liked him," Rafe said.

I smiled. "You'd win that bet." And if I kept it at that, maybe I wouldn't have to tell him that Mother had suggested Mendoza marry me in Rafe's absence.

"Prob'ly wished you were marrying him and not me."

He'd win that bet, too, but I didn't say so. "She was upset," I said instead, tolerantly. "She thought you'd run off rather than marry me. I knew you hadn't," except in a few very low moments I should just not mention, "but there was no telling her that."

"She didn't have to offer you to him like a piece of pie on a plate," Rafe grumbled.

I sighed. "Who told you about it? My brother?"

"Tammy," Rafe said, and made an effort to mimic her voice, too. It was less high-pitched and breathy than mine. "'It's a good thing you got back when you did. Her mother was trying to marry her off to someone else before lunch was over.'"

Great. "He wasn't interested," I said. "I wasn't, either."

"I know." He grinned. "It's the only reason I let him walk outta here."

"That's ridiculous. Why would I want him when I have you?"

"'Cause your mama liked him," Rafe said.

"My mother doesn't decide who I marry. And anyway, Mother has come to appreciate you."

He arched a brow. It's a very expressive brow, just so you know. He can say a lot with that little gesture.

"All right," I admitted, "so maybe 'appreciate' is too strong a word. But she let us get married. At the mansion. In front of all of Sweetwater. She even paid for it all."

Rafe grunted.

"This is silly," I said. "I love you. You're my husband. I'm having your baby. And I don't know the man. I met him once, for less than five minutes. You have no reason to worry. Besides, he isn't really my type."

"Yeah?" He leaned his posterior against the kitchen counter and folded his arms across his chest. I was reminded of a late night close to a year ago, when we'd stood opposite one another in this same kitchen, having a similar conversation. He was even wearing the same T-shirt: pale blue with a Corona logo. I had picked it out of the drawer earlier because it's one of my favorites. Lots of good memories attached to that shirt. "How's that?"

"He's too clean-cut. A little boring."

He arched a brow.

"That's probably what my mother liked about him," I added. "He'd be a compromise of sorts. Handsome and a bit exotic— kind of like you—but tame. Wearing a suit and tie. What she'd consider safe."

"I ain't safe?"

"Not to my mother. I don't think she trusts you."

"What about you?"

"I trust you implicitly," I said. "I knew you were coming back. And since you don't have any reason not to trust me, can we dispense with the conversation and go back to doing what we were doing when Detective Mendoza showed up?"

His lips quirked. "Want me to go outside and push the lawnmower around to get you in the mood again?"

I shook my head. "Not necessary." I was already in the mood. Still in the mood. Always in the mood. "Pregnancy hormones," I added.

The grin widened. "Whatever you gotta tell yourself."

"It *is* pregnancy hormones." And maybe just a little bit the fact that after seven months together, the last few weeks as husband and wife, I still couldn't get enough of him. Not to mention the blue T-shirt and the memories it evoked. But some of it was pregnancy hormones, too.

"Sure it is." But he didn't seem to care. And why should he? "C'mon." He reached for me. "Let's go back upstairs."

"Or we could just stay here."

"Works for me," Rafe said, and boosted me up on the edge of the table.

"Now that we got that outta the way," he said an hour later, after we had migrated upstairs and were on the bed, recuperating, "tell me about the dead guy."

I turned on my side to face him. "Not much to tell. Not beyond what you already heard downstairs. He was out jogging a couple of nights ago, when someone hit him over the head and killed him. On a path in Shelby Park."

"And he's the guy who used to own the house your friends are living in now?"

I nodded. "Virgil Wright. He and Stacy owned it. When they put it on the market, Aislynn and Kylie bought it. Stacy told me they sold it because Virgil had found someone else and wanted to move in with him, and Stacy couldn't afford to keep the house on his own. He tends bar for a living. I guess he doesn't make enough to support a house in that part of town."

"Not if the place he's living now is any indication," Rafe said.

"Not very nice, was it?"

"I've lived in worse. But it ain't a renovated Victorian in East End."

No, it wasn't. Not even close.

"You think he did it?" my husband added.

"Sent the letters? Why would he? Even if Aislynn and Kylie moved, it isn't like he'd get the house back. He still wouldn't be able to afford it."

"Killed his ex," Rafe said.

"Oh." I thought about it. "He might have, I suppose. Although that's a long time to wait. They broke up six months ago. Maybe longer. Why would he wait until now to kill him?"

"So's nobody would think he did it?" Rafe suggested.

"Maybe. Although I don't think Mendoza is stupid. Grimaldi said he wasn't. He'll probably investigate Stacy."

Rafe nodded. "And the new boyfriend. And your friends."

Most likely. Not that Aislynn and Kylie had any reason to want Virgil dead. Unless they thought he was the one sending the letters. Or they blamed him for selling them a house that came with a stalker.

"I don't think they would have involved me if they'd just committed murder the night before, do you? That would just draw attention to them."

Rafe shrugged. Not easy to do while lying down, but he managed. Muscles moved. Lots of them.

I smiled appreciatively.

He smiled back. "Ready for another round?"

Tempting though it was, I shook my head. "I think I need something to eat first. It's been a long time since lunch. And all I had were field greens."

"That ain't no way to feed my baby," Rafe said and put his hand on my stomach. "He wants a burger. Don't you, big guy?"

"Big guy?" I said.

We'd had an ultrasound a few days before the wedding, so less than a month ago, but it had been too early to determine the gender of the baby.

"Might be a she," Rafe said. "Though the way she's eating, looks more like a boy."

I didn't know whether it worked that way with unborn babies. I thought it probably didn't. They're all in there developing themselves, so they probably need the same amount of nutrients. When they come out, it's different, but as long as they're inside, I figure it's probably the same.

"Do you care?" I asked.

Rafe shook his head. "Long as it's healthy, it don't matter to me."

Me, either. Although raising a girl sounded like it might be easier than raising a boy. I've been a girl. Girls like dolls and dresses and hair bows and things like that. Things I understand. Boys like frogs and cars and dirt. All things I've taken care to avoid.

"I like frogs and cars and dirt," Rafe told me when I said so. "I don't mind another boy. I missed everything the first time."

Rafe has a twelve-year-old son named David. We only found out about him last November, when his biological mother was killed and my brother Dix, her executor, read her will. Rafe and David have developed a relationship since, even if it's just as much brotherly as parental. David already has a father who loves him, who has considered him his own since he adopted him at birth, and a mother to go with the father. Virginia and Sam Flannery are great, and we couldn't have asked for better parents for David. But yes, there was no denying that Rafe had missed out on pretty much every aspect of his son's childhood.

"I guess another boy would be all right."

He moved his hand in soothing circles on my stomach. "Do you want to find out? Or wait?"

"Knowing makes the decorating easier," I said, and watched his lips quirk.

"True."

"People will know what color blankets to buy."

"God forbid our baby boy has to deal with a pink blanket," Rafe nodded, his voice solemn, but his eyes alight.

I rolled mine. "There's no need for him to have a pink blanket if we know. Don't you want to know?"

"I don't care," Rafe said, and stopped breathing.

"What?" I asked after a few seconds, when he hadn't said anything more.

"He moved."

He—or she—did move occasionally. I felt it as little butterfly flutters in my stomach, like the baby was doing cartwheels inside. I hadn't realized it was possible to feel them on the outside, though. But if he thought he'd felt something, I wasn't going to dissuade him. Especially as he seemed so thrilled about it.

He looked at me with shining eyes. "He's really in there."

"Was there any doubt?" I'd been throwing up for months, so there had been no question in my mind.

"I guess it didn't feel all the way real," Rafe confessed, with a glance down at my stomach. "I could see you were getting bigger—"

I grimaced.

"—but until right now, I guess part of me didn't process there was a baby in there."

"There's definitely a baby in there," I said.

"Our baby."

I nodded. He scooted down and put his mouth against my belly, just east of the navel. "Hi, baby," he cooed. "I'm your daddy. How ya doing in there?"

Any woman would have melted. I ran my hand over the top and back of his head, feeling the short bristles of hair scratching against my fingers, and sniffed back tears.

He looked up at me and grinned.

"Just feeling lucky," I said.

"You could get lucky again." He lowered his mouth, and this time kissed my stomach. With intent.

There was no question in my mind that I could get lucky again. However— "Food. Remember?"

"Five minutes," Rafe said, moving south. "I'll do all the work."

"Just make it quick, please. I'm starving."

"Gimme a minute," Rafe said, "and I'll make your forget that you're starving." He proceeded to do just that.

An hour later we were sitting at a table at the FinBar, a block down the street from the real estate office, finishing up our burgers and fries. I was indulging in a milkshake—dairy is good for the baby—while Rafe was having a beer. And then the door opened, and who should walk in but Kenny Grimes and a friend.

I shrank in my seat. The last thing I needed was for him to yell at me again. Or worse, accuse me of stalking him.

Of course, if he yelled at me in front of Rafe, it was likely to be the last thing he ever did, but that didn't mean I wanted it to happen.

Luckily, he either didn't notice me sitting there, or he just didn't recognize me. Maybe he was too preoccupied with... let me be generous and call him a friend. A very solicitous friend, making sure Kenny was comfortable in the booth across the aisle from us.

Rafe—more observant than Kenny Grimes—noticed my wide-eyed look of panic, and arched a brow.

"Kenny Grimes," I mouthed.

"Who?"

"Kenny Grimes! Virgil's new boyfriend."

Across the aisle, the friend finished fussing over Kenny and slid into the booth opposite. Rafe glanced in their direction and turned back to me. "The black guy? Or the other one?"

"The redhead is Kenny," I said. "I don't know who his friend is."

Rafe nodded. "Looks rough."

Kenny? Or the other guy? I glanced over, and decided it could apply to both of them. Kenny looked rough in the worn-out sense, as he had earlier in the day. Bloodshot eyes, pale skin, drawn features. And his friend looked rough in the way Rafe does, like you wouldn't want to tangle with him in a dark alley. Big, black, with a shaved head and lots of muscles. And a surprisingly light and fluty voice. I couldn't hear the words, but I heard the tone, and it was soothing.

Probably trying to make Kenny feel better about the death of his lover. As if it's really possible to make someone feel better about something like that.

"So you're getting together with your friends tomorrow morning," Rafe said.

I nodded. Across the aisle, the black guy reached across the table to pat Kenny's hand. "To talk about what I've discovered so far."

Kenny allowed it for a second, but then he put both hands in his lap. His companion looked unhappy.

"Whaddaya think's gonna happen?" Rafe asked.

"I'm not sure," I confessed, turning my attention back to my own man instead of the ones across the aisle. "I haven't discovered much. I mean, I've learned a lot, but not much to do with the letters they're getting. I'm no closer to figuring out who's been sending them."

Rafe nodded.

"Kylie pointed the finger at Aislynn's parents, because they weren't happy when Aislynn 'turned gay.' But they live in Kentucky, and the letters were mailed here in Nashville, so unless they come to town regularly, it probably isn't them."

Rafe nodded.

"They're just in Bowling Green, though, so it's only an hour's drive. It could be them."

Rafe nodded.

"And Aislynn pointed the finger at Kylie's old girlfriend. She and Kylie were having lunch together today. Kylie and Lauren, I mean. At least I assume it was Lauren. Kylie was very careful not to introduce me."

Rafe nodded.

"I have no idea where Lauren lives. But she works in downtown, so it would be easy for her to drive across the river to East Nashville to post a letter every week or two. And for all I know, she lives in this neighborhood, too."

Rafe nodded.

"It might be her. If she's upset about losing Kylie and thinks if she scares Aislynn away, Kylie might come back to her. Or it could be Kylie herself, if she's tired of Aislynn but doesn't want to come right out and dump her. She doesn't seem all that disturbed by the letters. Aislynn is the one who's scared."

Rafe nodded.

"It could just be a malicious prank. Some people are weird that way. Kids playing around, or something. Or it could be something more serious. Some people are just plain weird."

"Tell me about it," Rafe said.

I might as well. "Take Elspeth, for example. You slept with her once, thirteen years ago, in high school. And she was completely obsessed with you until the moment she died. While you probably hadn't given her a thought since you zipped up your pants and staggered away."

His lips quirked. "Dunno if I'd put it like that, darlin'."

"Did you?"

He shrugged. "I told you she kept sending me letters in prison. Wasn't like I could really forget about her while she was doing that."

I guess not. "Just out of curiosity, did you ever think about me?"

His lips curved. "You didn't send me letters, darlin'."

No, I didn't. I hadn't slept with him in high school, either. Nor for that matter thought about him during the twelve years between his graduation and the morning he showed up in my life again, last August. But he had mentioned once that he'd liked me back then—from afar, since he knew that Dix and his friends would gang up on him if he looked at me wrong—so it was possible he might have spared me a thought now and then. Not that I could really blame him if he hadn't. But I was still curious.

He shrugged. "I mighta thought about you once in a while. Not much else to think about in prison."

Given some of the things that I hear go on in prison, the less said about that, the better.

"At any rate," I said, "people get weird and obsessive sometimes. If someone has developed an obsession with Aislynn—or for that matter with Kylie—"

"Or with the house," Rafe said.

I nodded. "There's no way we'd know about it if someone did. The letters come through the mail. There's no way to know who's sending them. So everyone's a suspect."

Rafe nodded. "What are you gonna tell 'em tomorrow?"

"I guess the truth. That I have no idea what's going on, and I don't think there's any way I can figure out who's behind it. If it was easy, they'd already know. You know?"

He nodded.

"Although..." I lowered my voice, with a glance across the aisle, "the fact that Virgil's dead is suspicious. Don't you think? Detective Mendoza must think so, or he wouldn't want to talk to

Aislynn and Kylie."

"I imagine so," Rafe said.

"Although that's just more reason for Aislynn and Kylie to sell and get the hell—excuse me, heck—out of the house. If someone's running around murdering people."

Rafe nodded. "Might be the safest for them. Or at least to take a trip somewhere for a week or two. Give the cops time to figure out whodunit and get the guy off the street."

"I'll be sure to mention that," I said. "A trip somewhere would probably be good for them, anyway. To reconnect."

"Just as long as they don't run into the kind of trouble we had on our honeymoon," Rafe said and slid out of the booth.

Eight

I followed suit. And no sooner had my feet hit the floor in the aisle between the tables, than Kenny looked up and over. His pale face flushed. "Are you following me?"

"Don't be ridiculous," I said.

"You were at my house. And then you called me. And now you're here."

His voice was getting louder and louder, not to mention more hysterical. Rafe turned around, brows lowered, but before he could do anything, the big, black guy had slid out of the booth and put himself between me and Kenny. "Is this lady bothering you?"

Up close, his voice was soft and lispy, and he looked ready to take me on to defend his friend's honor.

I rolled my eyes. "Nobody's following anyone."

"You're here," Kenny insisted. "You were at my house this afternoon. And you called me!"

"That doesn't mean I'm following you," I told him. "I live in the neighborhood, too. And we were here first!"

The plural made them both look at Rafe. I saw two throats move in unison as they swallowed. Even the big, black guy looked intimidated.

Rafe arched a brow. "Problem?"

Neither of them spoke. Maybe what they'd swallowed were their tongues. My husband has that effect on some people.

"No," I said. "Just a misunderstanding."

He nodded. "Coming?"

I nodded. It wasn't like Kenny would tell me anything. Not here and now. Maybe not ever. So I told them both to enjoy their meal, and followed Rafe out the door.

"So what do you think?" I asked when I was strapped in and we were on our way back home. Back in the old days—before my stomach took on the size and proportions of a basketball—I rode on the back of the Harley sometimes, but those days were over. My arms wouldn't be able to reach around my stomach and around Rafe's waist to hold on these days.

He glanced at me, in the process of navigating the traffic lights on Main Street. "About?"

"Them." I tilted my head to indicate the FinBar, and Kenny and his friend.

He shrugged. "Looked pretty normal to me, for a guy who's just lost his lover."

To me, too. Listless and despondent and close to tears. "What about the other one?"

"Looked like he was trying to make his move while he pretended to be supportive," Rafe said.

I nodded. "To me, too."

We drove in silence for a minute. It had gotten dark by now, and the lighted skyline of downtown was dead ahead. Until Rafe turned the corner of Fifth and Main, where my old apartment building was. The lighted windows of the downtown buildings reflected in the glass.

"Do you think he might have killed Virgil?"

Rafe quirked a brow. "You saying that because he's black?"

"No," I said, insulted. "I'm saying it because he was trying to make a move on a guy who lost his lover to violence two days ago. Don't you think that's a little suspicious?"

He shrugged. "Some people ain't got no manners."

No, they don't. At my colleague Brenda Puckett's funeral last year, the woman from across the street was already hanging on Stephen Puckett's arm, acting like the lady of the house.

"He had motive, though. He might have wanted Virgil gone, to clear his own way to Kenny."

"He might could," Rafe agreed, making a right turn onto

Dresden.

"Although I don't see what any of that has to do with Kylie and Aislynn's letters."

Rafe shook his head.

"What am I going to tell them tomorrow morning?"

"The truth," Rafe said as he signaled to turn the car onto Potsdam Street, in front of the Milton House assisted living facility, where Mrs. Jenkins had been living last fall, after Brenda cheated her out of her house. "There ain't no way to know who's sending the letters. If it was easy, they'd already know. But if they'll get outta the way for a few days, you'll keep looking."

"I suppose I could tell them that." And hope they'd see the sense in it.

"You can only do what you can do," Rafe said. "And if they wanna sell the house again, you make money."

I would. Assuming I could find someone to sell it to, and I guessed I probably could. Renovated Victorians on the historic register don't come along all that often. Even if this one had the slight stigma of having a stalker.

"I'd have to disclose the letters. Not sure anyone would want to buy it after that." I'm not sure I would. It was a nice house, but who needs the hassle? "And with Virgil gone, I'll never know whether he and Stacy were getting letters, too, before they left. And whether those letters had anything to do with what happened."

"Didn't you ask Stacy?"

I nodded. "He said they didn't. But with Virgil dead, who's around to contradict him?"

"You could ask Kenny." Rafe turned on the signal and aimed the car onto the driveway.

"I doubt he'll talk to me," I said, as we crunched over the gravel up to the front door. "You heard him. He accused me of stalking him."

Rafe didn't answer, just quirked a brow in my direction.

"You're right," I said. "That might mean he's been getting anonymous letters. Either that or it's a guilty conscience."

Rafe nodded and cut the engine. I opened my door and got out onto the gravel. "Maybe he killed Virgil," I said across the roof of the car. "Maybe he'd rather be with the black guy."

"You know what they say about black men," Rafe agreed, as he slammed his own door and headed around the car. I couldn't see him clearly in the dark—we'd forgotten to turn on the porch light before we left—but I could hear from his tone of voice that he was amused. What they say about black men—that they're well-endowed—is a standing joke between us.

I waved it aside. "Yeah, yeah. You're all that and a bag of chips. Moving on—"

But I didn't get to move on, because as soon as he got close enough, he grabbed me around the middle and swung me around so my butt was against the car and my front was against him. The baby poked against his stomach, but it didn't slow him down. "You weren't so dismissive earlier," he told me, as he leaned in to nuzzle the side of my neck.

I hadn't been, no. I wasn't feeling dismissive now, either. My knees turned weak and I hung on to his shoulders as I tilted my head to the side to give him better access. And that's when I saw the figure sitting on the porch swing.

Rafe felt my jolt of surprise, and in less than a second had gone from amorous husband to protective TBI agent. "Who's there?"

The figure moved. I watched from behind Rafe as it—she—stood up from the porch swing and moved to the stairs. It was only when she stepped down, out of the shadow under the porch roof, that I recognized her. Black clothes, pale face framed by long, black hair, quivering lips.

"She's gone," Aislynn whimpered. "Kylie's gone."

Five minutes later we were sitting around the kitchen table, where Rafe, Detective Mendoza, and I had sat a few hours ago.

Unlike Mendoza, Aislynn was a quivering mess. Her Goth-girl makeup had run, giving her the look of a raccoon, and her eyes and nose were red and puffy. The box of tissues I had provided took care of the former, but not the latter. After wiping away the black smears, she sat there clutching a soggy tissue, alternately dabbing at her eyes and her nose. Both were running.

"Tell us what happened," Rafe said.

Aislynn took a shaky breath. "The cop came."

"Detective Mendoza?"

She nodded. "He asked us questions about the letters. When they started coming. Who we thought might be sending them."

"Did you tell him about Lauren?"

She avoided my eyes. "He was from the police. I didn't think it was a good idea not to say something."

"You did the right thing," I told her. "What did he say?"

Aislynn clutched her tissue so hard I was surprised water wasn't dripping on the table. "He asked Kylie about her. About Lauren. Where she lived. What their relationship was. Whether Kylie thought there was any chance that Lauren was sending the letters."

"What did Kylie say?"

"She said no," Aislynn said miserably. "And after he left, she yelled at me. She said Lauren would never do something like that. That I was jealous."

And that might be the case. Aislynn herself had told me so when she brought up Lauren's name earlier.

"Did he ask about the last time Kylie had seen Lauren?" I asked.

"They work together," Aislynn answered. "They see each other all the time."

"I meant outside of work."

"He asked," Aislynn said. "Kylie told him she hadn't had anything to do with Lauren since they broke up last summer."

That might also be true. Then again, it might not. I had no proof one way or the other that the woman Kylie had had lunch with today was Lauren. It might have been someone else.

Or Kylie could be lying.

Or maybe she just didn't consider lunch during the workday 'outside of work.'

"Then what happened?" Rafe wanted to know.

Aislynn turned to him. "He left. The cop. And Kylie yelled at me. She said I shouldn't have said anything about Lauren. That I was jealous. And then she tried to call Lauren—to warn her about the cop, I guess—but Lauren didn't answer. So Kylie got in the car and left."

"To go find her?"

"I assume," Aislynn said. "She didn't tell me what she was doing." She sniffed and dabbed her nose with the tissue.

"How long ago was that?"

It couldn't have been too long. Mendoza had left here around six, and it was just after nine now. Certainly not long enough to put out an APB on her.

Aislynn shrugged. "A couple hours?"

"Have you tried calling her?"

Aislynn nodded. "She isn't picking up."

"Prob'ly still angry," Rafe muttered. Aislynn flinched.

"You did what you had to do," I told her, with a quelling glance at Rafe. "It's always a good idea to be honest with the police. And it's only been a few hours. I'm sure she'll show up."

Aislynn looked unconvinced.

"Did Mendoza tell you about the murder?"

Aislynn nodded. "Something about the guy who owned the house before us being dead. The cop asked us if we knew him."

"And did you?"

She shook her head. "I don't think so."

"Did Kylie?"

Aislynn blinked. "She said she didn't."

Then it was probably true. She hadn't said anything about recognizing Virgil's or Stacy's names back in December, when we'd been filling out the paperwork for the house. I couldn't remember the buyers and sellers ever coming face to face—we'd closed at different times, in different places, so we hadn't been sitting around the closing table together—but Kylie had certainly known their names. And there was no way to know whether she and Aislynn hadn't taken a drive past the house at some point before it was theirs, and had run into Virgil and/or Stacy then. They might have met before.

"Did Kylie ever say anything about suspecting anyone of writing the letters?"

"She pointed the finger at my parents," Aislynn said, her voice stronger now with indignation. "My parents would never do that! They love me!"

"Kylie said they weren't happy when you became involved with her."

Aislynn admitted they hadn't been. "But they wouldn't do something like this! Besides, they live in Kentucky. The letters were mailed here."

"Bowling Green's only an hour away," I pointed out. "It isn't a long drive."

She scowled. "I know exactly how long it is. My parents haven't been in Nashville since May. We had dinner together before they went to a show. And they wouldn't come to Nashville without seeing me."

Maybe not. Although my family had been known to make the drive to Nashville—about the same distance as the drive from Bowling Green—without taking the trouble to see me.

Of course, if someone had suggested the idea that any of them were behind a series of creepy anonymous letters, my reaction would have been the same as Aislynn's. I would have refused to believe it.

I abandoned the subject for the time being. "Just out of

curiosity, where does Lauren live?"

"Something Park," Aislynn said vaguely. "I think it started with an S."

"Sylvan Park? Sevier Park? Shelby Park?"

"Maybe Shelby Park?"

"Shelby Park is right down the street from you," I said. Right in the middle of the East Nashville neighborhood. Close to the post office. And it was where Virgil had been killed. "Are you sure?"

But Aislynn wasn't. "It could have been Sylvan Park. Or... what was the other thing you said?"

I told her, and she shook her head. "I don't know. Maybe I was wrong. It might not have been an S."

In that case the field was wide open. Charlotte Park, Richland Park, Centennial Park. Neighborhoods with the word 'park' in them all over town.

"How did you get here," Rafe asked, since we hadn't noticed a vehicle in the driveway.

"Walked," Aislynn said.

There was a beat, while we both considered Aislynn traipsing through the Potsdam neighborhood, on her own, in the dark. I've gotten to feel pretty comfortable here, especially with Rafe at home—the neighbors all know him, and nobody's going to risk incurring his wrath by bothering me—but I wouldn't have chosen to walk around at night. Chances are nothing would have happened if I did, but why take chances?

"I'll drive you home," Rafe said.

Aislynn glanced at me.

"Maybe she should just stay here," I suggested, trying to interpret Aislynn's expression. She either didn't want to go home with Rafe, or she didn't want to go home at all. Maybe she was afraid Kylie would yell at her again. "I have to go over there in the morning anyway. She may as well spend the night and ride back with me then."

"Whatever you want," Rafe said and got to his feet. "Scuse me. I'm gonna make a phone call."

He reached for his phone as he headed out of the room. Aislynn watched him go, and then turned back to me.

"Anything you didn't want to say in front of him?" I asked. "If so, now's the time to tell me."

She glanced at the opening to the hallway. We could hear the murmur of Rafe's voice from the front of the house, and then the sound of the front door opening and closing. "Is he going somewhere?"

"Probably not," I said. "More likely he wants some privacy for his phone call."

"Who is he calling?"

I told her I had no idea. "Not Kylie. He doesn't have her number."

He was probably calling Detective Mendoza, to tell him what had happened. Good relations between law enforcement agencies, and all that. Or maybe he was calling Detective Grimaldi, so she could notify Mendoza. Or maybe it had nothing to do with Aislynn or Kylie at all. Maybe he was calling a friend.

"Come on," I told Aislynn. "Let's go upstairs and get you situated. Unless you'd like to go home? I'd be happy to take you. It doesn't have to be Rafe."

Not that he was likely to let me drive off on my own at this time of night. If I insisted on going—if Aislynn wanted to go—it was more likely to be both of us driving her home.

But Aislynn shook her head. "I don't want to go home and have Kylie not be there."

"Kylie might be there," I said, leading her out of the kitchen and down the hallway to the stairs. "She might have gotten home by now."

"What if she hasn't?"

Well, then she hadn't. "Are you afraid of being alone?"

"Can you blame me?" Aislynn wanted to know, as we started

up the stairs. Through the window, I saw Rafe's silhouette outlined against the darkness of the yard, phone to his ear. "Those letters were creepy. You said so yourself. And if Kylie isn't there, I'll be alone in the house!"

I hadn't thought about that. I had figured it more for a game of tit for tat. "What if she comes home and you aren't there? Won't she be worried?"

"I left a note," Aislynn said. "And I have my phone. If she calls, I'll answer. That's more than she's doing."

"Maybe I should try to get in touch with her."

Aislynn shrugged and looked around the landing. "Where's my room?"

I led her to the door of what had been Marquita Johnson's room back when Rafe's grandmother lived here and had a live-in companion. More recently, my brother had stayed there on the occasion of what should have been my wedding day, when Rafe hadn't shown up for the nuptials and I needed moral support through the night.

I knew all about missing lovers. The difference was that by bedtime, Rafe had been gone twenty-four hours, and we had every reason to believe something bad had happened to him. Kylie might be back home. We had no reason at all to think anything bad had happened to her. Or at least I didn't have reason. Aislynn might.

"Oh, no," she said when I asked. "I was just afraid she'd spend the night with Lauren and I'd be alone in the house."

"So you're not worried that anything has happened to her?"

She looked surprised. "Oh, no. What would happen to Kylie?"

Any number of things, I imagined. Including what Aislynn was afraid might happen to her, if she spent the night alone in the house she shared with Kylie.

Or maybe she was just afraid of being alone.

She didn't have to worry about that here. We'd be right

across the hall. All night long. And Rafe is a light sleeper. If she stirred, he'd know.

I got her set up in Marquita's room, with clean sheets and towels, and a new toothbrush so she could brush her teeth. Before she went to bed, I made her call Kylie again, but there was no answer. Then I tried calling Kylie too, from my phone, and got no answer, either. When Rafe came upstairs, I made him call Kylie, just in case she wasn't taking calls from anyone she knew. She might have reasoned that Aislynn had contacted me, and that I was calling to find out what was going on. But if Rafe called—from a number she didn't recognize—I thought she might answer.

She didn't.

"You don't think anything's happened to her," I asked Rafe softly when we were snuggled up in bed together, "do you?"

He hesitated. "Dunno."

"Do you think something might have?" I kept my voice soft so Aislynn wouldn't be able to hear me. She was on the other side of the landing, so it wasn't likely she would, but better safe than sorry.

"Dunno. It might could."

It might.

Something about this whole situation felt weird to me. Maybe it was just that Aislynn's fear of being home alone had transferred itself to me, or maybe it was something else. I snuggled a bit closer, and felt his arm tighten around me. Maybe he was feeling the weirdness, too. "Who did you call?"

"Mendoza," Rafe said.

"At this time of night?"

"He's a cop. He don't mind." And a glance at the clock showed me that it wasn't actually that late. It had just been a long day with a lot of revelations.

"What did you tell him?"

"What she told us," Rafe said, meaning Aislynn. "He said

he'd have a car drive by and check if she's home. I woulda done it myself, but I didn't wanna leave the two of you alone here while I went out."

"I appreciate that. Has he gotten back to you?"

"Not yet," Rafe said. He was starting to sound drowsy. "And I don't know that he's gonna. But I figure he oughta know what happened."

"That was nice of you."

"Professional courtesy," Rafe muttered. "He'd a done the same for me."

Good to know. "I love you. Go to sleep."

The only answer was a soft snore. I snuggled in and went to sleep, too.

Nine

If Aislynn stirred during the night, I didn't hear her. If Rafe stirred, I didn't hear him, either. When I woke up, he was still wrapped around me, with a hand splayed on my stomach. He likes to sleep spoon-fashion, with his nose buried in my hair. It's nice.

And like most men, he wakes up ready to go. That's nice, too, especially when—like now—my hormones were pinging off the wall from the baby.

After a refreshing little interlude, it was finally time to talk. "Did anything happen overnight?"

He shook his head.

"She didn't move? Mendoza didn't call?"

"Nobody did nothing," Rafe said, stretching. I watched as muscles bunched and relaxed under his skin. In case you were in doubt, he's extremely nice to look at.

"That's good, right?"

"Means your friend's body didn't turn up at the morgue."

I shuddered. "That's definitely good."

"She's prob'ly home," Rafe said, relaxing back down beside me again. "Either worried about her girlfriend, or wishing she wouldn't have been stupid last night."

"You think she was stupid last night?"

"Some people are," Rafe said. "I don't know her."

"I guess I should get ready and go over there." I glanced at the clock. Just before eight. "I need a shower first."

"I'm gonna put in a couple hours in the gym," Rafe said. "Some of the boys'll prob'ly be there. I can usually count on'em giving me a workout." He grinned.

Since the boys—the young TBI recruits he was training—

were on average ten years younger than he was, and determined to beat him, I imagined he could.

"You can get in the shower first." I was never really ready to get out of bed these days. It takes a lot out of a woman, growing a baby.

"Don't mind if I do. I'll be quick." He rolled out of bed and padded toward the door to the bathroom. I watched until he was gone—I always watch—and then I closed my eyes again.

Fifteen minutes later, he was shaking me. "Darlin'. Time to wake up. You're gonna be late."

"Shit. I mean... shoot." I kicked like an overturned beetle for a moment before I got myself turned sideways and over to the edge of the bed. "Help me up."

Rafe chuckled, but he extended a hand and hauled me to my feet. And then he pulled me into his body and held me for a second. He was still damp from his own shower, with a wet towel riding low on his hips, and I was in a hurry, but as usual I put everything else aside and just enjoyed being close to him.

Until he let me go and swatted my butt. "Go on. I left you a little hot water."

"You better have." I scurried for the bathroom. The last thing I saw before I closed the door—and it gave me a moment's pause—was that he dropped the towel.

By the time I got out of the shower, he'd dressed and gone downstairs. I could hear him moving around in the kitchen, and smell coffee. And Aislynn must be down there with him—either that, or he was on the phone again—because I could hear his voice.

I did a quick blow-dry on the hair and threw on some clothes before heading downstairs. By now, it was already almost nine, but I figured with Aislynn here, and with Kylie not answering her phone, it wasn't the end of the world if I didn't make the nine o'clock appointment time.

And Aislynn was here, sitting across the table from Rafe drinking coffee. When I looked surprised—I hadn't realized caffeine was an approved poison—she told me, "I only drink coffee once in a while."

"It doesn't matter to me," I said, although I'd kill for some coffee. I'd been off it for five months because of the baby, and it was hard to get up in the mornings. I poured myself a glass of milk from the fridge instead, and sat down with them. "Any word from Kylie?"

Aislynn shook her head. "She's still not answering her phone."

"She might be asleep."

Aislynn shrugged.

"Has this ever happened before? That she doesn't answer her phone when you call?"

"When we've had an argument," Aislynn said. Which wasn't cool, as far as I was concerned. You don't punish your lover—or your boyfriend/girlfriend or spouse—for an argument by not picking up your phone. What if something was wrong?

If Rafe tried to pull a stunt like that, he wouldn't like what I had to say about it afterwards.

I glanced at him, wondering whether I should say so. He met my eyes, and I kept my mouth shut. There was no need to say anything. He knew, and was beaming the message back to me that I'd better not try to pull anything like that, either.

As if I would.

"We should get going," I said, finishing my milk. Aislynn got to her feet, obediently, and went to gather her belongings.

"Virgil's visitation starts at eleven," I told Rafe while I waited. "I thought I might go."

He nodded.

"You're welcome to come along if you want."

"No offense, darlin', but I think I'll pass. I ain't that big on funerals."

I wasn't, either, but I thought there was a chance that something interesting might happen at this one. If nothing else, a showdown between Kenny and Stacy over the casket. Perhaps an arrest, since the murderer often attends the victim's funeral. Aside from which, someone ought to represent LB&A at the proceedings. Granted, it was more Tim's place than mine, as broker and as Virgil and Stacy's former agent, but if I left it to him, I'd miss out on whatever happened.

"I'll probably be home around one or two. Then we can decide what we want to do with the rest of the day."

"I vote we go to bed early," Rafe said, as Aislynn's footsteps sounded on the stairs.

"Didn't you sleep well?"

"I slept fine. There are other things we can do in bed than sleep." He grinned.

I grinned back. "Of course there is." And by then, after attending a funeral, I'd probably need some of those other things.

Aislynn clomped into the kitchen in her army boots, and I told Rafe, "I'll stay in touch."

He nodded. "Let me know if you need anything. If not, I'll see you this afternoon."

I told him he would, gave him a quick peck—since Aislynn was watching; otherwise I would have made it a proper kiss—and headed out.

The drive was quick and painless. There wasn't a lot of traffic early on a Saturday morning. Ten minutes after we left Potsdam Street, we pulled up in front of Aislynn and Kylie's house.

Kylie's blue Volvo was parked in the driveway. "Looks like she got home safe," I told Aislynn, and steered my own blue Volvo over to the curb.

She nodded, and didn't even wait for me to cut the engine before she opened her door. I got out and dropped the key in my purse while Aislynn scurried into the yard, past the car, and up to the front door, digging for her key. While she got it out and into the lock, I made my own way to the Volvo and put a hand on the hood. It was cool. Whenever Kylie had come home, it wasn't in the last few minutes.

The door opened and Aislynn disappeared inside. I headed for the front door, and was halfway there when I heard her scream.

I covered the rest of the distance at warp speed, especially considering the shoes I was wearing. I had given up on really high heels when my center of gravity changed—it was hard enough to balance the basketball on my stomach without tipping forward while I was barefoot—but Mother would never forgive me if I wore flats for anything but exercise. So I had compromised on a couple of pairs of wedges for this summer. Not much heel to speak of, but an extra inch in height from the sole, and sexy straps across the instep and ankle.

Anyway, I ran in my wedge sandals: up the steps, across the porch, and through the door, leading with the stomach. And found Aislynn standing in the doorway to the office, where Kylie and I had sat just two days ago looking at poison pen letters, screaming her head off.

I pushed her aside and took in the office at a glance.

It was a mess. The books were off the shelves, and the knick-knacks were scattered across the floor, many of them broken. Papers from the desk had sailed everywhere. Drawers hung open or had their contents dumped in piles on the floor. And in the middle of it lay Kylie, the back of her head red and sticky.

My stomach heaved, and I stumbled back outside while I fumbled for my phone. My first call was to Rafe—"I need you!"—and my second to 911. They kept me on the phone while they dispatched the ambulance, so by the time I heard the sound of sirens coming up the street, Rafe had already brought the Harley to a screeching halt behind the Volvo and was on his way through the yard.

By then, I had conquered my squeamishness—more or less—and gone back inside the house to A) shut Aislynn up, and B) see if there was anything I could do for Kylie.

She was alive, but unconscious, so that was the good news. And the bad news too, I guess, since alive was good, but unconscious wasn't. It was better than dead, though, so I'd take it. And while I'm not an expert, I felt for her pulse, and had no problem finding it. Hopefully that meant she wasn't in danger of dying.

Aislynn's screams changed to hiccups once we determined that Kylie would live. By the time Rafe burst through the open door and the ambulance came to a squealing stop outside, she had herself pretty well in hand. So did I. The knowledge that I wasn't looking at another dead body had done wonders for my peace of mind.

I told the 911 operator that the ambulance had arrived, and disconnected. Then I looked at Rafe. "Thanks for coming."

He nodded, taking in the room. "You OK?"

"Fine. A little shook up when I called you."

"She OK?" He glanced at Kylie's immobile body.

"She seems to be. She's breathing and her pulse is strong, but she's unconscious. Concussion, maybe. I didn't know what to do for her, so I just left her alone. Rather than do the wrong thing, you know? In case I shouldn't have tried to move her, or whatever."

He nodded. "The EMTs are on their way in. Let's get outta their way."

He extended a hand. I took it and let him haul me up. Getting to my feet took more effort every day. Good thing he was strong.

We hustled Aislynn out the front door just ahead of the EMTs coming in, and put her on the porch swing. I took a seat next to her and patted her hand, while Rafe went back inside to communicate with the EMTs. That TBI badge works wonders, even when the guy wielding it is wearing gym shorts and a sleeveless T-shirt.

Or maybe especially when the guy wielding it is wearing a sleeveless T-shirt. One of the EMTs was female.

"This is my fault," Aislynn sobbed. "If I'd been here last night, this wouldn't have happened."

"You don't know that," I told her, although between you and me, I suspected she might be right. A burglar might think twice about entering a house where there are two people. Then again... "And if you'd been home alone last night, that might have been you in there, instead of Kylie."

Aislynn whimpered, and then got to her feet when the EMTs came through the door with Kylie on a stretcher. We stood and watched as they carried it down the stairs and over to the driveway, and then they flipped down two sets of legs with wheels, and rolled it the rest of the way to the ambulance.

Aislynn twitched her hand out of mine. "I want to go with her!"

"I don't think they'll let you," I told her, but she wasn't listening. "Aislynn!"

She didn't stop. I turned to Rafe, who had just come out onto the porch. "They won't let her ride in the ambulance, will they?"

He shook his head. "Go find out where they're going. Then you can follow 'em in the car. I'll stay here and wait for the cops."

"Did you call the cops?"

"Not yet. I just got here as fast as I could." And it wasn't easy to maneuver the Harley, wear a helmet, and make a phone call at the same time.

"I appreciate that." I leaned into him for a moment, enjoying the warmth and solidity of his body. "Although I'm sorry to ruin your workout."

"I can work out another day," Rafe said and gave me a push. "Go."

I went. Over to the EMTs, who were arguing with Aislynn

about why she couldn't go in the ambulance with Kylie.

"It's against the rules, miss. No civilians in the bus."

"But I don't want her to ride on her own!"

"One of us will sit with her," the female EMT said patiently. "She won't be alone. And we'll get here there as fast as we can. It won't be a long drive."

Aislynn bit her lip, clearly not convinced.

"Come on." I took her arm. "I'll drive you there. We'll stay with the ambulance the whole way. I promise."

"But I want to stay with her," Aislynn said stubbornly.

I shook my head. "You can't. And the longer you stay here and argue, the longer until they can leave, and the longer until they get her to the hospital."

She sent me an unfriendly look, but finally allowed herself to be towed away. The female EMT hopped into the back of the ambulance with Kylie, and the male EMT shut the doors before swinging himself up into the driver's seat.

The ambulance rumbled to life.

"Come on." I hustled Aislynn over to the Volvo. "Hurry."

We sorted ourselves into our seats as the siren started. Aislynn winced. I turned the key in the ignition and followed the ambulance as it peeled away from the curb and headed down the street, lights flashing. Up on the porch, Rafe had his phone to his ear. He lifted a hand as we shot out of sight.

The trip to the hospital was quick. A little quicker than was comfortable, since I had to follow in the wake of the ambulance the whole way there. Rafe drives like a bat out of hell under most circumstances. He wouldn't have had any problems. I'm usually a pretty cautious driver, and getting more cautious the more pregnant I get. The baby is closer to the surface now than it used to be, and just the idea of having to stop fast, and slamming my stomach into the steering wheel, is scary.

When we arrived at Vanderbilt Hospital, the ambulance shot,

screaming, into the ambulance entrance. Aislynn and I had to go around the building to the ER. I let her out at the doors, and took off to find a parking space. By the time I made it inside, she was arguing with the nurse at the duty desk about wanting to see her girlfriend.

"I'm sorry, miss," the nurse kept repeating. "Only family allowed. And not yet."

We'd been here before, Aislynn and I. In this place, and this situation. This was where Kylie had ended up after the traffic accident in December, and the hospital staff hadn't been helpful about giving Aislynn information then, either. Now it was six months later, and gay marriage had become legal, but Aislynn and Kylie weren't married. Guess it was up to me to save the day again. I sighed—silently—and went to the rescue. "I'm Kylie's sister. She was here six months ago, after a traffic accident. You should have her in your records from then. I'm probably there, too. Savannah Martin."

I showed her my driver's license while she pecked at her computer.

"You have different last names," she told me.

"Marriage," I answered, flashing my brand new wedding ring.

It must have satisfied her, because she didn't say any more about it. "Any changes in her insurance since the last time she was here?"

I glanced at Aislynn. She shook her head. "No," I said.

She tap-tapped some more. "If you'll take a seat, someone will be out to talk to you shortly."

"Thank you." I grabbed Aislynn by the arm and hauled her away. "They probably don't know anything yet. She just got here."

We ended up in two uncomfortable plastic chairs over by the wall, where we had a good view of the swinging doors into the ER. Aislynn got busy gnawing on her fingernails. Since they were lacquered black, I didn't imagine it could be good for her, but I didn't say anything about it. We were in a hospital. If she poisoned herself, presumably they'd know what to do for her.

It got on my nerves after a few minutes, though, and I cast about for something to say. "Kylie's been married once, right?"

Aislynn nodded, but didn't take her thumb out of her mouth.

"Did you ever meet him?"

She shook her head.

"Why not?"

"It was before we met," Aislynn said. And promptly stuck her finger back in her mouth.

"She told me about him. Although I can't remember..."

"Damian," Aislynn said.

I nodded. "Was Mitchell her married name? Or did she go back to her maiden name after the divorce?"

"Does it matter?" Aislynn wanted to know.

Not really. I was just making conversation to pass the time, and to stop her from her cannibalism. Although it might be helpful to know Kylie's maiden name when I was pretending to be her sister.

"Mitchell was Damian's name," Aislynn said when I explained my reasoning, but not without an eye roll. "Kylie's maiden name was Williams."

"Is Damian here? Or did she move to Nashville after they got divorced?"

"Kylie's always lived here," Aislynn said, which I took to mean that yes, the marriage had been local and Damian was still around. "But he doesn't need to know that she's in the hospital. They aren't married anymore."

That hadn't been on my mind at all, actually, but now that she mentioned it, and sounded adamant about it, I was curious. "Do they see each other these days?"

Aislynn shook her head. "Kylie felt bad about leading him on. When she married him, she didn't realize she was gay."

I nodded. She had told me that. And that it had been a remark of her ex-husband's—about how she seemed to prefer her girlfriends' company to his—that had spurred the realization.

"He wouldn't be behind this, would he?"

Aislynn looked shocked.

"Is he still upset about what happened?"

"I don't think so," Aislynn said.

"What do you think happened?"

"To Kylie? Someone broke in and hit her."

Obviously. Or more likely, someone broke in while the house was empty, and Kylie came home and found him or her in the process of ransacking the office, and then he or she hit her. Most burglars have enough sense not to break into a house when people are home.

Aislynn and Kylie's house had sat empty all day long, though. It made a lot more sense to break in then, when they were both at work. Anyone who knew anything about their schedules would know that Kylie worked regular business hours and Aislynn's waitressing job was in Brentwood, a thirty minute drive from the house. It wouldn't have been hard to check that she was there. Just stop by and look.

Yes, late morning would have been a much safer time for a foray into the house than evening. Especially since the backyard was fenced and private for someone to come and go without being seen.

And that reminded me... "Do you know a guy in a plaid shirt?"

Aislynn stared at me.

"Blue and green plaid. Sort of light." And yes, I did realize how stupid the question was. All someone in a plaid shirt had to do, was take off the plaid shirt, and he'd no longer be someone in a plaid shirt.

"I'm sure we do," Aislynn said. "I think Kylie has a plaid

flannel shirt that she uses in the winter. And I have a plaid skirt."

Not quite what I'd been looking for. But rather than telling her the reason I asked—since I didn't want to worry her any more than this incident with Kylie already had—I just thanked her and didn't say anything else about it.

Ten

The doctor came out a few minutes later, to update us on Kylie's condition. He turned out to be the same ER doctor who had been here in December, when she had her car accident, and also the same guy who had been here when Tim was shot in February. His name was Simon Ramsey, and he was a good-looking guy in his thirties who either recognized us, or pretended well. His smile was warm and familiar and reassuring.

"She's stable. Still unconscious. Lost a bit of blood but nothing extraordinary. She has a concussion, of course."

We both nodded, although he addressed most of his remarks to me. I was pretty sure he had figured out, last time were here, that I wasn't really Kylie's sister, but maybe he didn't remember that part.

"We'll be keeping her sedated for a while to give her brain time to recover. We'll probably bring her out of it tomorrow morning, and we'll see if she regains consciousness on her own."

"What if she doesn't?" Aislynn wanted to know, gnawing on her bottom lip.

"Then we'll just have to wait a little longer until her body's ready. But there's nothing too badly wrong with her that I can see. We gave her a CT-scan to rule out brain injury, and it came back clear. We've stitched her up. It looks to me like it's just a matter of time before she wakes up on her own, but we'll give her until tomorrow to rest."

We nodded. Doctor Ramsey looked from me to Aislynn and back.

"You can see her if you want, although she won't know you're here. And there's no sense in staying with her. Come back in the morning."

I nodded.

"Can I see her before we go?" Aislynn asked.

So we went and saw Kylie, who was pale and bandaged and unconscious, and hooked up to various beeping and whooshing machines. Then I took Aislynn out of there and put her back in my car. "She'll be all right. You heard what he said. He was the same doctor who patched her up last time, and he did a good job then. She'll be fine."

Aislynn nodded, sniffing into another tissue. "I feel so bad. If I hadn't gotten upset yesterday..."

Then it might have been her in a hospital bed right now, and not Kylie. But since I'd already said that, I didn't bother repeating it.

"You can't think like that," I told her instead. "Kylie would probably prefer it this way. I'm sure she'd rather be hurt than have you be hurt. And anyway, if she had been answering her phone, or if she'd called you before going home, she might not have been there alone. She might have picked you up first, and then it would have been the two of you coming home together."

And if so, the burglar might have heard them coming and decided to book it out the back door rather than waiting for Kylie to walk in and then bash her over the head with something.

I wondered whether she'd gotten a look at the guy—or girl. Head-bashing is an equal opportunity crime, and once she woke up, maybe we'd get lucky and she'd be able to tell us something about whoever had done this to her.

Back at the house, there was a lot more activity than there had been when we left. Rafe's Harley was gone, but Detective Mendoza was there, overseeing a group of crime scene techs in white coveralls. A Metro PD crime scene van was parked at the curb along with a gray sedan. I assumed the latter was Mendoza's. And in spite of it being Saturday, he was dressed in another killer suit, complete with shirt and tie. Aqua shirt, teal tie today.

When he heard our footsteps on the porch stairs, he turned, and gave us a killer smile. "Ladies."

Aislynn liked women and I'm happily married to the greatest guy in the world, but I'm sure we both sighed appreciatively. He was just so very pretty.

Then I shook it off. "Detective. We've been at the hospital."

Mendoza nodded. "So your husband said. Everything OK?"

I gave him the rundown. Aislynn, meanwhile, was peering around the doorjamb, watching the crime scene team at work. I could have told her that she'd have a mess to clean up once they were done—fingerprint powder takes a lot of vacuuming—but I was more interested in whatever Mendoza had to say. "Any idea what happened?"

"No more than you do, I imagine." He glanced at Aislynn. "The door was locked when you arrived?"

Aislynn nodded.

"Did you check the back door?"

We hadn't. We'd just walked in, found Kylie, and raised the alarm.

"Is something wrong with the back door?" I asked.

Mendoza shook his head. "But if the front door was locked, it's possible the culprit left that way."

"That reminds me..." I glanced at Aislynn. She was still more interested in the crime scene than the conversation. I took a step to the side and lowered my voice. Mendoza followed, looking politely interested. "Yesterday afternoon, when I was driving by here, I saw a man in the yard. Or maybe a woman. Wearing a plaid shirt."

Mendoza arched his brows.

"I didn't get a good look, OK? He was just on his way around the corner of the house when I saw him. Or her. I pulled over and went into the backyard, but I didn't see anyone. I figured he might just be a neighbor cutting through the yard, but now I'm not sure. It could have been someone casing the place, I guess.

Although if he was, why didn't he just break in then? The house was empty."

"It was broad daylight?" Mendoza suggested.

"The backyard is private. And fenced. Nobody can see what's going on."

"Then that's likely where our burglar entered," Mendoza said. "I'll make sure we dust for prints in the back of the house."

There was a pause.

"Did you find the weapon?" I asked. "Whatever Kylie was hit with?"

He nodded. It was nice of him to be so forthcoming, actually. He didn't have to. Then again, maybe he figured Aislynn would tell me everything later. And he probably planned to tell her. "Snow globe."

"The one with the Eiffel Tower in it? That's too bad." I had noticed it the other night. It had been nice: big and sturdy.

"It was intact," Mendoza said. "Sitting on the bookshelf on the other side of the room."

I blinked. "He put it there after bashing her over the head with it?"

"Must have. Unless you moved it?"

I shook my head. "Last time I saw it, it was on the desk. That was two nights ago."

"It was on the shelf this morning. With blood all over it. We've packed it up to be tested, but there's not much doubt it's the weapon."

"Virgil Wright wasn't killed with the snow globe, was he?"

"No," Mendoza said. "The murder weapon in that case was a rock. It was found at the scene. Too rough to take fingerprints. We'll try for trace DNA, but by the time we're likely to get anything useful back from the lab, I'm sure we'll have the murderer in custody anyway."

Must be nice to be so confident.

"But you think you can get fingerprints from the snow

globe?"

"Unless the burglar was wearing gloves," Mendoza said. "And since he was in fact a burglar, it's quite likely he was. But we'll check."

"Are you planning to go to the visitation?" I glanced at my watch. It was already past noon. With the trip to the hospital, the time had totally gotten away from me.

"I was," Mendoza said, "until this. Now I have to talk to Ms. Turner. Are you going to the visitation?"

I told him I thought I might.

"If you learn anything you think I should know," Mendoza told me, "give me a call." He nodded. "Excuse me."

He turned to walk back to Aislynn. I thought about offering to stay with her—she had that quality of making us all want to protect her; I'm sure Kylie felt the same way—but I decided against it. I really did want to get to the visitation, and Aislynn was an adult, she could handle this herself. Besides, I was pretty sure she'd already told me everything she knew. Which amounted to zilch, since she didn't know anything.

So I told her I was leaving, and to call me if she needed anything. She looked at me with huge doe eyes, and I steeled myself. "Maybe you should run up to Bowling Green when you're finished talking to the detective. Spend the night with your parents. You probably don't want to stay here, and you won't be able to see Kylie until tomorrow anyway."

Aislynn sank her teeth into her lip, and I added, "You're welcome to come back and stay with us again. But I thought maybe you'd like to see your mother and father."

She turned to Mendoza. "Would that be all right?"

"As long as you tell me where you're going," Mendoza said, "so I can get in touch with you if I need to, I don't see why not."

I left them to work out the details, and headed for the Volvo.

Virgil Wright's visitation took place at the Phillips-Robinson

Funeral Home in Inglewood, where Brenda Puckett's memorial had also taken place almost a year ago. Unlike then, there were no TV cameras, and no reporters accosting me for a sound byte as I made my way across the parking lot to the front door. And while Misters Phillips and Robinson had opened every room in the place for Brenda's funeral last year, Virgil Wright hadn't drawn that kind of crowd. A handful of people were gathered in a room to the right as I came into the lobby, and that was the extent of it.

I made my way there, and stopped in the doorway, looking into a room full of gay guys.

And I do mean that literally. There wasn't a single woman in the room, and while it isn't always easy to tell from the outside whether a man is gay, not one of them spared me a look.

That might have been partly because of the stomach. Most guys, even the heterosexual ones, usually take care not to ogle a pregnant woman. But I really think it was more a case of keeping an eye on the tableau taking place by the casket.

Kenny was there, somberly attired in a navy blue suit and tie, with a black armband. His friend from last night was standing a few feet away, cracking his knuckles.

Meanwhile, another man was facing them across the coffin. He had his back to me, so it took me a second to recognize the brown hair and slight build.

In fact, it might not have been the hair and build I recognized at all. It might have been the voice.

"I have the right to be here. He was my lover, too."

A whisper ran through the room as everyone craned their necks. I moved a few steps into the room.

"Was," Kenny said tightly. "A year ago. Not anymore."

"I still loved him," Stacy said. "Maybe we weren't together anymore, but that doesn't mean I didn't care. Or that he didn't."

"This is *my* memorial for *my* lover!" Kenny said.

"He was *my* lover before he was *your* lover!" Stacy answered.

Both their voices were becoming shriller the longer they were at it. He added, "And *I* can't have a memorial for him, because *you* took him away from me!"

"He was sick of you by then!" Kenny said.

Uh-oh.

I waited for Stacy to go for Kenny's throat, but it didn't happen. Instead he shot back, "And he was sick of you now!"

There was another audible gasp, and Kenny's pale face flushed a deeper red than I would have thought possible. "That's not true!"

"What?" Stacy said tauntingly. "Didn't he tell you he was tired of you? He told me!"

Uh-oh.

I had joked about Kenny and Stacy getting into a cat-fight over the casket, but I hadn't actually expected it to happen. It had been a joke. I swear.

Kenny howled something. I'm not even sure what it was, it was so high pitched and hysterical. He threw himself forward, reaching for Stacy, who danced out of range. The guy from last night grabbed Kenny around the waist and tried to haul him back, but it was too late. Kenny attempted to crawl over the coffin to get to Stacy, and in the process, the coffin tipped over. Everyone in the room screamed. I'm pretty sure I screamed, too. If Virgil could have screamed, I'm sure he would have. I winced to think about what was going on inside that coffin at the moment, and I didn't envy the funeral home employee who had to put it right.

And then pandemonium continued as Stacy pushed past me and knocked me back against the wall on his way out the door, running like a gazelle in black leather pants and biker boots.

"Get him!" somebody screamed, and there was a stampede on the door, and a bottleneck as everyone tried to get out at the same time. People grunted, shoved, and swore, and propelled each other through the opening. I'm sure casualties resulted.

Kenny—released from the embrace of yesterday's dinner partner—flew past me without a glance. The dinner partner thundered after.

In the silence after the storm, I looked around. The room was empty. It was just me and the overturned coffin, and funeral flowers scattered all over the floor. Many of them were flattened, from being trampled by the throng, and the scent was overpowering. Through the window, behind the somber red velvet curtains, I could hear whooping and hollering from the parking lot, like a pack of hounds scenting a fox.

I gave Virgil a silent apology, and then I got out of there as quickly as I could, before the attendants showed up and discovered the carnage. I wasn't sure I could explain what had happened, or that I wanted to.

I ended up explaining to Detective Mendoza, though. He had told me to tell him anything untoward that happened at the funeral, and this definitely qualified.

After I'd run through the chain of events, there was a pause. "Really?"

"Yes," I said, steering the car with one hand and holding the phone with the other. "Really. I barely got out of there with my life. When I drove away, Stacy had barricaded himself inside his Jeep while the mourners were rocking the car back and forth to try to get him out."

Mendoza sighed. "I guess I better dispatch a couple cars to break it up."

"That would probably be a good idea," I agreed. "If they get their hands on Stacy, I'm afraid they'll kill him. And while I know that pays your salary, it would probably be best if they didn't."

Mendoza agreed that would be best, and disconnected the call, presumably to get a couple of squad cars over to Phillips-Robinson to break up the party, hopefully before Stacy took damage. I headed home to Rafe.

He was back to mowing. When I pulled into the driveway, I saw he had picked up where he'd left off yesterday and was pushing the mower back and forth across the grass, shirtless and in the gym shorts he'd put on this morning. When I pulled into the driveway, he squinted at me but kept going. And when I got out of the car and stood for a second to admire the view, he waited until he got close enough that he didn't have to yell, and then he announced, "Don't even think about it."

"You can't stop me from thinking," I told him.

"Well, then don't tell me you're thinking about it. I don't need the distraction." He turned his back and pushed the mower in the other direction. I watched the play of muscles under his skin and felt my mouth go dry and other parts go the other way.

"I'm thinking about it," I told him when he came back around.

He groaned. "I told you not to tell me that. I gotta get this done or we're gonna have weeds up to our knees."

"I don't mind if you don't."

"I mind," Rafe said. "I'm an upstanding citizen these days. I gotta house and a wife and a kid on the way. I gotta keep things looking good."

"From where I'm standing, things are looking very good." Hell—heck—just put a shirtless Rafe into the front yard, and nobody would even look at the grass. We'd probably have accidents as people—women—ran into the fence next door because they weren't watching where they were going.

"You're good for my ego," he told me on the third pass, "but you're trouble. What happened to the girl who always did the right thing as per her mama?"

"She married you. And now she wants her conjugal rights."

He shook his head. "I've got five minutes to go till I'm done. Just gimme that. After that you can have whatever you want."

"I'll hold you to that," I told him, and went to prepare a glass of iced tea, since I figured he'd be hot and thirsty when he came inside. I was hot, too, and I'd only been standing there a couple of minutes.

He was as good as his word. Five minutes later, he sauntered into the house, still shirtless, and elevated the temperature by at least twenty degrees just by being present.

I handed him the glass of tea and watched him tilt his head back and dispatch it. His throat moved smoothly as he swallowed. I swallowed, too.

He was laughing as he reached around me to put the glass on the counter. "Still holding that thought?"

"It comes back," I confessed. "Pretty much every time I see you." Especially if he was flaunting skin. Then again, he could be fully dressed, in a winter coat and gloves, and I'd still want him.

"You poor thing." He leaned in to nuzzle my neck, one hand on each side of me, braced against the counter.

"It's terrible. I need help."

He chuckled. "I've got what's gonna help you."

"I know you do." I looped my arms around his neck and let him carry me upstairs.

"We're having dinner with Tammy," he told me an hour later, after I'd had enough help to make me feel nice and relaxed.

We were still in bed, facing one another, and he was up on one elbow twisting a strand of my hair around his finger.

That's something I do—to my own hair—when I'm lying. But I didn't see any reason why he'd lie about this.

"That's fine."

"At the FinBar."

We'd been there yesterday, but Grimaldi didn't know that. "OK."

"She's bringing Mendoza."

I blinked. And blinked again. "You mean... like a date? A double date?"

Wasn't Grimaldi dating my brother? Or wasn't she at least

sort of involved with him, even if it wasn't strictly a dating relationship?

And for that matter, wasn't Mendoza still married?

"I'm sure it don't mean nothing," Rafe murmured, as he continued to play with my hair. And of course the fact that he felt the need to point out that it didn't mean anything, gave the impression that it did. "Just two colleagues going out together with friends."

"Friends who are married."

"A friend who's also in law enforcement, and his wife."

When he put it like that, it made more sense. However— "What about Dix?"

"He's in Sweetwater," Rafe said. "Ain't he?"

"I assume he is. He hasn't told me differently."

"Then he prob'ly doesn't even know." And wouldn't, the implication was, unless I told him.

"That's not the point," I said. "I thought he and Grimaldi... you know."

"Your brother and Tammy are friends," Rafe said. "Maybe they're more than friends. Neither of'em has ever said anything to me about it, so I don't know. There's something going on there, but I dunno how serious it is."

I didn't, either. It wasn't something Dix would talk to me about—a big brother doesn't discuss his sex-life (or lack thereof) with his little sister—and Grimaldi just wasn't the type to indulge in girlish confidences. I'd spent enough time with them—together and alone—to be reasonably sure that there was something romantic going on between them, but I didn't know how serious it was.

Was he moving too slowly for her, maybe? She was tired of waiting, and so she was going out with Mendoza instead?

Or was it the girls? My brother has two daughters. Maybe the idea of taking on someone else's children was hard for Grimaldi to handle.

Or maybe it was my mother she objected to. And if so, who could blame her?

Grimaldi had been part of Rafe's and my wedding, that Mother arranged, last month. Mother might have gotten on Grimaldi's nerves. In fact, she was certain to have gotten on Grimaldi's nerves. Maybe Grimaldi had decided she couldn't under any circumstances tolerate being related to my mother. It amazed me every day that Rafe had been willing to take her on. Especially as she'd made her disapproval of him abundantly clear. She would disapprove of Grimaldi, too. And might have let Grimaldi know it.

"I can hear the gears turning," Rafe said, tapping my temple. "Don't worry about it, darlin'. Not till you know there's something to worry about."

"If we're having dinner with Grimaldi and someone other than my brother, there *is* something to worry about."

"They work together," Rafe said, "Could be they have dinner all the time."

If so, Grimaldi had never mentioned it.

She'd been my maid of honor less than a month ago. And she hadn't told me she was dating someone else?

"I don't like this," I said.

"We'll figure it out." He slipped the hand that had been fiddling with my hair around my neck and pulled me toward him. "C'mere. I'll give you something else to think about for a while."

I wasn't sure I wanted anything else to think about. My mind was fully occupied with this, and wanted to twist and turn it, and think about the ramifications.

But I knew what he was offering, and it isn't anything I'd ever turn down. I leaned forward and let him take my mind off things for a bit longer.

Eleven

Rafe was insistent that we had to get to the FinBar before Grimaldi and Mendoza did. It wasn't until we got there, beating Grimaldi and her 'date' to the punch, that I realized why. As he headed for a booth in the back corner, and put himself with his back against the wall, I saw the issue: if we'd gotten here last, he'd have had to sit with his back to the room, and he doesn't like to do that. Grimaldi doesn't, either, and when she came in and saw that we'd already taken the front-facing seats, she didn't look happy.

That was OK with me. She had Jaime Mendoza trailing her, and the sight of him made me angry.

For the record, I had nothing against Mendoza. He seemed like a decent sort. He'd complimented my husband on his handling of the insane serial killer a month ago. He'd handled my mother beautifully when she invited him to marry me, and he'd done it without making me feel rejected. He was managing Virgil Wright's murder case as well as anyone could expect, at least as far as I could tell. Grimaldi had told me he was a good cop. And he was extremely easy on the eyes. I had no problem with him, other than that he was here as Grimaldi's date.

Although I must say they didn't look or behave like two people on a date. Grimaldi wasn't dressed up at all, but arrived in the same severe business suit she must have worn to work all day. So did Mendoza, if it came to that. Then again, I'd had dinner with Grimaldi and my brother when she'd been wearing that same suit, and I was pretty sure that, at least, had been a date.

They sat down across from us, both of them clearly bothered by the fact that they had to keep their backs to the door.

Three cops walk into a bar... scrolled through my head, and I grinned.

Grimaldi looked at me. "Something funny?"

"Just watching the three of you jockey for position. We left early so Rafe could get the seat with his back to the wall. You have to admit it's more likely someone will be gunning for him rather than the two of you."

Grimaldi shrugged. "Police work has been known to create enemies."

"Ten years undercover creates more."

She didn't seem to have an answer for that. Mendoza looked at Rafe. "Ten years undercover? How did you pull that off?"

Very carefully, I thought. In fact, it wasn't until he got involved with me that his cover was blown. Sometimes I felt bad about that, about the fact that I'd cost him his career and had almost gotten him killed along the way. The rest of the time I was just grateful that he was out now, and wasn't risking his life every day.

They got to talking about it, and I sat back and listened. And watched, for any sign of a special intimacy between Grimaldi and Mendoza. Hand-holding under the table, sideways glances, playing footsie. But if there was anything like that going on, I didn't notice.

The waitress arrived in the middle of the conversation to take our drink orders, and seemed to be quite overcome by the testosterone hovering over the table. It took her two tries to get her voice to work, and when it did, she didn't seem quite sure which of them to look at. "Something to drink?"

Rafe ordered a beer, and I asked for sweet tea. Mendoza waited for Grimaldi to order—beer as well—before he asked for a Coke.

The waitress could barely drag her eyes away from him. "Are you ready to order?"

Rafe chuckled. "I'll have a burger. Darlin'?"

I'd had a burger too, yesterday, but today I wasn't in the mood. "Chicken Caesar, please."

Grimaldi ordered another burger, and Mendoza a Philly cheese steak. The waitress came close to stumbling over her own feet as she walked away.

"Can't take you anywhere," I murmured to Rafe.

He chuckled. "It ain't me getting the attention this time, darlin'. That was all for tall, dark and handsome over there."

Mendoza grimaced. "It's a curse."

I could well imagine it might be. I look OK, and I get my own share of attention from men, but I'd gotten sick and tired of how some women behaved around Rafe when I took him out somewhere. They acted like I wasn't even there, so they could slaver over him.

"Does it bother you?" I asked Grimaldi.

She looked at me like I'd lost my mind. So that either meant that it didn't, and she was wondering why I'd even think it might, or she didn't care, because this wasn't really a date and Mendoza was on his own.

"Have you spoken to Dix lately?" I asked, as the men went back to talking shop, or more specifically, talking about Rafe's years undercover and Mendoza's time as a cop. Male bonding, law enforcement style, I guess.

I must say the idea bothered me some. The bonding, I mean. Not because Rafe doesn't deserve friends—he does, and he has very few, since spending your life deep undercover isn't conducive to forming deep friendships. Not with the people who have to rat out next week or next month. But he was making friends with Grimaldi's date. When Grimaldi's date ought to be my brother!

"We talk every couple of days," Grimaldi told me.

That sounded promising. "Have you been in Sweetwater since the wedding?"

"I've been working weekends this month," Grimaldi said

calmly. "And seeing as your brother works during the week, there's been no good time."

It was a good excuse, but that might be all it was: an excuse. "You didn't make it down for the Fourth of July picnic."

"I worked on the Fourth," Grimaldi said. "Holidays are big business for murder cops."

"People kill each other on holidays?"

She nodded. "More so than the rest of the time. Tempers get short when families get together."

No kidding. My patience is usually stretched pretty thin whenever I have to deal with my mother.

Although at the moment Mother was still on her best behavior around Rafe, and had been downright friendly during the picnic. I didn't know how long it would last—probably not forever—but I wasn't about to look that particular gift horse in the mouth.

"And the heat doesn't help," Grimaldi added. "It makes people cranky."

"I would have thought it made them lazy."

She shook her head. "It all contributes to making them angry. And when some people get angry they take it out on other people."

I glanced at Rafe and Mendoza, still in conversation. "Do you think that's what happened to Virgil Wright? The heat got to someone and they hit him over the head with a rock?"

Grimaldi glanced sideways too, before she answered. "According to the boyfriend, Mr. Wright ran the same route every evening. Someone who knew that about him, could easily have lain in wait in the only part of that route that was private and offered the murderer cover while he committed the crime."

"Why would someone kill him? Was he rich?"

"He was doing all right," Grimaldi said. "White collar job. Good salary and a bit of savings. Most of it from the sale of the house last winter, and from not spending the proceeds to buy another. But it wasn't like there was a greedy nephew next in line for the fortune. That only happens in books."

"Who inherits the money he's got?"

"In general? Because I have no specific information about Mr. Wright's case."

"Sure," I said. "In general. I guess."

"Unless there's a will, and most people our age haven't bothered with one, it's next of kin. Spouse, if there's a legal marriage. Children. Parents. Siblings."

I nodded. "Virgil wasn't married, and I don't think he had any children. I guess that would make his parents his heirs."

"Unless he'd written a will in favor of his lover," Grimaldi said.

"Meaning Kenny? I guess he might have. If they were that serious about each other. Although as far as I know they've been together less than a year."

"You and your husband haven't been together any longer," Grimaldi pointed out.

"No. But we knew each other before."

Grimaldi shrugged. As well she might, since Rafe's and my acquaintance in high school hadn't stretched much beyond a word or two in the hallway, if he thought nobody was close enough to listen.

"Now that Rafe and I are married," I said, "if anything were to happen to me, I guess he'd inherit everything I own?" A run-down, seven-year-old Volvo that Bradley had paid for, and a lot of designer dresses and high heeled shoes I couldn't fit into at the moment...

"Why ask me?" Grimaldi wanted to know. "I'm a cop, not a lawyer. The person you should ask is your brother."

I shot a glance at Mendoza, who was still talking to Rafe, and showing no interest in what Grimaldi and I were saying. "Speaking of my brother..."

She didn't roll her eyes, but she looked like she wanted to.

"Really?"

"I'm just worried, that's all. And curious. I thought you and Dix were... you know..."

"Your brother and I are friends," Grimaldi said firmly.

I lowered my voice, with another sideways glance. "And you and Detective Mendoza are...?"

"Colleagues." Her expression challenged me to disagree with her.

"So this...?"

"Isn't a date." She lowered her voice, too. "He's still married, you know. And not about to do anything that would jeopardize his ability to spend time with his son. He may have screwed up in the past, but he's toeing the line at the moment."

Ah. "Sorry," I said. "But if he wasn't married...?"

She sat back against the seat. "You do realize that my love life is none of your business, don't you? I didn't ask you questions about your relationship with Mr. Collier."

"You didn't have to," I said. "I volunteered information. Probably more information than you wanted to hear."

She didn't contradict me, and I added, "And I'm worried about my brother."

It's possible I might have imagined it, but I think her steely gaze softened. "You don't have to worry about your brother."

"He likes you." And if she was going out with someone else, whether she called it a date or not, then yes, I needed to worry.

"And I like him," Grimaldi said. "But he hasn't even been widowed a year yet. And he has two daughters to worry about."

"Abigail and Hannah are fine," I said. "I'm sure dealing with Sheila's death was easier for them than for Dix. They're so young."

"Losing a mother is hard for any young girl," Grimaldi said, and since her own mother had died young, I figured she knew.

"I wasn't saying it hasn't been hard. But they're children. They have a lot of other things to focus on. School and friends

142 | JENNA BENNETT

and things like that. Dix lost his wife and his co-parent."

"Precisely why he isn't ready to move on yet," Grimaldi said.

"Just tell me what I'm supposed to tell him about this!"

"This?"

I indicated the restaurant, the table, and Detective Mendoza.

"You don't have to tell him anything," Grimaldi said. "I already told him I was having dinner with you tonight. He said to give you his best."

"Did he offer to drive up and join us?"

"He had plans," Grimaldi said. "Pizza and the latest Disney Princess movie with his daughters."

"Did he ask you to join him?"

Her expression warned me that I was crossing the line, but she answered. "As a matter of fact, he did. And I told him I couldn't. I'm on call this weekend."

"But you could go out to dinner with us?"

"Here," Grimaldi said, "I'm within fifteen minutes of any fresh body that turns up in Davidson County. At your brother's house, I'm an hour away."

So she had a point. And scored a few more when she added, "And when I'm there, I'm not doing something I want to stop doing. I enjoy your brother's company. It's nice not to talk shop. If I ever get serious about a man, I can tell you right now, he won't be involved in law enforcement."

"I guess my husband is safe from you."

"Your husband has always been safe from me," Grimaldi said. "Not that I would have gotten anywhere if he were my type. It was obvious from the first time I met you both you had no interest in anyone else."

Good to know, although it was a little disconcerting that everyone but me had realized it long before I did. Not that Rafe was interested in me—I had known that, although it took me a while to realize the extent of his interest—but that I was in love with him. That had taken a lot longer than I'm comfortable admitting, since it makes me sound like a dunce for not seeing something that was right in front of my nose, that everyone else was seeing, clear as day.

But I digress. "In case you wondered," I told Grimaldi, "if you consider a lawyer to be uninvolved in law enforcement, I'd love it if you and my brother worked things out. You'd make a much more interesting sister-in-law than Sheila. Rest her soul."

Grimaldi looked daunted. I hadn't realized I had the ability to do that. And it hadn't even taken much effort on my part. "Thank you," she said. "I think."

"Besides, if Dix marries you, maybe Mother will go a little easier on Rafe. Since he won't be the only unsuitable spouse in the family."

Grimaldi arched her brows.

"You know what I mean," I said. "Mother probably has her eye on some vapid blonde for Dix, just like she had her eye on Todd for me. He deserves better than a wife my mother picks out for him. I'm sure he loved Sheila, and it isn't like it was an arranged marriage or anything like that. He met her and married her on his own. But Mother liked Sheila better than she liked any of the rest of us. If he isn't careful, she'll saddle him with a Sheila-clone."

"I'll keep that in mind," Grimaldi said and looked up. "Here's the food."

It was. And since it was, I let the conversation lapse, even though I was pretty sure she'd been looking for a way to stop talking to me, and the food was just the excuse she needed.

The discussion moved on to Virgil Wright, and from there to Aislynn and Kylie and the anonymous letters.

"Your friend decided to drive up to Kentucky to spend the night with her parents," Mendoza told me between bites of Philly cheese steak.

Grimaldi eyed him critically. "You let a suspect leave the state?"

"Just across the state line to Bowling Green," Mendoza said. "She was so incoherent I couldn't get anything out of her. I figured a day to calm down might be the best thing for her. Maybe tomorrow, she'll make more sense."

"If she comes back," Grimaldi muttered.

"She'll come back," I said. "Her girlfriend's unconscious in the hospital. Of course she'll come back. And what do you mean, suspect? Surely you can't suspect Aislynn of killing Virgil? Why would she? And have you seen her? She can't weigh more than a hundred and fifteen pounds. She'd never be able to hit anyone hard enough to kill him."

"She's a waitress," Grimaldi reminded me. "They're usually pretty strong from carrying all those trays. But I wasn't thinking she'd killed Mr. Wright. I was more interested in the possibility that she might have put her girlfriend in the hospital."

My jaw dropped. "Aislynn? Hit Kylie? Why?!"

"A couple of possible reasons," Grimaldi told me, while Rafe looked on, amused. I guess he'd already figured this out for himself. Everyone's mind but mine worked along the same track. "You said they had an argument and then one of the women went to talk to her ex. The same ex the other woman suspects her of wanting to get back together with. What was to keep the woman who stayed home from hitting the woman who got back..."

"Please. Just call them Aislynn and Kylie. The woman who left and the woman who came back make me confused."

Grimaldi sighed. "Kylie left to talk to her ex-girlfriend. When she came back, she and Aislynn may have gotten into an argument that ended with Aislynn hitting Kylie and then tearing the place up to make it look like a burglary."

"But she spent the night with us," I said.

"It could have happened before she arrived at your place."

"But she said she walked there. That would have taken at least an hour. Maybe more like an hour and a half."

"Or she took a cab," Grimaldi said, "and told you she walked."

Well... yes. She might have done that.

I turned to Mendoza. "Do you think she hit Kylie?"

He shrugged, his mouth full of sandwich. I looked at Rafe, who winked at me.

"You guys are depressing," I said. "Always looking for hidden agendas everywhere. Always thinking that people are lying."

"Thinking that people are lying's saved my life a time or two," Rafe reminded me calmly. "I'll just keep thinking that, if it's all the same to you."

And since there was nothing I could say to that, I just forked up some lettuce and started chewing.

Twelve

We went out for breakfast the next morning. Just Rafe and me this time. To the Pancake Pantry in Hillsboro Village, where the line snaked around the corner of the building. And after I had built up my strength on Belgian waffles and strawberries, I made him take me up the road to Vanderbilt Hospital, so we could check on Kylie.

Dr. Ramsey was working again this morning, and greeted me like an old friend. He even remembered Rafe, since had Rafe had been with me the time Tim got shot. In fact, it was Rafe who had kept pressure on Tim's shoulder—with a T-shirt he'd ripped off his own body—while I called for the ambulance. I think having a bare-chested Rafe bending over him had done just as much to keep Tim alive as the EMTs did.

Anyway, Dr. Ramsey was on duty, and updated us on Kylie—or 'your sister,' as he called her. I avoided looking at Rafe, but I knew he was arching a brow at me.

"She's resting comfortably," Dr. Ramsey said. "Heart and brain wave functions are normal. Everything seems fine. We're cutting down on the meds to see if she'll wake up on her own." He glanced at his watch. "She should be about ready to come out of it."

He gestured us to follow.

"Is anyone else here?" I asked, as we trailed him down the hall toward Kylie's room. "Her girlfriend? The police?"

"The girl with the black dreadlocks?" He shook his head. "I haven't seen her since yesterday. Her husband stopped by after visiting hours last night, but since he wasn't on the list of visitors, he didn't get in."

"Husband?"

Dr. Ramsey stopped in the middle of the hallway. "That's who he said he was. Your sister isn't married?"

"She was," I said. "They got divorced a couple of years ago." And as far as I knew had nothing to do with one another anymore.

"You don't have any contact with him?"

I could say in all honesty that I didn't. "I wonder who told him she was here. I doubt it was Aislynn. She and Kylie got involved after Damian was history. And Kylie wasn't in any condition to call him yesterday." Or anyone else, I assume. Like her parents.

Dr. Ramsey shook his head.

"I wonder who notified him."

"I wonder if it really was her husband," Rafe murmured.

I turned to him. "What do you mean?"

"It mighta been whoever hit her, coming back to make sure the job was done."

A caterpillar with very cold feet crept down my spine. "You mean, whoever hit her thought he'd killed her, and when he realized he hadn't, he came back to finish the job?"

Rafe shrugged.

"Surely that's a bit melodramatic," Dr. Ramsey said.

I was about to tell him that in my world—our world—things like that happened regularly, but before I could, Rafe had spoken up again. "Better safe than sorry, doc. After all, someone did hit her in the first place."

Dr. Ramsey nodded. "I'll append a note to her file that no one gets in except family and law enforcement. And that she has no husband."

"I'll talk to Mendoza about putting a guard on the door till she's outta here," Rafe added. I nodded my thanks, just as we arrived outside Kylie's room.

Dr. Ramsey pushed the door open, into the same beeping, pulsating world as yesterday. Kylie looked the same: pale and still on the bed.

I forgot that Rafe hadn't seen her before. It didn't occur to me at all—until he went stone still next to me.

I glanced at him, and saw that he'd turned a shade paler, staring at her.

Uh-oh. I reached for his hand, and he turned to me. It took a second, and then he got his voice to cooperate. He had to clear his throat first. "She looks like you."

I nodded, but it was Dr. Ramsey who said, "There's a strong family resemblance."

That statement hung in the air like a dying fish for a few seconds, before I said. "We drive the same kind of car, too. Hers is a few shades darker than mine."

"The twin bond," Ramsey nodded sagely.

I bit the inside of my cheek. He was a nice man, and I felt bad for deceiving him, but I needed to know what was going on. And Aislynn, not being legally married to Kylie, needed to know, as well. Saying we were sisters had seemed like a good idea at the time, although now it felt uncomfortable.

Not to mention that while we did resemble one another, superficially, we didn't look anything like twins.

To get past the awkwardness, I crept forward to the bed and peered down. "Is she doing all right?"

Dr. Ramsey glanced at the various beeping and whooshing machines. "Nothing wrong that I can see. Her head will hurt when she wakes up, but we can give her something for that. At the moment, it's important to see if she'll come out of it. If she won't, we might have problems."

"You mean, she might stay unconscious for longer?"

He nodded. "I can't see any reason why she will, but with head injuries, it's sometimes hard to tell."

"But you X-rayed her head, right? There's nothing wrong? No bleeding or anything?"

"Just a concussion," Dr. Ramsey said. "She should come out

of it just fine, and in a week or so, be good as new. Let's see if she can hear me."

He stepped over to the other side of the bed and leaned in. "Ms. Mitchell? Kylie? Can you hear me?"

We waited, but there was no response. The machines kept beeping and Kylie kept sleeping.

Dr. Ramsey took a step back. "You try. Maybe a familiar voice will make a difference."

Sure. Even if mine wasn't as familiar as he obviously assumed it would be.

I took a breath and leaned in. "Kylie? It's Savannah. Can you hear me?"

We waited. "Kylie?" I tried again. "Are you in there?"

"Her eyebrows moved," Rafe said.

I looked, and yes, she was wrinkling her brows. Only about a millimeter, but wrinkling. "Kylie?"

She pursed her lips.

"Good," Dr. Ramsey said approvingly. "Keep talking to her. Let's see if we can get her out of it."

"Hi, Kylie," I said obediently. "It's Savannah. Rafe is here, too." I glanced at him. "It's Sunday morning now. You've been sleeping a long time. We're worried about you. Can you wake up and tell us what happened?"

Her eyebrows drew together again. "Is she confused?" I whispered to Dr. Ramsey.

He shrugged. "Could be. Could be she's trying to remember. Could just be a muscle thing as she's trying to wake up."

OK, then.

"Just keep talking to her. Ask her to open her eyes."

I kept talking to her, and kept asking her to open her eyes. It took a small eternity, or at least it felt like one, but five or ten—or twenty—minutes later, her eyelashes fluttered.

"There you go," Dr. Ramsey said, pleased. "Good girl, Kylie. Open your eyes."

Her eyelashes fluttered some more. But eventually she did get around to opening her eyes. They were vacant at first, staring up at the ceiling. Another eternity passed while she blinked and tried to get her bearings. Her head moved slowly from one side to the other as she took in the room and the people in it. Rafe didn't rate a second glance. She obviously didn't know who he was. She watched Doctor Ramsey for a while, with that little wrinkle between her brows, probably trying to place him.

"Hi there, Kylie," he said, his voice friendly and undemanding. "I'm Doctor Ramsey. Remember me? We met last year."

If she did, she didn't respond. Having identified him to her satisfaction, she moved on to me, and this time her eyes registered recognition.

"Hi, Kylie," I said, moving a step closer and taking her hand. It was hooked up to a contraption that measured what I thought was her heartbeat, but at least there were no needles going into it. "How do you feel?"

She tried to move her lips, but nothing came out.

"We've been worried about you," I told her. "Do you remember what happened?"

She blinked, and then moved her head slowly from side to side.

"That's not unusual," Dr. Ramsey said softly. "A blow to the head can cause temporary memory loss."

I glanced at him. "Will she remember later?"

He shrugged. "Maybe, maybe not."

Helpful. Not.

"Someone hit you," I told Kylie. "On the back of the head. At home. Maybe someone who was looking through the office when you came home?"

Her eyes turned blank for a second as she thought it through, and I could almost feel her probing for the memory of what had happened. A look of frustration crossed her face when she couldn't find it.

"It's OK," I told her, patting her hand. "It'll come back to you. Just give it time."

The corners of her mouth turned up, and she curled her fingers around mine. Her lips moved.

"What?" I asked, leaning down.

There was hardly any breath at all behind the word, and no sound, but I'm pretty sure I heard her right. "Aislynn? She's fine. I'm sure she'll be here soon."

She'd have to be. Or Grimaldi would rub Mendoza's nose in the fact that he'd let her leave the state.

Kylie looked frustrated.

"She went up to Bowling Green to spend the night with her parents," I added, trying to explain what had happened, so she'd understand why Aislynn wasn't here. "Your house is a crime scene. The police were all over it, trying to figure out what went on. And she was probably afraid of staying there by herself. She spent the night before with us."

Kylie's gaze moved from me to Rafe, behind me.

"Remember Rafe?" I smiled. Of course she didn't—she'd never met him before—but since we were supposed to be sisters, I'd just have to pretend that my 'sister' knew my husband.

Rafe, bless him, can always be trusted to think on his feet. He gave her a smile. "Hi, Kylie. I'm sorry this happened to you."

Kylie moved her attention back to me. I think she approved.

She also looked exhausted, so I let go of her hand. "We just wanted to stop by and see how you were doing. You'd probably like to rest some more."

She managed a nod. The tip of her tongue came out to moisten her lisp. "Aislynn," she whispered again.

"I'm sure she'll be here soon. It's a long drive from Kentucky."

Kylie looked frustrated.

"Take a nap," Dr. Ramsey told her, patting her hand on top

of the covers. "By the time you wake up again, I'm sure she'll be here. And you might remember more about what happened after some more rest."

Kylie looked like she wanted to argue, but she lacked the strength. So she just closed her eyes and relaxed back into the pillows.

Dr. Ramsey headed for the door, waving us ahead of him. Outside in the hallway, he turned to face us. "That went better than I expected."

Really? "She doesn't remember anything."

"I didn't think she would," Dr. Ramsey said, and went into a long explanation about how the brain and memory are affected by trauma. "She might remember something later, or she might never remember exactly what happened."

"That'd be a shame," Rafe remarked, and I nodded.

"As of right now, the police have no idea who attacked her. It would be great if she could identify someone. Or at least give a description, if she didn't know the guy. Or woman."

"Only time will tell," Dr. Ramsey said philosophically, which wasn't a whole lot of help. I mean, I liked the guy, but he wasn't telling me what I wanted to know at the moment.

"Are you going to call the police and tell them she's awake?"

"I figure they'll show up here sooner or later," the doctor said. "Until then, my first responsibility is to my patient. And she needs to rest."

So the answer was no. I glanced at Rafe, who gave me an almost imperceptible nod. He'd call Mendoza. Why, I didn't know, since Kylie didn't seem to know anything, but the police needed to know that she was awake and mostly aware.

"We might stop by again later on," I told Dr. Ramsey, who informed me that I was on the approved visitor list and could come by anytime I wanted. "If I'm not here, just let the duty nurse know you're here to see Ms. Mitchell."

I nodded. "Any idea how long you're planning to keep her?"

"At least another day," Dr. Ramsey said firmly. "I'll be here in the morning tomorrow. I'll check on her then, and see how she's doing. If she's better, and has someone at home who can take care of her, she might be able to go home tomorrow afternoon. If not, we'll repeat the process on Tuesday."

She could come stay with us for a few days, I supposed, if nothing better came along. We had plenty of room. Although Kylie would probably prefer to be home in her own bed. Hopefully Aislynn would be back from Kentucky soon, and would take care of it.

We said goodbye to Dr. Ramsey and made our escape. I waited until we were in the elevator before I leaned into Rafe and told him, "Thanks for backing me up in there."

He put his arm around my shoulders. "You told him you're Kylie's sister?"

"Back in December, when she had her car accident. They wouldn't tell Aislynn anything about what had happened. Two gay girls, you know how it is. Or maybe you don't. They can't be each other's legal next of kin. Or at least they couldn't back then. Maybe they can now."

Rafe nodded.

"But Kylie and I look enough alike to be related, so I told them I was her sister. It wasn't like they could prove otherwise. And she looks more like me than Catherine does."

My sister Catherine takes after my father's family. The Martins tend to be short and dark. Dix and I take after Mother's family, the Georgia Calverts. We're taller and blond. Like Kylie.

Rafe nodded. "You're sure this didn't have nothing to do with you, right?"

"This?" I peered up at him. "You mean, Kylie being hit over the head and ending up in the hospital? I don't see how it could. She was at home. Her home, not mine. There's no way anyone would expect me to be there."

Rafe nodded, but still looked worried. The elevator lurched

to a stop at the garage level, and the doors slid open. We stepped out, right into the path of a woman with messy brown hair and a worried look, dressed in dumpy jeans and a frumpy T-shirt. It took me a second—all right, more than a second—to recognize the put-together business woman I'd seen two days ago. The elevator doors were closing when I swung on my heel and stuck my arm into the narrowing crack.

"Lauren!"

"Shit," Rafe muttered, probably at the sight of my arm in danger of being crushed by the sliding elevator doors.

The woman inside blinked. "Do I know you?"

Not yet, but that was about to change. I reached in and yanked her out of the elevator.

"Hey!" she protested.

"Sorry," I said, "but you're Lauren, right? I saw you on Friday. You were going out to lunch with Kylie."

She folded her arms across her chest. "So?"

"So you're going up to see her, aren't you?"

"Yes," Lauren said, the single syllable laced with a heavy dose of 'what's it to you?'

"We just came from there," I said, "and we have a couple of questions."

She sneered. "Why should I answer questions for you?"

I looked at Rafe. He rolled his eyes, but pulled his TBI identification out of his pocket and showed it to her. She sneered at it, too. "What's the TBI got to do with this?"

"Not much," Rafe told her, "but my wife is a friend of Kylie's. And I do have the power to arrest you, so it would probably be best if you'd just tell her what she wants to know."

"You don't worry me," Lauren said, but she didn't walk away. Behind her, the elevator doors shut and the car started moving as someone else summoned it from another floor. "Well? What do you want to know?"

It's hard to think when someone's that pushy.

"I guess first of all what you're doing here."

"My friend was attacked," Lauren said. "Why wouldn't I be here?"

"Did the police contact you?"

She nodded.

"I guess they asked you about Friday night?"

"I didn't see Kylie Friday night," Lauren said. "I had a date."

"So when Kylie came to your place, you weren't home?"

"*If* she came to my place," Lauren said. "You don't know that she did. I don't, either. I wasn't there."

Point taken, even if she sounded a touch defensive about it.

"When did you find out what had happened?"

"The police called me in the middle of the day yesterday. I would have been here then, but the detective I spoke to said she'd be unconscious until this morning, so I should wait."

"And you did?"

She shrugged. "No sense in sitting beside her bed if she's out cold."

I guess not, although if it had been Rafe, I would have been here. Even if only to watch him breathe. They'd have had to throw me out when it was time to close up for the night.

I glanced up at him and saw that his eyes were amused. He knew what I was thinking.

I turned back to Lauren. "I don't suppose you have any idea who knocked her out? I know you didn't speak to her on Friday night," or so she claimed, "but you did have lunch together. Did she mentioned anything that was going on?"

"Just about the letters," Lauren said, and sneered again when I looked surprised. "We were friends. We talked about things."

"You used to be more than friends, didn't you? Until she met Aislynn?"

"We dated," Lauren said with an off-handed shrug that didn't quite come off. "It wasn't really serious on either of our parts. And when she met the little waitress, they clicked."

That sounded like something my mother would say. Calling Aislynn 'the little waitress' instead of using her name—which she had to know; Kylie and Aislynn had been together for a while—reduced her to something instead of someone. Or so it seemed to me. "I guess you didn't approve," I said.

Lauren tossed her head. "Of their relationship? I thought she was too young and immature. That Kylie would regret getting involved with her."

"They seem to be doing OK so far. It's been almost a year, hasn't it?"

"Something like that," Lauren said, in a tone that indicated she wasn't happy to have that fact pointed out.

"I don't suppose you have any idea who might have written the anonymous letters?"

"Kylie thought it was her girlfriend's parents," Lauren said.

"What about you?"

"I figured it was the waitress," Lauren said with a shrug. "It seemed like something she'd do. Immature and spiteful."

"Why would she?"

But Lauren had no answer to that. She just didn't like Aislynn, and that was the only reason she needed. We let her head upstairs to see Kylie. And while I'd wondered when Aislynn was going to get there—since I thought it was sort of strange that she wasn't—now I hoped that she'd take her time instead. The thought of the two of them—Lauren and Aislynn—coming to blows over Kylie's hospital bed was a frightening, and very real, possibility. And Kylie—like the corpse of Virgil Wright—might go flying, with direr consequences. Virgil had been beyond pain when he'd tipped over. Kylie was still very much alive, and breakable.

Thirteen

"What did you think?" I asked Rafe when we were in the car and headed up Hillsboro Road toward downtown.

He glanced at me. "About?"

"Any of it. Kylie. Lauren. The fact that Aislynn isn't here."

"The fact that your friend kept saying her name?"

"She was just wondering if Aislynn was OK," I said. "Wasn't she?"

Rafe shrugged.

"You don't think Lauren was right, do you? That Aislynn wrote the letters, and when Kylie figured it out, she tried to kill her?"

"Dunno," Rafe said. "You're the one who knows them. You'd know that better than me."

I should. But he's got that criminal mind, always suspicious of other people's motivations, while I tend to take things at face value. I rarely look for hidden agendas, and Rafe always does.

"Would they have called me to talk about the anonymous letters if Aislynn was the one who wrote them?"

"You told me," Rafe said as he made the turn onto Division Street, "that Kylie was the one who wanted to contact you, and that Aislynn didn't want her to."

Yes, Kylie had said that.

"I'm confused," I said. "Why would Aislynn write threatening letters to herself?"

"It happens. Kids do it sometimes to get attention. Or write love letters to themselves so the other kids will think someone's interested in them."

"She's not a kid," I said.

"Young, though. And Lauren said she's immature."

"I think that might be because Lauren is older than Kylie," I said, "and she probably felt threatened by Aislynn."

Rafe thought about that for a moment as we made our way past the Music City Center—the new convention center downtown—toward the bridge linking East Nashville to the SoBro area. "Could be she was worried that her girlfriend's feelings had changed. She mighta started writing the letters just so Kylie would pay her more attention."

"Possible," I allowed. "I know she was worried about that. Lauren thinks Aislynn is immature and that Kylie needs someone older. And Aislynn thinks the same thing. That Kylie thinks she's immature and wishes Aislynn was older. More like Lauren."

"Tangled web," Rafe said.

I nodded. "Confusing. And I don't see where Virgil's murder comes into it at all."

"Maybe it don't," Rafe said, as we headed up and over the bridge. To the left was the downtown skyline and to the right the old Metro General Hospital, perched on a cliff overlooking the Cumberland River; now the site of a couple of new condo buildings. "Maybe they're two different things."

That made a lot more sense. Although at the same time, it didn't. "Isn't that too much of a coincidence?"

"Dunno," Rafe said, cresting the bridge and heading down the other side, toward Nissan Stadium, where the Tennessee Titans play. Thank God it wasn't football season yet. Sunday mornings in East Nashville during football season are gridlocked.

We crossed the interstate and headed up Shelby Avenue.

"Where are we going?" I inquired, when he didn't signal to make the turn on South Fifth.

"I thought we'd take a walk in the park."

"You mean you want to look at the crime scene?"

He shrugged. "I thought maybe you did."

I did, as a matter of fact. And for a change, I was even dressed for it, in Capri pants and a T-shirt and semi-sensible shoes.

We entered the park at the Shelby Avenue entrance, and drove around the baseball fields, the same route Grimaldi had said Virgil had taken the night he was killed. We found a parking space in the lot at the bottom of the hill, on the edge of the lake and across from the small island with the duck habitat. Rafe turned the car off and got out to open my door. "You OK walking from here?"

"Of course," I said, and took the hand he extended. "It's just up the hill, isn't it?"

He nodded. "If it's the path I'm thinking of, it is. Let's go take a look."

We went, hand in hand along the edge of the water and then around the side of the hill. About halfway up, before we got to the golf course at the top, a path snaked into the growth on the right.

"This?" I asked Rafe.

He nodded. "You OK?"

"Fine. Let's do it." I let go of his hand and headed into the trees.

The path was narrow, so we had to go single file. The ground was mulched, but not paved like the road we'd just been on. And there were tall trees all around, blocking out the morning sun, casting us into semi-darkness. It wasn't cool, though. It never is in Tennessee in July. The moisture in the air made the T-shirt cling to my back and made little pieces of mulch stick to my feet.

"This is nasty," I told Rafe over my shoulder. "I'll never understand why people choose to be outside in this."

He chuckled. "Some people like to sweat."

"Some people sweat nicely." Like him. He glistens. I turn pink and moist, like a pig's snout. "Some people don't."

We walked another few feet.

"Dark in here," I added.

"The better to kill you," Rafe told me. I shot a startled look over my shoulder, and he grinned. "Not you. But it's a nice, private place if you wanted to get rid of someone."

It was. And that was probably why the murderer had chosen this path to commit his dastardly deed. Especially if it was part of Virgil's usual route.

"So it was probably premeditated."

"Looks that way," Rafe agreed, trudging along behind me, looking around. "I don't see a lot of rocks. He had to go find one and then wait for Virgil to come running up the path. Not like anybody would be hanging out in here otherwise."

"Drug deal gone wrong? Virgil accidentally came upon something criminal, and the criminals killed him?"

"No drug dealer in his right mind would wanna do business here," Rafe said. "It's outta the way, and there's kids and dogs and people jogging. Besides, you've seen'em. They hang out on the street corners where we live."

They did. The buyers, anyway. And then the dealers would drive by and do business out of the windows of their cars.

"So whoever killed Virgil was waiting for him," I said. "Unless it was just some nutcase who wanted to commit murder and didn't care who he killed."

"Those don't come along that often," Rafe told me. "Most killers have a type. Even Huron," the serial killer from last month, "only killed young women."

"So maybe this was a serial killer who only kills 30-something gay guys. Or joggers. Men with muscles. Watch out."

He arched a brow. "How d'you know he had muscles?"

"He jogged," I said. "I assumed he kept in shape. Stacy had muscles."

Rafe scowled.

"He was wearing a towel," I said.

"I know."

"It's not like I could avoid noticing what he looked like."

"I know."

"He's gay. I'm sure he was more excited to see you than me."

"No doubt," Rafe said, "but he still shouldn'ta opened the door like that."

"He probably likes to stir people up. I told you what happened at the visitation yesterday, didn't I?"

He shook his head.

"It must have slipped my mind in the excitement." I gave him the rundown and watched him, unsuccessfully, try not to laugh.

"Wish I coulda seen that."

"It was quite something. Horrible, of course. That poor coffin. Talk about undignified."

"It didn't feel nothing," Rafe said, his voice uneven. "The guy inside didn't, either."

"I know that. It's still awful. Anyway, Stacy started it. Probably on purpose."

Rafe arched a brow, and I added, "It took guts—or stupidity, or something—to show up there in the first place. It was Kenny's memorial for Virgil. Stacy's the ex. He must have known he wouldn't be welcome."

"He mighta been telling the truth," Rafe said. "Maybe he still cared."

"That doesn't mean he had to behave inappropriately. And crashing someone else's funeral for a dead ex-lover, is inappropriate."

Rafe just shrugged, so I guess he didn't see the big deal. Maybe I thought the deal was bigger than it was, being my mother's daughter. Mother has a lot to say about inappropriate behavior. Especially mine.

"Anyway," I said, "that's what happened. And whatever Stacy's motivation for being there, he started it. When Kenny challenged him, he could have backed down. Left. Said something conciliatory. But instead he egged him on. Deliberately. I heard him giggle when Kenny charged him."

"Maybe he was just squeaking," Rafe said. "In fear."

Sure. "When I left there, he was barricaded in his Jeep, and the rest of them were trying to tip him over. I called Mendoza, and he said he'd send a couple of cars to break it up. I wonder if they arrested anyone."

"You saw him last night," Rafe said. "Why didn't you just ask?"

I'd forgotten, truth be told. In all my concern over Grimaldi's possible date with someone other than my brother, I'd forgotten all about Stacy's plight.

"We should probably call him anyway. And tell him that Kylie is awake, and that Lauren came to see her."

"And that Aislynn didn't," Rafe said. But instead of digging out his phone, he looked around. "This looks like a good spot."

While I'd just been moving forward, intent on putting one foot in front of the other and on the conversation, he'd actually been looking around. I stopped, too. "For what?"

"Murder," Rafe said. "See how the path curves around this big tree?" He reached out and put his palm against it. "If I was gonna kill somebody, here's where I'd wait. On the other side of the tree. And when the guy I was waiting for came up the path, I'd step out."

I tried to picture it. It made sense.

"A couple words," Rafe said, "maybe an argument, and as the guy tries to brush past me, or run back the way he came, a quick tap to the head."

He lifted his arm and mimed a quick strike down.

"It was probably more than a tap," I told him. "I don't think a tap would kill someone."

"Depends on who's doing the tapping," Rafe said. "You can kill somebody with a single blow if you're strong enough. And if the angle's right."

"Angle?"

He motioned me down the path ahead of him. "You ever meet him?"

"Virgil?" I shook my head. "Not to my recollection. We didn't close together in January. And I don't remember either him or Stacy being home when we were at their house. Although I admit my mind was on other things then."

Namely, the fact that Rafe had shown up at my mother's house on Christmas Eve to tell me that he'd retired from undercover work and was ready to settle down. We'd lived together from then on, and my days—and nights—were filled with much more pleasant concerns than real estate. I'd done my job, of course, making sure that Aislynn and Kylie did their due diligence in home inspections and surveys and the like, but I'd walked around in a haze of love and lust, and couldn't remember many of the details of most of the month of January.

"Does it matter?" I added.

He shrugged. "If he was tall, and he was hit standing up, whoever hit him had to be pretty tall, too. Especially if it took only one blow to kill him. It's hard to get that kind of velocity if you're a half a foot shorter and hitting up."

I'd take his word for it. "But?"

"If he was on the ground," Rafe said, "anybody coulda killed him. It's a lot easier to hit down than up. You get some help from gravity."

That made sense. "What makes you think he was on the ground?"

"Couple things," Rafe said, as I saw the end of the path ahead of us. "Did you see the handprints in the dirt on the side of the path?"

I shook my head.

"That prob'ly happened the night of the murder. It'd stopped raining by then, but the ground woulda been wet. By the next morning, it woulda been dry."

I nodded. "That could have happened if someone hit him from behind, though. Couldn't it? One blow to drop him, and another to kill?"

"Could," Rafe agreed. "I dunno whether he was hit more'n once. Did anyone ever tell you?"

I didn't think anyone had, and said so.

"Also, there was some bark rubbed off a couple trees. One on each side of the path. Like somebody'd strung a wire, maybe."

"You think the police noticed?"

"Mendoza don't strike me as stupid," Rafe said, "so he musta seen it, too."

I nodded. "So someone may have strung a trip wire across the path, and when Virgil came running, he fell. And caught himself on the edge of the path. And then someone picked up a rock and killed him."

We passed from the mulched path onto the paved road, and from under the canopy of trees into sunlight. I took a deep breath, and it wasn't until I did that I realized how much the atmosphere under the trees had affected me.

"Something like that," Rafe said, and took my hand now that we could walk side by side again. "You all right?"

"I will be. It's just sad, to think of that happening. Just where we were standing, someone died. Someone killed someone else. In a very nasty way."

Rafe nodded. "Sorry, darlin'. Maybe this wasn't a good idea."

"I'm all right," I said. "It's just disturbing to think about. Who'd do something like that?"

Mine had been more of a philosophical question, but Rafe took it literally.

"Someone who couldn't do it while he was standing up," he said. "When we practice hand-to-hand in the gym, it's all about taking your opponent down. If you can get him on the ground and get on top of him, it don't matter how much bigger and stronger he is."

"That's interesting. So the killer could have been someone much smaller and weaker."

"Coulda been," Rafe agreed. "I'm bigger and stronger than you are, but if you could drop me, you'd have the advantage over me."

"I can drop you anytime I want to," I informed him.

He grinned. "Oh, yeah?"

"Yes." I smiled back. "Want to have sex?"

"Sure. Now?"

I looked around. "I'm sure there's a private spot around here somewhere. I get to be on top, right?"

"Whatever you want," Rafe said.

"See how easy that was?"

It took him a second—it's that male brain; once you dangle the prospect of sex in front of it, it's all it can focus on—and then he chuckled. "Touché. So no sex?"

"We can have sex. Let's go home first, though. There are too many people here."

He nodded.

"Do you think somebody might have offered Virgil sex, and that's why he was on the ground on his hands and knees?"

"You never know," Rafe said and hustled me toward the car.

Fourteen

We were standing by the car, ready to get in, when someone ran past. I caught a glimpse of red, and turned. "Kenny!"

The jogger slowed and glanced over his shoulder. When he saw it was me, for a second I thought he might keep going—and then it would be interesting to see whether Rafe would let him go, or whether instinct would kick in and he'd go after Kenny and bring him back. But then Kenny slowed down. Reluctantly, but he slowed.

"Oh," he said. "It's you again."

"What are you doing here?"

He was bent over, hands braced on his thighs as he tried to catch his breath, and the sun lit up that head of red hair and made it gleam like a copper penny. "What's it look like I'm doing?" he wanted to know. "I'm running."

Yes, but... around the same park where his lover had been killed just a few days ago?

My disbelief must have communicated itself to him even though I didn't say a word, because he straightened and moved his hands from his thighs to his hips. "What are *you* doing here?"

"Walking," I said, with a look at Rafe. He arched a brow at me.

Kenny glanced at him, but didn't say anything.

"I'm sorry about what happened at the funeral home yesterday," I added.

His face darkened. "You were there?"

"Someone had to represent LB&A." And I hadn't seen Tim in the throng chasing Stacy out the door. "Virgil was one of our clients."

"Bastard," Kenny muttered, probably not in reference to his

dead lover.

"It was awkward," I agreed

He sent me a fulminating glance. "It was a freaking disaster."

That, too. "I hope everything turned out OK with the... um... deceased."

"No thanks to that nutcase!" Kenny growled.

"When I left, he was barricaded in his car. Did he get away?"

"The police came," Kenny said. "Two cars. With sirens and everything. I tried to get them to arrest him, but they said they couldn't. That he hadn't done anything illegal. As if knocking over a coffin isn't illegal!"

Technically, it was Kenny himself who had knocked over the coffin trying to wrap his hands around Stacy's throat, although I'd readily admit he'd been driven to it.

"I don't suppose there was any truth to what he was saying?"

"No!" Kenny said. "We were in love! We were talking about making it legal!"

"Getting married?"

He nodded. "We've been waiting for that for a long time."

'We' meaning the gay community, I assumed, since he and Virgil had only been living together for six months or so.

"So there was no problem with your relationship."

"No," Kenny said. "We were happy. My family liked him. We got along well."

"So why would he tell Stacy he was unhappy?"

"He wouldn't! He didn't!"

"So you're saying Stacy lied?"

"Of course he lied!" Kenny shrieked. "Virgil and I were happy! Stacy was jealous!"

That was certainly possible. Although going to his late ex-lover's funeral to tell the grieving boyfriend that the deceased had been tired of him... that argued for something more than just jealousy. It was malicious and vindictive, and as we say in the South, ugly. Kicking Kenny while he was down.

"But the police let him go."

Kenny nodded, disgusted. "They said there was nothing they could do. That he hadn't broken any laws. That I could get a restraining order if I wanted, but that they couldn't do anything about him otherwise."

There probably wasn't much point in that. And I didn't think Stacy would be bothering Kenny again. The funeral had just been too tempting for him, probably. And maybe he'd told the truth: he still did care about Virgil, and wanted to be there. And then he'd seen the chance to take some of his own grief out on Kenny, and had taken it.

"I never met Virgil," I said. "When he and Stacy were selling the house, Tim Briggs represented them. I represented the buyers. So I never met him. What did he look like?"

Kenny looked at me like he suspected I'd lost my mind, but he answered. "He looked like a black guy. You know, brown skin, black hair."

Huh. It hadn't even crossed my mind that Virgil wasn't Caucasian.

"So he looked like the friend you were with at the FinBar the other night?"

"Claude?" Kenny shook his head. "Virgil was taller. And thinner. He was a runner."

"He wasn't getting anonymous letters, was he?"

"No," Kenny said.

"Sending them?"

"Of course not! What's that about?"

"One of the girls who bought his and Stacy's house was attacked Friday night. And hit over the head with a paperweight." A rock, pretty much. "They've been getting anonymous letters."

"That's crazy," Kenny said. "And anyway, Virgil was dead on Friday. He didn't hit anyone over the head with anything."

"That's why I asked if he'd been getting anonymous letters."

Since he'd also been hit over the head with something.

Although that could just be a coincidence. Lots of people are killed with blunt force trauma to the head. Very few of the homicides are related. It's just an easy way to get rid of someone, I guess. Just snatch up the nearest blunt instrument and swing it.

"No," Kenny said. "We haven't been getting anything weird in the mail. Not before he died, and not after."

He looked around. "Are we done here?"

"We're just talking," I said. "Feel free to push off anytime you're ready."

He pushed off, without so much as a goodbye. I turned to Rafe, who'd been very quiet throughout this whole conversation. "That was interesting."

He nodded. "Ready to go?"

"I suppose we should." I opened my door and slid into the car. "What did you think?"

"That you oughta give up real estate and become an interrogator," Rafe said and turned the key in the ignition. A blast of hot air burst from the air conditioning vents, and then turned cool.

"No, thank you. And anyway, he didn't tell us anything we didn't already know."

"He told you Virgil didn't get, or write, anonymous letters," Rafe said, pulling the car out of the parking space and rolling off down the road. I kept an eye out for Kenny, and saw him ahead of us, going up the hill toward the path.

"I'm not sure we can trust what he says. He might not even know if Virgil was getting anonymous letters. Virgil might not have told him."

"Why wouldn't he tell him?"

"Maybe Stacy was right," I said. "Maybe Virgil was tired of Kenny."

"You think?"

"It's more likely that Kenny was telling the truth and Stacy was upset and jealous, but it's possible."

Halfway up the hill, Kenny turned onto the path through the woods. "Does that strike you as odd?" I asked.

"That he's out here running the same path where his lover was killed a few days ago?" He shrugged as he turned the car in the opposite direction around the lake. "Makes me wonder why they weren't running together Wednesday night, if they both ran. But grief takes people different ways. Could be his way of coping. Getting back on the horse."

I supposed. Maybe Kenny was planning to stop in the middle of the path and say a prayer for Virgil.

Or maybe he was a murderer returning to the scene of the crime. Stacy could be telling the truth about Virgil being tired of Kenny. He might have told him so on Wednesday night, then gone for a run thinking he'd give Kenny time to process the news. But instead of staying home and processing, Kenny got in his car, got to the park first, parked, hid, and bashed his lover over the head before returning home to pretend he hadn't left at all.

"I wonder who inherits Virgil's money," I said.

"Did he have money?"

"Grimaldi said he had a good job and had some savings from selling the house. It's probably not a lot, but it could be enough for someone to want it."

"He don't look like he's hurting," Rafe said, nodding in the direction of the path and Kenny.

"No. But you can't always judge by what someone looks like. He lives in a nice house, but it could be mortgaged to the rafters." Although I hadn't found any evidence of that when I'd looked him up the other day. "Or," I added, "he could have a gambling problem and owe a fortune to loan sharks."

"Gambling's illegal in Tennessee," Rafe said.

"All the more reason to keep it quiet. For Kenny to inherit, Virgil would have had to make a will benefitting him, though.

They aren't married, so they aren't each other's next of kin."

Rafe nodded. "If something happens to me—"

"Don't say that!"

He glanced at me. "Something's gonna happen to all of us sooner or later, darlin'."

"Later," I said. "Much, much later. You aren't undercover anymore. You're safe now."

"Shit happens to people who ain't undercover, too. Just look at Virgil."

"I'm not going to get tired of you and hit you over the head," I told him. "If I do get tired of you," and I didn't see that happening soon, or ever, "I'll divorce you, like civilized people do. Give me a break, Rafe. We haven't even been married a whole month yet. Just let me enjoy it for a while without having to worry about something happening to you so I inherit, all right?"

He shrugged. "I was just gonna say that if something happens to me, you gotta make sure my grandma's taken care of. And David. And the baby."

"Ginny and Sam will take care of David," I said, "but of course I'll make sure your grandmother and the baby are taken care of. And if something happens to Ginny and Sam, I'll take care of David, too. And if something happens to me, you'll have to make sure my family gets to know the baby, all right?"

"Nothing's gonna happen to you." He turned the car out through the big stone gates marking the entrance to the park.

"Something could happen to me. I could die in childbirth. Or a traffic accident. Or get sick or something. Promise."

"If something happened to you, your mama would get her hands on that baby so fast your head would spin. I wouldn't stand a chance of keeping it."

"Don't be silly," I said. "My mother would never take our baby away from you."

"You wanna bet?" He shook his head. "I don't wanna talk

about it. Nothing's gonna happen to you. To either of us. You're gonna have the baby, and we're gonna raise him—or her—together. Nobody's gonna take him away from either of us."

"I'll drink to that," I said, although there was nothing whatsoever to drink in the car. "Let's just go back to Virgil and Kenny. They weren't married when Virgil died, so Kenny doesn't inherit whatever Virgil owned."

Rafe nodded.

"Whoever Virgil's next of kin is, inherits. Unless Virgil had a will, and then it's whoever he named in the will."

Rafe nodded. "No way to figure out if he did or not, I guess."

"Detective Mendoza might know," I said. "And he might be willing to share if you ask nicely."

"Me?"

"He seems to like you. Fellow law enforcement and all that."

He slanted a disbelieving glance at me, as if I'd accused him of inappropriate behavior, and I added, "The two of you seemed to find plenty to talk about the other night."

"He was telling me about his kid," Rafe said. "The ex-wife has primary custody, but he gets to see him pretty much whenever he wants. But he's afraid she's gonna marry again once the divorce is final, and what's gonna happen when she does."

I could well imagine. That would worry me, too. I'd had a miscarriage while I was married to Bradley, and had been devastated at the time, but once we split up, I was very glad that we didn't have children together. And now that he was in prison, I was even happier about that. "I'm sure she won't keep his son from him."

"Depends on how pissed off she is about what he did," Rafe said.

"What did he do?"

He glanced at me. "Cheated. She hired a private eye to catch him, and the guy did. And now they're engaged and just waiting for the divorce to be final so they can get married."

"Sheesh," I said. "So the guy who proved to Mendoza's wife that Mendoza was cheating is going to be her next husband and the kid's stepfather? That's got to hurt."

"You know it," Rafe said, and turned on the signal for the turn onto Potsdam. "Anyway, we were talking kids. His, mine, and the one on the way."

Male bonding over children. Who'd have thought?

"The one on the way is also yours," I reminded him.

"I know. It just don't seem real yet."

"Maybe when we have the ultrasound and find out if it's a he or a she, it'll seem more real to you."

He shrugged and changed the subject. "Almost home. Whaddaya wanna do the rest of the day?"

"I promised you sex," I said, "so we should probably get that out of the way first."

He arched a brow. "Don't do me any favors."

"I was looking at it more like you doing me the favor."

The corner of his mouth turned up. "Yeah?"

"If you'd oblige."

"I think I might could do that," Rafe said, and turned into the graveled drive.

So we had sex, and then we had a nap, and then we had something to eat, and while we were doing that, Rafe's phone rang. He answered, and I spent a minute or two nibbling on turkey and Swiss cheese while I listened to him say things like, "What the hell?" and "Have you lost your fucking mind?" and "That ain't gonna end well."

The conversation ended with, "Don't do nothing till I get there. Nothing. You hear me?"

The phone quacked, and I assumed the answer was in the affirmative, because Rafe didn't say anything else, just stabbed the End button with enough emotion to make me suspect he'd rather be drilling that finger into somebody's chest while he screamed in his face.

"What?"

He got to his feet. "Sorry, darlin'. I gotta go."

"What happened?"

He grimaced. "That was Jamal. He's got himself a situation."

"What kind of situation?" I put my sandwich down, the better to concentrate on the conversation. It wouldn't be a long one, I could tell, so I'd have to get what I needed quickly.

"Gang," Rafe said, shoving his feet into sneakers.

"That doesn't sound good." Jamal's brother had died as a result of gang violence, and that was why Jamal had wanted to join the TBI.

Rafe shook his head. "Somebody approached him. Somebody from the neighborhood, who knew his brother."

He pulled open the kitchen drawer where he'd stashed his gun when he came in. I watched as he shoved it into the holster at the small of his back. While he did that, I thought about what I knew about Jamal, other than the dead brother thing.

It wasn't much. We'd only met a few times. He'd worked just as hard as everyone else when Rafe went missing in June, and had been willing to do whatever it took to find Rafe and bring him back. He seemed like a nice kid, outgoing and a natural leader.

"It was something about an action against another gang," Rafe said, adjusting the T-shirt he was wearing so it covered any sight of the gun and holster, "the one that was responsible for killing Deondre."

"Deondre being Jamal's brother?"

He nodded. "This guy from the neighborhood thought Jamal might wanna be a part of it. Jamal said yes, and now he's calling me to tell him what to do."

"You don't know anything about gangs, do you?"

"Not much," Rafe said.

"What are you going to tell him?"

"I already told him he's lost his mind. And I'm gonna tell him again when I see him. But he thinks this could be a chance to put some of these guys behind bars."

"The ones who didn't shoot his brother?"

"He blames them just as much," Rafe said, stuffing a last few bites of sandwich into his mouth and washing them down with milk. "If Deondre hadn't been in a gang, none of it woulda happened."

He had a point. Or Jamal did.

"But is he ready for this?"

"Hell, no," Rafe said.

"So are you going to talk him out of it? Or offer to help?"

"Right now I'm just gonna talk to him." He put the empty glass on the table with a decisive thunk. "Don't do anything stupid while I'm gone."

"I might go back to the hospital," I told his back as he headed for the door. "See if Aislynn ever showed up. And if Kylie remembers anything more about what happened Friday night."

He glanced at me over his shoulder. "Just be careful."

"Always," I said, and waited for the front door to latch and lock before I got to my feet and began to clean up after lunch. Outside, the Harley roared to life and, a second later, tore down the driveway with a spurt of gravel.

Fifteen

Vanderbilt Hospital looked just as it had when I left earlier this morning. Different nurse on duty at the desk, so I had to go through the process of explaining who I was—or rather, who I wasn't—again. After that, I was directed to my 'sister's' room, where everything also looked the same.

Dr. Ramsey was nowhere to be seen. Busy with other patients, I guess, or maybe just done for the day. Or off somewhere having lunch.

Lauren was also gone. Kylie was alone, looking pale and wan, but slightly more alert than earlier. When she heard me at the door, she turned to look at me.

"Oh," she said, her voice still a little raspy, but stronger than earlier, "it's you."

It was obvious I wasn't who she'd been hoping to see, but I didn't comment.

"Rafe had to go to work," I said instead. "I thought I'd come back and see you one more time today."

I pulled a chair up to the bed and folded myself into it. "Are you feeling any better?"

"My head hurts," Kylie said, "but they're giving me something for it." She lifted her hand weakly to indicate an attached IV.

"You're talking much better now."

She nodded. "I had some food. Soup and Jell-O. And I've had visitors."

"We saw Lauren on our way out this morning," I said, and added, when she looked surprised, "I recognized her from when I saw her on Friday. The two of you were going to lunch, remember?"

She said yes, but I had no idea whether she actually remembered or not. Chances were she did. It would have been just the minute or two immediately before being hit she'd have lost.

"She said she didn't see you on Friday night," I added. "That she was out on a date when you got to her house."

She looked puzzled.

"Don't you remember?"

She shook her head.

"Do you remember talking to her?"

"I'm not sure," Kylie admitted. "I remember talking to her, but it could have been earlier. At lunch. The drugs are making it hard to concentrate."

"Have the police been here?"

"That good-looking detective stopped by. The one who told us about the dead man."

"Detective Mendoza," I said. "Did he have anything new to report?"

She shook her head.

"What about Aislynn? Has she been here?"

A shadow crossed her face. "No."

"Really?" Maybe I shouldn't have been, but I admit to being surprised. I had understood—or thought I understood—why she didn't want to stay in the house alone last night. Kylie had been attacked there, and then there were the threatening letters. And I'd understood why she'd wanted to go home to her parents. She was young, alone, and scared. But I was surprised she hadn't come back. I had never questioned her devotion to Kylie. "Have you spoken to her?"

"I called," Kylie whispered, "but she didn't pick up."

I'd have to call, too, later. And see if she'd pick up for me. Now didn't seem like a good time. Who knew how long Kylie would be up for talking? I should take advantage of it while she did.

"Did anyone tell you that your ex-husband was here last night?"

Her eyes opened wide. "Damian?"

"That's who he said he was. Dr. Ramsey told me. But it was after visiting hours and you weren't awake, so he didn't get in to see you. Detective Mendoza didn't mention it?"

She shook her head. "Why would Damian come here?"

"I have no idea," I said. "I'm not even sure it was Damian." Although if it wasn't, it was someone who knew that Kylie had been married to Damian Mitchell. "You didn't call him?"

"I was unconscious," Kylie said.

"Would Aislynn have called him?"

She shook her head. "Damian and I split up long before I met Aislynn. She's never even met him. She wouldn't have any idea how to get in touch with him."

"Someone must have." Unless it hadn't been Damian at all. Unless it had been the person who had broken into the house and hit Kylie when she came home and found him. "Maybe you should ask Dr. Ramsey to describe the guy, and see if the description matches."

"Or I could just call Damian and ask," Kylie said.

I suppose she could. Although I didn't tell her to. "Why don't you just lie back and rest for a while," I suggested instead, "while I tell you about the funeral yesterday."

"You went to a funeral?"

"Virgil's funeral," I said. "The guy who owned the house you live in before you did. The guy who was killed on Wednesday."

She wiggled down in the bed, one careful inch at a time. "You went to his funeral?"

I nodded. "I don't think I ever met him. He wasn't ever there when we came to see the house, that I recall. Do you remember meeting him?"

She shook her head.

"But LB&A represented him and his partner in the sale.

Someone had to do it."

"So what happened?" Kylie wanted to know, getting comfortable against the pillows.

"Well, after he sold the house to you, he and his boyfriend split up. And Virgil moved in with another guy..." I detailed the whole relationship, all the way up to the showdown at the funeral yesterday. When I described the coffin falling over, Kylie gasped, but by the time I got to Stacy in his Jeep in the parking lot, surrounded by a dozen or more guys rocking it back and forth in an effort to get him out, she was shaking with feeble laughter.

"I called Detective Mendoza," I said, "and he sent a couple of squad cars to break things up, but apparently no one was arrested. Causing a scene at a funeral doesn't seem to be a prosecutable offense."

"I'll have to remember that," Kylie answered weakly. She seemed amused, but that amusement was taking energy, and she didn't have much to spare.

"I should probably leave you to get some rest." I made to get up from the chair, and she put out a hand.

"Wait a second."

I sank back down. "What?"

"I'm worried about Aislynn."

Of course she was. I was, too. "I'll call her," I promised. "Maybe she'll pick up for me. And if not, maybe I'll try to track down her parents. They probably have a landline."

"The number's in the Rolodex in the office."

"Your home office?"

She nodded.

"I'm sure your house is locked," I told her. "And I doubt anyone remembered to bring your purse when we rushed you out of there yesterday morning."

She looked around for it—I didn't see it, and it appeared she didn't, either—and turned back to me. "There's a hide-a-key on the back porch. Inside the thermometer."

"Really?" An image of the guy in the plaid shirt flashed before my eyes. "Who knows about that?"

"Just Aislynn and me," Kylie said. "And a couple of people we've told."

"Lauren?"

She shrugged. I took that to mean yes. "Your ex-husband?"

"No," Kylie said. "I haven't spoken to Damian since we moved into the house."

"Your parents?"

"Of course."

"Have they stayed in touch with Damian?" And was it possible that they might have told him?

Kylie shrugged.

"How long have you had it?"

"It was there when we bought the place," Kylie said.

So presumably the previous owners knew about it, as well. Stacy and Virgil. And whoever they'd told. Like maybe Kenny and Kenny's friend, the bald guy.

For all I knew, half of Nashville might know about the hide-a-key thermometer.

"I'll see if I can get in touch with Aislynn," I said. "And if I can't, I'll go to your house and use the hide-a-key to access the Rolodex and call her parents."

Kylie nodded.

"Do you want me to bring you your purse when I come back tomorrow?"

She shook her head. "I think I'm being released in the morning. Just make sure the key is in the thermometer so I can get in when I get home."

"Do you need a ride?"

"No," Kylie said. "If I can't get hold of Aislynn, Lauren will take me home."

"Are you sure that's a good idea?"

"If Aislynn's left," Kylie said, "it doesn't matter."

"I don't mind driving you," I told her. "I did in December, remember?"

"I don't want to impose on you again," Kylie said. "Maybe I'll call Damian."

I shook my head. "Don't do that. We don't know how he's involved in this. And I don't mind. I have a flexible schedule. I'm happy to pick you up and take you home. There's a sales meeting I have to go to at nine, but after that I'm free. If I don't get in touch with Aislynn, I'll make sure I'm here to get you."

She thanked me. I said goodbye and took myself off. And once I was in the car and on my way toward East Nashville, I dialed Aislynn's number.

The phone rang. And rang.

She didn't pick up.

It's illegal in Tennessee to text and drive, so I took a second to flick on the little microphone icon and then spoke a text message instead.

It's Savannah. I'm just coming home from seeing Kylie. She's worried about you. So am I. Please give me a call.

The auto correct tried changing Savannah to Samantha and Kylie to Julie. Once we got that sorted out, I sent it off and kept driving. And waiting for a response that didn't come. By the time I pulled up in front of Aislynn and Kylie's house in East Nashville, Aislynn still hadn't gotten back to me.

The first thing I did was ring the doorbell, just in case she had come back to Nashville this morning—or hadn't gone to Bowling Green at all yesterday. When there was no answer, I wandered around the house, through the gate, and into the backyard to look for the hide-a-key in the thermometer on the deck.

It was just a couple of days since I'd stood here, wondering where the guy in the plaid shirt had gone. I hadn't noticed the thermometer then. I had to look for it now. It was hanging, demurely, on the wall next to the door, blending into the pale gray paint and trim: a small, white strip that looked like any other thermometer I'd ever seen. According to the mercury, it was approaching ninety-five, which sounded accurate. Obviously, it was a working thermometer as well as a hide-a-key box.

It took me a few moments to figure out the mechanism. First I tried opening the front, like a door, from the left and right, but that didn't work. Finally I figured out that the bottom opened, and dropped down. A key was tucked into a little tube that disappeared up inside the thermometer and latched on up there.

I shook the key out in my hand and inserted it in the knob, which was gray and sticky from the fingerprint powder the crime scene crew had used. Inside, I locked the door behind me—you never know when someone might decide to join you if you leave the door open for them, and uninvited company was the last thing I wanted in an empty house. Then I put the inner workings of the thermometer on the floor next to the door and looked around.

Everything in the family room looked normal. There were books on the shelves, magazines on the table, and pillows on the couch. It was just the doorknob, inside and out, and the key itself that showed evidence of fingerprint powder. Everything else was in its proper place and showed no sign of having been tampered with.

I headed from the family room down the hall to the front of the house, looking around as I went.

Everything else looked normal, the way it had when I was here on Thursday night. The house felt empty, but I stopped at the bottom of the stairs and called up. "Aislynn? Are you here?"

There was no answer, and no sound of movement upstairs. I went up anyway, and stuck my head into the master bedroom. The bed was made and the curtains pulled. The towels on the towel bars were dry. Nobody had showered here this morning.

Downstairs, I checked out the kitchen—empty, with no dirty dishes in the sink and no evidence that anyone had been here in the past twenty-four hours. Same for the dining room. It didn't look like the crime scene crew had done any investigating in any of these rooms. Nobody was hiding behind the shower curtain, and the towels downstairs were as dry as their master bathroom counterparts.

At last I came to the parlor-cum-office at the front of the house. It also looked the way it did when I last saw it. A big, fat mess, in other words. Now amplified by the work the crime scene crew had done. There was fingerprint powder everywhere: on the edges of the desk, the door knob and jamb, the drawer pulls, the light switch...

A small, dark stain on the rug made my stomach lurch for a moment, until I reminded myself that I'd just seen Kylie, and she was alive and well. The rug would have to be shampooed, though. Or replaced. Blood is very difficult to get out of fibers.

I hadn't paid a lot of attention yesterday morning. All of my focus had been on Aislynn and Kylie and on swallowing back nausea. Now I took a good look around and compared the room now to what it had looked like Thursday night, when I'd sat here with Kylie.

Several of the drawers had been upended and the contents dumped on the floor. I saw gaping manila folders labeled in Kylie's neat handwriting, mixed with paid bills, old bank statements, and tax forms.

There were lots of interesting things there, for your standard burglar. Bank account numbers, social security numbers, credit card numbers, PINs... And that might be one explanation for what had happened. Someone had broken in looking for something like that. To do a spot of identity theft, or just to clean out someone's bank account.

The other explanation was the anonymous letters. I didn't see any of them in the mess. Not a single letter or a single envelope with that distinctive, spiky handwriting.

Not that that meant anything. Detective Mendoza could have

taken them with him when he was here earlier in the evening. Or they could have walked out in the afternoon, with the man—or woman—in the plaid shirt.

Someone would have to go through this mess to make an inventory of what was missing. That would fall to Kylie, most likely, when she felt up for it. Or Aislynn, if she came back. Although this office, and the organization of it, struck me as being more Kylie's doing than Aislynn's. Aislynn was more of a free spirit. If it was up to her, there probably wouldn't be any paper statements, nor for that matter any records of any kind.

The Rolodex was still on the desk, threatening to fall off one corner. I rescued it, and started flipping through. The Turners' number in Bowling Green was the first one I looked up, and once I found it, I pulled out my phone and dialed.

A half a minute passed. Then another. I was about to give up when a breathless woman's voice came on the line. "Yes?"

"I'm sorry to bother you," I said politely.

"Oh, it's no bother. We were sitting on the porch having some sweet tea."

A proper Southern pastime on a lazy Sunday afternoon in the middle of summer.

"Mrs. Turner?"

She murmured in the affirmative.

"My name is Savannah Martin," I said. "Can I speak to Aislynn?"

"'May I.'"

"Excuse me?"

"It's 'may I speak to Aislynn?'"

Of course it was. "I'm sorry," I said. "May I speak to Aislynn?"

"She's not here," Mrs. Turner said.

"Has she left already? Is she on her way home?"

"Home from where?" Aislynn's mother asked. "We haven't seen Aislynn for months."

Shit. I mean... shoot.

I thought about clarifying—asking whether she was sure Aislynn hadn't driven up yesterday afternoon and spent the night with them—but of course she was sure. If her daughter had been there, she'd know. And telling her that Aislynn wasn't where she was supposed to be, would only serve to worry her.

So I pretended that nothing was wrong. "Would you have any idea where I could get in touch with her?"

"This is her cell phone number," her mother said, rattling it off. It was the same number I had myself, the one Aislynn wasn't answering. "She works at a restaurant called Sara Beth's in Nashville."

In Brentwood, if you wanted to be technical, but I didn't say so, just pretended to take down the information. I'd try calling Sara Beth's in a minute. It was a pretty good idea, actually.

"She has a roommate," her mother said. "Her name is Kylie. This is her number."

She gave me Kylie's cell phone number, which I also already had. I thanked her anyway, while I noted the fact that Aislynn's mother called Kylie Aislynn's roommate and not her girlfriend or lover or significant other. Denial, or something else?

"So you haven't seen her lately?" I asked when she'd finished giving me numbers.

"Not for a few months. We were down in Nashville for a theatre performance in May, and we had dinner with her before the show. But I haven't seen her since."

She sounded sincere.

"I appreciate it," I told her. "I'll try the numbers you gave me. If you hear from her, would you mind telling her that I'm looking to talk to her? My name is Savannah."

She assured me she would, and I let her get back to her sweet tea and, presumably, her husband.

The number for Sara Beth's wasn't hard to find, either. It was in the Rolodex. I dialed, and waited. And waited some more.

Finally, a recording came on. "You've reached Sara Beth's Café, in the Brentwood Commons Shopping Center. Our business hours are from 11 ^AM to 9 ^PM Monday through Friday, and 11 ^AM to 6 ^PM on Saturdays. We're closed Sunday. Please come back during our regular business hours."

So that took care of that. Aislynn wasn't working today, and if she was at Sara Beth's, she was camping out in a closed restaurant, probably subsisting on a diet of field greens and McDonald's French fries. And not answering the phone.

I kept looking through the Rolodex, and made a note of Damian Mitchell's phone number. It was probably left over from before Aislynn and Kylie got together. The name and number were written in the same neat cursive as the file folders strewn across the floor, while the numbers for the Turners and Sara Beth's Café were written in a spikier, less even hand.

I flipped through the Rolodex for anything else of interest, but didn't see any other names I recognized. Kylie must have removed Lauren's info card once she and Aislynn got together.

Kylie's purse was on the floor, sideways and gaping open. It was a brown leather satchel, that I recognized from Friday afternoon when she was going to lunch. Some of the contents had spilled out, or perhaps the burglar had dug through the purse after knocking Kylie over the head.

The mental image of that was a bit disturbing.

And maybe it hadn't happened that way. Maybe the bag had opened and the contents escaped when Kylie collapsed. Maybe the burglar had hit her and beat it as fast as he could.

I squatted on the floor next to it, and picked through the stuff, looking for anything of interest, but it all looked much like the contents of my purse, or the purse of any other woman of around thirty in the US. A couple of lipsticks. A mirror—luckily not broken in the fall. Two tampons in a discreet case. A small package of tissues. A wallet—and a quick look inside showed me the edges of a couple of bills, as well as the corners of credit cards. Only Kylie would be able to tell whether one or more of them was missing, but chances were that the burglar would have taken all the money if he wanted money at all, and he wouldn't have picked and chosen between the credit cards. If money was something he was interested in, he would have just taken the whole wallet.

I tucked it all back in the purse and set it upright next to the wall. Nothing of interest there, that I could see. And while I hated to leave Kylie with all this to clean up, a lot of it was confidential papers, so I didn't feel like I could take it upon myself to clean up, either.

Besides, I'd have a hard time trying to figure out where a lot of it belonged.

A thought occurred to me, and I got to my feet and headed back up the stairs to the second floor.

When the house was renovated—by Virgil and Stacy or whoever came before them—the entire second floor had been turned into a master suite. And while that probably sounds excessive, let me just explain that this was a Folk Victorian cottage, one-and-a-half stories tall, with maybe fifteen hundred square feet on the first floor and a much smaller space in the middle of the upstairs where the ceiling height was such that it was possible for a normal adult to stand upright. Rafe might have felt a little squeezed.

The master suite might have been four hundred square feet, maybe. Probably a little less. A large bedroom with skylights, a 10 x 10 walk-in closet, and a slightly bigger bathroom. There was no shower curtain here. It was all floating glass, bright and open. I could see everything from just inside the door, and nobody was hiding anywhere.

I made a beeline for the closet and pushed the door open. One side was dedicated to business suits in black, gray, and navy blue. The other had flowing gypsy skirts, beaded blouses, and lots of crazy colors. Colors and designs the conservative Kylie wouldn't be caught dead in. It didn't take genius to see which part of the closet belonged to which woman.

And Aislynn's clothes were there, hanging in neat rows with no obvious gaps where anything had been removed. A fact that made me breathe easier. I couldn't tell Kylie where her girlfriend had gone, but at least I didn't have to report that Aislynn had moved out of the house in Kylie's absence. That wasn't the kind of news I would have wanted to impart.

With that possibility at least off my mind, I headed back down the stairs. I made sure the front door was locked, and then I locked the back door, too, and shoved the key back inside the thermometer. It still said ninety-five degrees.

On my way to the car, I stopped at the mailbox.

Of course I knew there hadn't been any mail delivered today. It was Sunday. But I thought it possible that no one had picked up the mail yesterday, between one thing and the other, and so it would still be in the box.

And so it was. An electric bill, a circular from a local grocery store, coupons for pizza, a letter from St. Jude's Hospital, and a square envelope, addressed in a spiky hand, ripped open at the top. Addressed to Aislynn Turner.

I peered inside. I wouldn't have been surprised if the envelope had been empty. If whoever opened it had kept the letter. But it wasn't. There was a piece of paper inside, the usual 92 brightness Xerox copy paper.

I unfolded it and read the message.

YOU'RE NEXT, it said.

Sixteen

I admit it, I felt a shiver go down my spine, and the letter wasn't even addressed to me. I could only imagine how Aislynn must have felt, reading it.

She had told Mendoza she was going home to her parents, but she hadn't gone there. Now that made perfect sense. I wouldn't have gone to Sweetwater either, if someone was gunning for me. I might not even have gone home to Rafe, although he's quite capable of taking care of himself—and me— so I might have risked that. Especially as, if he'd found out I was in danger and I hadn't come to him, he'd have killed me himself.

But I wouldn't have involved my mother or siblings. Or anyone else I cared about.

Maybe she really was hunkered down at Sara Beth's, waiting for Monday morning and her coworkers to come in.

Or maybe the anonymous letter-writer had her, and that was why she hadn't shown up at her parents', and why she hadn't come to the hospital to see Kylie. Not because she chose not to, but because she couldn't.

I pulled out my phone and dialed Mendoza's number. It rang and rang until finally his voicemail picked up. "You've reached Jaime Mendoza with the Metro Nashville PD. I can't take your call right now. Please leave me a message and I'll get back to you as soon as I can. If this is an emergency, please call 911."

It wasn't an emergency—or probably not what Mendoza would consider an emergency—so I waited for the beep and told him to call me when he had a minute. Then I disconnected and called Tamara Grimaldi instead.

"Good," I said when she answered, "you're working."

Her voice was dry. "I'm not sure if that's good or bad, but

yes, I am."

"I tried to call Mendoza, but he didn't answer."

"Afternoon off," Grimaldi said. "He's probably spending it with Elias."

Elias must be the kid. And it was hard to blame him for not answering the phone if he had an afternoon to spend with his son. Especially as he'd taken the time to visit Kylie this morning. "I have something for him. If I give it to you, can you make sure he gets it?"

"What is it?" Grimaldi wanted to know.

"Another anonymous letter." I explained where I was, why, and how I'd checked the mailbox. "I think all the other letters are gone. At least I didn't see them inside. Granted, the place is a bit of a mess. But they weren't in the piles of paper I could see. I think whoever wrote them must have come back for them. Maybe he thought there was something there that we could trace to him."

"We?" Grimaldi said.

"You. Whatever. You know what I mean."

"I think Jaime probably got them on Friday," Grimaldi said, "and they're already at the lab, but if you have another—one that hasn't been handled by so many people—that's great."

"I've handled it. And I figure Aislynn probably did." I explained about the ripped envelope and how it wasn't likely to have been anyone else reading the mail. "She's gone. Nobody knows where she is. She told Mendoza she was going to go spend the night with her parents in Bowling Green, but she didn't go there. She didn't come to us. She hasn't been home, and she hasn't visited Kylie in the hospital. I'm worried."

"I'm sure she's fine," Grimaldi said bracingly. "Just lying low until she doesn't have to be in the house alone."

"Kylie won't be much help even when she gets there. She's flat on her back with a concussion."

Grimaldi did the sort of shrug I could hear. "I'm in the

office," she told me, "if you want to come downtown with the letter now."

I might as well. I wasn't doing anything else, and I was only a mile away. "I'll be there in ten minutes."

"I'll be waiting," Grimaldi said and disconnected.

She was as good as her word. When I walked into the lobby of the police headquarters building—quiet now on a Sunday afternoon—she was there, leaning on the counter where the duty cop was sitting, chatting. "This is her," she told him when I came in.

He nodded. "I still need to see your ID, ma'am."

I produced it, and signed the log he put in front of me, and then Grimaldi and I headed upstairs to her office.

Once there, she took a seat behind her desk and snapped on a pair of latex gloves. There was already an empty space cleared in the middle of the desk. "Put the letter here."

I pulled it out of my purse and put it on the desk. Carefully, by the edges, so I wouldn't add any more fingerprints than the ones I'd already added.

Grimaldi sprinkled the envelope with fingerprint powder and blew it off.

"Got a couple of good ones here." She fumbled for tape.

"Probably mine. And Aislynn's."

She nodded. "We'll see. Yours are on file. We'll have to get hers."

"That could be tricky. I told you I have no idea where she is."

"She'll turn up," Grimaldi said, moving fingerprints from the envelope to little index cards on the back of pieces of tape. "OK. Let's take a look at the letter."

I moved to open the envelope, and she shook her head. "I've got it."

She took the envelope by the edges and shook the letter out, then used a couple of pens to unfold it. "Hmmm."

"Scary," I said.

"Could be. Depends on what it refers to."

"I assumed it referred to what happened to Kylie. Or maybe even to Virgil Wright."

"And you could be right," Grimaldi said, busy with her powder and pieces of tape again. "We've got a couple of prints here. Just about in the position I'd expect them to be if someone took the letter out of the envelope and held it up to read."

"So mine and Aislynn's."

She nodded. "Most likely. But we could get lucky."

"The post mark is East Nashville again," I pointed out. "Just a few blocks from where Aislynn and Kylie live. For the letter to arrive on Saturday, it must have been mailed on Friday."

"Sounds reasonable."

"I spent Friday talking to a bunch of people. Aislynn and Kylie themselves, Stacy Kelleher, Kenny Grimes, Tim..."

She arched her brows. "Surely you don't suspect Mr. Briggs of sending the letters?"

"There isn't much I would put past Tim," I told her. "He could have been hoping for another house to sell. But no, I guess not. Aislynn and Kylie wouldn't call him. They'd call me." As in fact they had.

"Your point?" Her fingers stayed busy with the letter and envelope.

"I talked to people on Friday. About the letters. On Friday night, someone broke into Aislynn and Kylie's house to take the letters back. Maybe it was because he or she realized that someone was looking into it. That it had turned into something more than just private poison pen letters sent to an individual. Or individuals."

"Could be," Grimaldi agreed. "That means it'd be one of the people you talked to. Or someone they talked to."

Kenny Grimes's dinner date came to mind. Although if that guy had hit Kylie over the head, she'd probably be dead.

Or there was Kenny himself—although why he'd send

threatening, anonymous letters to the current owners of his lover's former house was beyond me. He might have had a reason for wanting to get rid of Virgil, though, and the letters might just be a part of that. A red herring, so to speak.

And Stacy—ditto. Although if he was retaliating for Virgil leaving him, he sure had waited a long time to do it. And the letters made no sense from his perspective, either, although again, they could just be a red herring to detract from the real reason someone wanted Virgil dead.

Kylie may have explained who I was and what I was doing to Lauren during their lunch on Friday. If Lauren had been writing the letters—to scare Aislynn away so she could get Kylie back; a reason that actually made sense—she might have decided it was a good idea to get them back before someone connected them to her. She had said she'd been out on a date on Friday night, but who knew where she'd really been?

If she still loved Kylie, would she hit her, though?

Or maybe Kylie had been writing the letters to get out of her relationship with Aislynn, and Aislynn had found out, and Aislynn had hit Kylie. And now she was in the wind, afraid of being arrested for assault or attempted murder.

Or maybe Aislynn had been writing the letters to herself, to get out of her relationship with Kylie without having to admit she wanted to break up, and now she'd taken the opportunity to leave.

That made sense, except for the fact that all her clothes were still at the house.

"I have no idea who's behind this," I told Grimaldi. Or maybe 'whimpered' would be closer to the mark.

She glanced up at me. "We'll figure it out."

"I don't see how. It doesn't make any sense. It could be any number of people writing the letters, for any number of reasons, but I don't see what the letters have to do with Virgil's murder."

"Maybe nothing," Grimaldi said.

"Don't you think it's too much of a coincidence if they aren't connected?"

"Maybe," Grimaldi said, "maybe not. In real life, crimes aren't always neat."

I guess not. "It seems like they should be, though."

Grimaldi shrugged.

"Does Mendoza have any suspects?"

She gave me the beady eye.

"We saw Kenny this morning," I said. "Rafe and I. In Shelby Park. He was jogging. Down the same path where Virgil was killed Wednesday night."

This time she arched her brows.

"Does that seem a bit callous to you?"

"He might think it'll help," Grimaldi said. "To see the place where his boyfriend died. Just in case something of him lingers there."

I suppressed a shiver. "If something lingers, we didn't notice it. And if it does, I'm not sure I want to know."

Grimaldi gave me the eye.

"Rafe said he thought someone might have strung a wire or something across the path, to trip Virgil and make him fall. He said there was bark rubbed off a couple of trees."

"Jaime noted the same thing," Grimaldi said.

Good for Mendoza. "So Rafe was right."

"So it seems," Grimaldi said. "I'm sure he explained to you how it's easier to deliver a killing blow to someone who's on the ground versus someone who's upright."

Not in those words, but— "Yes," I said. "He did."

She nodded. "Anything else?"

I thought about it. Aislynn, Kenny, the letter... "I don't think so. Will you make sure those fingerprints get to the lab?"

"Yes, Ms.... Savannah," Grimaldi said patiently, "I will."

I grimaced. "Thank you."

We sat in silence for a moment. "I'm not sure what to do," I confessed.

"About?"

"All of it. Any of it. Aislynn being gone. Kylie being in the hospital. Virgil being dead."

"It's not yours to do anything with. We'll take care of it."

I must have looked mutinous, because she added, "Go home and enjoy a quiet evening with your husband. I've got this."

"I can't," I said, getting to my feet. "He isn't home. One of the boys called. He's gotten himself in trouble, so Rafe went to get him out of it."

Grimaldi got up, too, either to walk me out or to take her fingerprints to the lab. "One of the rookies? What kind of trouble?"

"Gang," I said. "Someone invited him to be a part of some kind of retaliation against another gang, and I guess he figured it was his chance to be a hero and arrest them all."

"Your husband will talk him out of it."

Undoubtedly. Either that, or he'd offer to join them.

"I'm just worried about Aislynn," I said as we got to the door and passed through and out into the hallway. "She's out there somewhere, I don't know where, and I'm worried. She hasn't even visited Kylie in the hospital. If she isn't careful, Kylie is going to think she doesn't care and go recuperate at Lauren's house instead."

"Maybe that's what Aislynn wants," Grimaldi said.

"What if it isn't? What if this guy snatched her and is keeping her somewhere?"

"I think what happened last month is playing with your mind," Grimaldi told me, kindly. "I'm sure no one has kidnapped and is torturing her. She drove off on her own, didn't she? She's probably just lying low at a friend's house so she doesn't have to be alone in her own. I don't blame her for being nervous. Her house was broken into and her girlfriend attacked. It's understandable that she doesn't want to be there. Especially after this last letter."

It was. Very understandable. And maybe Grimaldi was right: Rafe's kidnapping last month had made me jump to conclusions. Aislynn was probably just camping out with a friend. That didn't explain why she hadn't gone to see Kylie in the hospital—unless my other theory was right and Aislynn had hit Kylie—but either way, she was gone of her own free will and not because someone else was holding her.

I took a deep breath. "Thank you."

"No problem," Grimaldi said. "I'll put out an APB on her, OK? It's too soon to report her as a missing person, and there are reasons to think she's not missing, but this way, if anyone sees her they'll let me know."

"I appreciate it."

"Don't mention it," Grimaldi said. "If these fingerprints turn up anything of interest, I'll let you know. Meanwhile, just go home and enjoy your husband. I'm sure he'll be there soon."

He probably would be. Maybe I'd stop at the grocery store on my way and surprise him with a home-cooked meal. We'd been going out to eat a lot lately. Maybe I'd be domestic tonight, and cook.

"I'm sure he'd appreciate that," Grimaldi said when I mentioned it.

I squinted at her. "Do you cook?"

"When I have time. Mostly I eat out."

If she ended up marrying Dix, that could be a problem. Sheila had practically been a professional cook. Or at least a full-time stay-at-home mom.

Of course, if Grimaldi married Dix, who was going to do the cooking was likely to be the least of the problems they'd face. If she moved to Sweetwater, she'd have to give up her job. She might have to work with Sheriff Satterfield at the Maury County sheriff's office, and the mere idea of that was making me bug-eyed.

But on the other hand, Dix had a law practice in Sweetwater, not to mention two girls in school, and a sister, brother-in-law, mother, and best friend in town. I didn't think it made sense for him to pack up and move to Nashville, either.

I wondered if they'd thought about it, and that's why their relationship seemed to move forward at a snail's pace.

None of my business. I shook it off. "I guess I'll head out. Let me know if you hear anything."

Grimaldi told me she would, and we went our separate ways: she to the lab, and me down in the elevator to the lobby, where I handed in my visitor's badge and was allowed to leave the building without being detained.

It was still just as hot outside. The sidewalk was steaming, and the blacktop felt squishy under my feet. Maybe it was too hot to cook.

I stopped at the grocery store anyway. And I bought a rotisserie chicken and some salad fixings and rolls and more ice cream, since you can never have too much Mocha Double Chunk. On my way out, I tossed in a pound cake and a pint of strawberries, too, and then I had to go back for a container of whipped cream, since strawberries and pound cake isn't complete without a dollop of whipped cream.

Rafe wasn't home yet, so back at the house I changed into something more comfortable (and less sweat-soaked), and then got to work cutting and slicing and dicing. The air conditioning was blasting, and so was the radio, and I was singing along with Shania Twain when I heard the rumble of the Harley outside. After a few seconds the rumble stopped, then silence. The radio was loud enough that I couldn't hear the key in the lock. I didn't hear Rafe's footsteps until he appeared behind me and slipped both arms around my waist; hands splayed across my stomach.

He leaned in to nuzzle my cheek. "Looks good."

I tilted my head for better access. "Me or the food?"

He chuckled. "Both. But I was talking about the food."

"It'll be ready in about ten minutes. Are you hungry?"

"Always," Rafe said.

"For food?"

"That, too." But he dropped his hands from my stomach after one final caress, and headed for the fridge. "You mind?"

He held up a bottle of Corona.

I shook my head. "Knock yourself out." I hadn't been fond of beer even before I got pregnant. Beer is low class, as my mother always said. My own preferred poison—like hers—is white wine. But of course I can't have any of that at the moment, either.

Rafe popped the top of the beer and took a seat at the table. "Everything OK?"

"Fine," I said, shredding rotisserie chicken to put on top of the salad. "Why?"

"You're cooking."

"I cook sometimes. And I felt guilty because we'd been eating out so much."

He arched a brow, and I added, "Oh, fine. Grimaldi told me to go home and spend time with my husband. I figured I might as well cook, since I don't have anything else to do."

His eyebrows gyrated. "I know something we can do."

"Later. After I spent time doing this, the least you can do is eat it first." I distributed chicken onto the two plates and topped it with slivered almonds. "And anyway, you weren't here. I needed something to do that I could do alone."

"You know..." Rafe said, and I held up a hand.

"Don't go there. Please."

He grinned, but subsided. "What were you and Tammy doing?"

I told him about the trip to the hospital and then the trip to Aislynn and Kylie's house and the letter and trip to downtown while I put the salad and rolls on the table. I was still talking long after we'd sat down to eat. "I'm not sure what to think," I finished the narrative. "She's probably all right. Just spending time with a friend because she doesn't want to go home to an empty house. But it bothers me that she didn't come visit Kylie in the hospital. And that she's not answering her phone."

Rafe nodded. "Any idea where she mighta gone?"

"None. I don't really know them outside of selling them a house. We aren't friends. Friday was the first time I heard anything about Lauren, and I know nothing about Aislynn's friends. Maybe I should have asked her mother whether any of them live in Nashville now."

"If she's like most of us," Rafe said, "she prob'ly hangs out with people from work."

Probably. "Sara Beth's is closed today. I called. I'll have to wait until tomorrow to go down there and look for her."

"By then she mighta shown up," Rafe said, and put his fork down. "What's for dessert?"

"Funny you should ask. I have pound cake, strawberries, and whipped cream."

"And here I was hoping you'd say 'me.'"

Oh, really? "That could be arranged, too." The pound cake would wait. Not like it had to be kept warm.

"It's all right," Rafe said. "Pound cake sounds good."

Not as good as certain other types of dessert, but if he was willing to settle for pound cake for now, then he could have pound cake now, and me later.

"So what happened with Jamal?" I asked when we were sitting across from one another forking up strawberries and whipped cream.

He made a face. "The kid's wasted in the TBI. He should be a lawyer."

"Talked you into it, did he?"

"It makes sense. If he runs with the gang for this, he can feed us information we can use to arrest them. And he's willing to do it. Hell, he wants to do it!"

"Of course he does. He wants to be a hero. Like you."

He shook his head. "I was never a hero. I was a stupid kid who was given a chance to straighten out his life before it went too far off the rails, and I was smart enough to take it."

"And the fact that you almost singlehandedly took down the biggest SATG," South American Theft Gang, "in the Southeast, that was...?"

"Not singlehandedly," Rafe said. "I had plenty of help."

"You had plenty of support. Or at least you had Wendell, who'd pull your butt out of the fire if you needed it. But you were the one on the inside risking your life every day. By yourself."

He had no response for that.

"The rest of us think you're a hero. Jamal thinks you're a hero. Get used to it."

"He don't," Rafe said. "If he did, he woulda been a bit more respectful."

Maybe so. But... "He talked you into letting him do it."

He shrugged. "I'm gonna have to clear it with Wendell tomorrow. But he'll prob'ly say yes. And Jamal's gonna do it whether he gets an official nod or not. I'd rather have his back than know he's out there on his own."

"I'm sure Wendell will see it the same way," I said. "He cares about the three of them, too. They all worked around the clock to find you back in June."

He nodded. "Wendell's gonna do it. I might be working late nights in the next little bit."

"Just keep Jamal safe," I said.

Seventeen

We finally did get our second round of dessert, although by then it was more like a midnight snack. Or not midnight, exactly—I don't last until midnight these days—but it was bedtime. And when I woke up the next morning, Rafe had already left. I had a vague memory of being kissed goodbye, although it could just have been in my mind.

I staggered into the shower, and once I came out—considerably more awake—I sent him a text to let him know I was up and everything was all right. *You?*

It took a minute, and then I got a message back. *Meeting w/ brass re Jamal. Can't talk now.*

Of course not. I continued dressing.

By the time I had dried my hair and had breakfast, he still hadn't called back, so I picked up the phone and made another call, this time to Vanderbilt Hospital. The duty nurse told me that yes, indeed, Kylie Mitchell would be released as soon as Doctor Ramsey finished his rounds, and her 'sister' was welcome to come pick her up. I asked to talk to her, just to make sure she hadn't made other arrangements—just in case Aislynn had showed up—and was connected to her room.

It took a moment, and then I heard Kylie's voice. "Hello?"

"It's Savannah," I said. "The nurse said you're getting to go home today. Do you have a ride?"

She hesitated, but eventually admitted, "No."

"I'd be happy to come get you. Once the sales meeting is over, I'm not doing anything else."

She hesitated again, but finally said, "That would be great. Thanks."

"It's no problem. I guess Lauren had to work?"

"I didn't call her," Kylie said. "I just want Aislynn back. And that's not going to happen as long as Lauren's around."

Probably not. "It might not have been that good of an idea to leave Aislynn at home while you went to warn her about the police on Friday night." Since that had pretty much cemented Aislynn's fears about Kylie and Lauren.

I could practically hear Kylie's eyes rolling like marbles. "Is that what she thought I was doing?"

She didn't wait for me to confirm it, just kept going. "When she first told the detective that she thought Lauren might be sending the letters to get rid of her, I didn't believe it. And I said so, and it probably sounded like I was defending her. But Detective Mendoza seemed like he took Aislynn seriously, and he kept asking me questions about mine and Lauren's relationship and how she took being dumped, and of course she didn't take it well. Although I didn't really dump her. We weren't serious. Or at least I wasn't. I'd just gotten divorced from Damian, and I guess I was experimenting, you know?"

I murmured something appropriate while I glanced at my watch. If she didn't stop talking soon, I'd be late for the meeting.

"So I started thinking that maybe Aislynn had a point," Kylie said. "And that maybe Lauren might have had something to do with it. I wasn't going there to warn her. I was going to confront her."

"Does Aislynn know that?"

I imagined her shaking her head. "I didn't get a chance. When I got home, she wasn't there."

"So you do remember coming home."

"I guess I do," Kylie said, sounding surprised. Hard to tell whether it was real surprise, or whether she was putting me on.

"Do you remember what happened when you got there?"

"I parked the car in the garage, since I knew we wouldn't be going out again that night. And I came in through the back door. Out through the side door in the garage and up on the deck. The light was on in the parlor, so when I came through the door, I called Aislynn's name and told her it was me."

I nodded, not that she could see me.

"She didn't answer, but I heard a noise from the parlor, so I headed that way. I turned into the doorway... and that's the last thing I remember."

"Because someone hit you," I said. "I don't suppose you saw who?"

She hadn't. Of course not. That would have been too easy.

Although the narrative had taken care of one lingering possibility. Kylie had identified herself when she came into the house, and had called Aislynn's name. If Aislynn had hit her, it had been deliberately. No chance of an accident at all that I could see.

"You haven't heard anything from Aislynn, have you?"

"No," Kylie said. "I guess she's still with her mom and dad. Maybe they talked her out of wanting anything to do with me. She probably thinks I prefer Lauren."

I murmured something noncommittal. I could have broken the news that Aislynn wasn't at her mom and dad's, I suppose. That she hadn't gone to her mom and dad's in the first place, and that they hadn't seen her in more than a month. But I had to get to my meeting, and it wasn't the kind of news I wanted to impart over the phone. Better to wait until she'd been released from the hospital and we were face to face—or side by side—in the car, going home. Better done in person.

So I said, "I have to get going. But I'll be there around ten-thirty to pick you up, OK? Don't go anywhere without me. And if Aislynn shows up—" which she could conceivably do, "just have her text me that she's there and I don't have to come."

Kylie said she would, but her voice said that she wasn't holding her breath. I wasn't, either, as I headed out and over to LB&A for the weekly sales meeting.

It was something Walker Lamont, the former broker of

204 | JENNA BENNETT

LB&A, had instituted. Every Monday morning, every agent in the office—the ones selling real estate full time and the ones selling real estate only on the weekends, the ones selling millions of dollars worth of inventory a year and the ones selling very little—got together in the conference room and talked about new listings and new clients, what properties had closed since last week, and anything else of consequence.

The big deal this time, not surprisingly, was the news that one of our clients had passed away. "Virgil Wright," Tim said, from his throne at the head of the table. "He and his partner sold a property last January. Savannah," he nodded to me, "had the buyers."

Everyone turned to me, and I saw surprise on several faces. Heidi stopped masticating for a moment before taking another bite of the iced donut someone had brought in. I smiled politely. *Yes, even a blind bird occasionally finds a worm.*

"What happened?" someone wanted to know.

"He was mugged," Tim said, sounding for all the world like this was his deal and not mine; like he'd known anything at all about it before I brought it to his attention. "Jogging in Shelby Park last Wednesday night. Someone hit him over the head with a rock. It might be a hate crime."

There was a pause. "That's terrible," someone said. "Is there anything we can do?"

"The funeral has already taken place," Tim said.

I added, "Although an official condolence card might be nice." Especially since Tim hadn't bothered to show up, and since I hadn't actually had time to pay my respect and let Kenny know I was there before the scene with Stacy took place.

Tim said, "Have Brittany take care of it."

Sure. As if Brittany was likely to do anything I told her to do.

However, I just nodded and said I would.

"Anything else?" Tim wanted to know, looking around the table. Everyone was quiet. Heidi's chewing was very loud in the silence.

Tim rapped on the table. "Meeting's adjourned. Savannah, stay for a minute."

Uh-oh.

The last time he'd told me to stay after a meeting, he'd fired me, because he said my meddling in crime put LB&A in a bad light. Rafe had talked him into rehiring me a week or two later. I hoped we weren't going to go through that again.

But no. He just wanted to explain to me why he hadn't made it to the funeral on Saturday. "See, there was this guy I met..."

I raised my hand. "Say no more." It made perfect sense that Tim would prioritize sex with a stranger over going to a client's funeral. If it had been a well-attended funeral—well-attended by media, I mean—I'm sure he would have been there, ready to get his face on camera, but since this hadn't been that kind of occasion, this didn't surprise me at all.

And anyway, to give him the benefit of the doubt, he might not like funerals. I don't either, particularly, but I've been well-brought-up, so I attend against my own desires.

He leaned back on the chair. "You went?"

I nodded.

"How was it?"

"It was a funeral," I said. "Lots of sad and angry people." And then a knock-down, drag-out fight.

"I heard the police were called." His blue eyes glittered maliciously.

Great. So what he wanted was an eye-witness account. "Who told you that?"

He shrugged. "Is it true?"

"I didn't see them," I said, even though I'd called them myself and knew they'd arrived.

"I hear there was a fight."

I sighed. "Where did you hear that?"

Tim waved his hand airily. "I had a drink at South Street last

206 | JENNA BENNETT

night. Stacy was there."

Of course he was. "Was he damaged?" Part of me wished he was. I could excuse his behavior if I had too—overcome by grief, still in love with his former lover—but he had behaved atrociously. If he couldn't control himself, he shouldn't have been there.

"A bruise," Tim said, waving an elegant hand in the direction of his cheekbone. "He said the police chased them off before they could hurt him."

Good for Stacy.

"So were you there? Did you see it?"

I said I was, and then I had to give Tim a detailed description of what had happened. If I tried to fluff over a point, he asked me questions until he'd gotten every morsel of information out of me. When I was wrung dry, he giggled.

"Is that it?" I wanted to know. "Because I have to go pick up a friend from the hospital and take her home."

"Sure. Go." He waved his hand.

"Thank you ever so." But I didn't say it loudly, just took my purse off the floor next to my chair and got out of there. I didn't even backtrack to the front desk to tell Brittany to arrange for that condolence card for Kenny. It would wait. At the moment, I just wanted to get as far away from Tim as I could, in record time.

Kylie was waiting when I got there, in a wheelchair in her room, dressed in the same clothes she'd worn Friday night when we brought her here. I looked closely, but I didn't see any blood. Still, I could imagine she was quite ready to go home, take a shower, and change.

I gave her my best smile. "Ready?"

She nodded. And although she was ready to go, she didn't look great. Her face was pale, and she looked like she were in pain.

"Let's go talk to the nurse and get you out of here." I moved behind the chair and wheeled it into the corridor and down to the desk. There, a nurse took over and came down to the parking garage with us. She helped me get Kylie transferred from the chair to the front seat of the car, and got her seat reclined, and then she wheeled the empty chair back into the elevator and was gone.

I got in and started the car. "I bet you can't wait to get home."

Kylie nodded weakly.

"Are you going to be OK by yourself, or do you want me to stay with you?"

"I want Aislynn," Kylie said.

I'm sure she did. "I haven't heard from her. Have you?"

She shook her head. Carefully.

"After I drop you off, I can go down to Brentwood and see if she's at work. Is she supposed to work today?"

Kylie shrugged. "Go now."

"Now?" I looked both ways before heading right on Hillsboro Road. It was the way to Brentwood, but I could still take Kylie to East Nashville. I just had to choose one direction over the other when I got to the interstate.

"Sure. We're halfway there."

"But don't you want to go home and to bed?" I signaled to turn on Wedgewood Avenue.

"I want Aislynn," Kylie said.

OK, then. I headed for the interstate, and took the exit south, for Brentwood. It wasn't even ten minutes before we pulled into the Brentwood Crossings shopping center.

I cut the engine on the car and turned to her. "Do you want to wait here?"

Kylie shook her head. "I'll come with you."

"I wish you wouldn't. You look like you should rest. Why don't you just let me go in and see if she's there? It'll only take a minute."

"I want to come," Kylie said, and unbuckled her seatbelt.

Fine. I unbuckled mine, and walked around the car to help her get out. We headed for the door to Sara Beth's. Slowly.

Very slowly.

I held it and let Kylie go in first. And then I moved to grab her, since there was nothing to hold on to just inside the door, and the last thing I wanted was for her to collapse on the hard stone floor.

She turned to me. "She's not here."

I looked around.

No, she wasn't. Or not where I could see her.

"When I was here on Friday, she was in the back room." Eating French fries.

Kylie glanced at me. "You were here on Friday?"

"You turned me down for lunch," I said. "I had to eat somewhere, and this seemed like a good choice."

The waitress from Friday's lunch was working again today, and when I beckoned, I got the very distinct feeling she wasn't happy to see me. Instead of coming over, she called out, "Sit anywhere you like."

"We're looking for Aislynn," I called back. Hey, if she was going to be impolite, I'd be impolite right back. There was a time when I wouldn't have considered yelling across a half-full restaurant, but those days were gone.

"She's not here."

The waitress turned away. I arched my brows. "Excuse me a moment," I told Kylie

She nodded. She looked ready to drop, honestly. I put her on a chair at the nearest empty table to wait until I got back, and then I wove my way through the tables over to where the waitress was pouring organic green tea in glasses for two of her customers. "Excuse me."

I resisted the temptation to tap her—rather harder than

necessary—on the shoulder, but my voice was laced with a fair amount of attitude.

"I told you," she said over her shoulder, "Aislynn isn't here."

"Is she supposed to be here?"

The waitress glanced at me. "What do you mean?"

It wasn't a particularly difficult question. At least I hadn't thought so. "Is she on the schedule?"

"No," the waitress told me.

"Have you heard from her?"

She shook her head.

"Do you have any idea where she is?"

She said she didn't.

"Are you sure?"

She gave me a glare. "Go check behind the curtain if you don't believe me."

I checked behind the curtain, just because she told me I could. I didn't expect Aislynn to be there, and she wasn't.

"When was the last time you saw her?"

"What are you?" she demanded. "The relationship police?"

I wanted to say something cutting—just as soon as I'd come up with it—but I kept my temper. Shrieking like a fisherwoman is uncouth, and probably wouldn't get me the information I wanted. "Just a concerned friend. We haven't heard from her since Saturday afternoon."

"Maybe she wanted a break," the waitress said.

"Break from what?"

"Duh." She rolled his eyes. "Her life."

"What was wrong with her life?"

But she retreated back into herself. "It's not for me to say."

"Actually," I told her, "if you know something, I'd appreciate it if you'd tell me. There's an APB out on her, and if she doesn't show up soon, I'm sure it'll turn into a full-fledged alert."

She stared at me as if I'd suddenly sprouted a second head.

"She's been gone almost forty-eight hours. Her parents

haven't heard from her. Her girlfriend hasn't heard from her. Her friends haven't heard from her. So if you know anything about where she is, you'd better tell her to get in touch with someone before the police bring out the big guns."

I meant it as a metaphor, but she turned a shade paler. Since she was already pale—one of those vampire types—she turned almost transparent.

"Do you know where she is?" I pressed.

"No." Her voice cracked. "How would I know anything about that?"

"I don't know. You work together? Maybe she confided something in you?"

She shook his head, but I wasn't sure I believed her. "Listen," she added, "you gotta go. I have work to do. And if the boss hears that the service was slow, she's gonna be mad."

"Fine." I dug a business card out of my bag and put it on the counter. "If you hear from Aislynn, would you let me know?"

"Sure." The waitress didn't even look at it, or at me. "Excuse me."

She took her two glasses of green tea and pushed past me, leaving the card there. I turned to watch her, and caught Kylie's eye. She was listing to one side, almost like she was sliding to a prone position. I hurried back to her.

"Come on. Let's get you home."

"I'm fine," Kylie said, but I had to take half her weight on our way out the door. "I'll be fine once I get in the car."

She'd be better once she got in the car, but I didn't think she'd be fine for a few days, at least. Although I didn't argue about it. I just supported her over to the Volvo and got her arranged in the passenger seat. Once I had the car started, and the air conditioning blasting, and was ready to back out of the parking space, Kylie said, "Wait a minute."

"What?" I put the car back in park but left the engine (and AC) running. "Are you feeling sick?"

She shook her head. "Just tired. And in pain. What did she say?"

"Who...? Oh, the waitress? That she hadn't heard from Aislynn and didn't know where she was."

"Do you think she was telling the truth?"

"I have no reason to think she was lying," I said. And added, "Although she might have been lying about something else."

She rolled her head on the seat to look at me. "What's that?"

"I asked her if Aislynn was on the schedule today. You know, scheduled to work. And she said no. But she's alone in there. On Friday, it was the two of them. And she said something about the boss being upset if she learned that the service was slow."

"There's supposed to be two of them," Kylie murmured. "Aislynn's had to do it alone before when someone's called in sick, and she always comes home wiped out. It's too much work for one person."

So either someone else had called in sick today, or Aislynn was supposed to be there.

"I wonder why she lied."

"Maybe she didn't," Kylie said. "Maybe it was someone else's day to work and they called in sick."

"A bit of a coincidence, though, don't you think?"

She shrugged.

We sat in silence for a moment.

"I guess I should get you home," I said. And then I'd come back here, and lurk in the parking lot until the waitress left. And follow her. Just in case she'd take me to Aislynn.

"I'm all right here for a while," Kylie said. She snuggled into the seat.

I squinted at her. "Do you know something I don't?"

"I don't think so. But I want Aislynn back. Maybe she'll show up here."

Maybe. Or maybe the waitress would lead us to her, once she

left.

I snuggled into the seat, too, and prepared to wait.

Eighteen

Of course it wasn't that easy. We got hungry after a while, so I had to leave the car and make my way across the parking lot—a large parking lot—to the fast food place on the other end. I would have driven, but I didn't want to risk missing something, not to mention losing my parking spot.

Then I trudged back with two containers of sweet tea and two salads. Kylie just picked on hers, although I wolfed down all of mine. Along with the tea.

And of course the inevitable happened: we had to go to the bathroom. That's usually the outcome of drinking a half gallon of sweet tea.

I've said it before: I'd be hopeless at stakeouts.

Or rather, I *am* hopeless at stakeouts. This wasn't the first time I'd had the bathroom problem. Once, almost a year ago now, I'd been sitting outside a warehouse in East Nashville, trying to get a look at the owner and debating whether or not to make a run to the nearest restroom when Rafe had rapped on my window and almost scared me into having an accident.

That didn't happen this time, but eventually we did succumb to nature's call. And since Kylie couldn't walk across the parking lot to the fast food place, I had to drive and help her inside. (She was OK in the stall on her own. I would have drawn the line there.)

Of course, by the time we got back to the area in front of Sara Beth's, someone had taken our parking space, and I had to drive around for a while looking for another. This one was less convenient, and by now I was worried that our quarry had gotten away during the bathroom run, too. The closed sign was up on the door.

"Uh-oh." I pointed to it. "Think she's left?"

Kylie blinked. "Maybe. Although she probably has to clean up. That could just be so nobody else walks in."

Could be.

"They're not supposed to close," Kylie added. "Between lunch and dinner. They're supposed to stay open all day."

So either the waitress just wanted a break while she recovered from handling the lunch rush on her own, or she was planning to shut up shop for a while, and maybe come back later. Only time would tell which.

We waited.

"There," Kylie said finally.

I looked up, and there she was, letting herself out of the restaurant and locking the door.

"Looks like she's had enough for now." The long apron was gone and the waitress was dressed in jeans and a black T-shirt with a skull on the front. Casual-wear for the young and hip.

We watched as she headed into the parking lot, weaving through the cars. Then she disappeared.

"Where'd she go?" I said.

"Probably into a car," Kylie answered.

I craned my neck, but couldn't see anything. "We should start moving, too. See if we can find her and follow."

Kylie nodded.

I started the car and crept out of the parking space. We rolled down the aisle between the parked cars, peering left and right.

"There," Kylie said.

At the end of the row, a small, seen-better-days economy car buzzed across the aisle, headed for the exit. It was too far away for us to see the driver, but the car had appeared in approximately the right spot at the right time, so I was willing to take a chance that this was our quarry. I slid up behind her at the light, and signaled to take a left.

"Can you see her?"

Kylie shook her head. I couldn't, either—or just as a rounded outline over the top of the seat. But the car itself gave a couple of clues to its owner. The bumper stickers—and there were many—proclaimed slogans like '*Bikes, not bombs,*' '*Share the road,*' '*Buy fresh, buy local,*' and '*No farms, no food.*' From that, I surmised that the owner might indeed be someone who would work in a health food restaurant.

The light changed, and off we went down Old Hickory Boulevard. I'd driven this same way on Friday, after lunch, on my way to see Stacy Kelleher. Imagine my surprise when we followed the exact same route this time.

When we approached the brick gates where Aislynn and Kylie had crashed last year, Kylie held her breath.

"It's OK," I said. "The brakes are fine today."

I tapped them to show her that the car responded by slowing down. She nodded, but didn't start breathing again until we were at the bottom of the hill, past the gates, and still proceeding at a safe and steady pace.

When the car ahead of us pulled into the same apartment complex where Stacy lived, I was only marginally surprised. Somehow it made perfect sense that it would. Here, after all, was the connection we'd been looking for. Aislynn's coworker knew Virgil's ex-boyfriend, thus tying the murder and the anonymous letters together. How, I didn't know, but at least it was a connection, and a place to start.

But then the compact went in the other direction beyond the gate.

"Huh," I said, staying back while I watched it disappear between two buildings. Two other buildings; not the one where Stacy lived.

"Aren't you going to follow?"

"In a second. I don't want her to see us." The Volvo crept forward, with my foot barely touching the gas pedal. "This is the apartment complex where Stacy Kelleher lives."

"Who's Stacy Kelleher?"

I glanced at her. "The guy who lived with Virgil Wright when they sold you the house you're living in. Virgil's boyfriend."

"Stacy's a man?"

I nodded. Up ahead, the compact came to a stop in a parking space. The engine shut off and after a second, the door opened. I held my breath, and let it out again when the waitress from Sara Beth's shoehorned herself from the small car. "At least we followed the right car."

"She could just be coming home for lunch," Kylie said.

Of course she could. However— "She was the only waitress there. Why didn't she just have the cook put something together and keep the place open? If there's one thing they had plenty of, it was food."

"Maybe she needed a break?" Kylie suggested.

Maybe. Or maybe there was something here that she needed to check on.

I tried not to imagine Aislynn chained to the wall in this woman's dungeon—aka second bedroom—but couldn't get the picture out of my head.

"Did Aislynn ever mention this girl?"

"I have no idea," Kylie said. "I've never met her. I don't know her name. She has mentioned this one girl she's worked with a lot, though."

"What has she said about her?"

I watched as the waitress locked her car and headed for the nearest building.

"Just that they end up working together a lot. Like, it always ends up being the two of them."

"Is that a problem? Doesn't Aislynn like the other girl, or something?"

If so, she certainly wouldn't be here. Not unless this woman really did have Aislynn chained to the wall in the spare bedroom.

"It isn't that," Kylie said as the waitress reached the bottom of the stairs and started climbing. "They get along just fine. I think they even lived together for a month or two when Aislynn first came to town. Before she moved in with me. She just thinks it's a little weird that she never ends up working with anyone else."

While we'd talked, the waitress had reached the top of the staircase and now she stopped and fumbled in her pocket. We watched her knock on the door before she inserted the key in the lock.

"That's weird," I said.

Kylie shrugged. "Maybe she has a roommate."

Or a guest. Or maybe she *was* the guest. We didn't know whether this was her apartment or someone else's. Maybe she'd had a booty call from her boyfriend, or for that matter from her girlfriend, and that's why she left work in the middle of the day and ran over here.

The door shut behind her, and I reached for my door handle. "Time to go."

And hopefully I wouldn't catch the waitress and her significant other in the act.

Kylie opened her door and twisted on the seat.

"You can stay in the car," I told her. "You shouldn't even be here. You should be home in bed. Dr. Ramsey would kill me if he knew I'd been dragging you all over creation like this."

"I want to come," Kylie said, grabbing the top of the car door and hauling herself to her feet. She stood there for a second, swaying, before she caught her balance. "If Aislynn is there, I want to see her."

Fine. She was an adult; she was responsible for her own actions. I closed my own door, walked around the car to offer an arm to lean on, and closed hers. Then we made our slow way across the parking lot to the stairs.

I don't mind admitting I didn't think she was going to make it. Standing at the bottom of that staircase looking up, made the second floor look as far away as the top of Mount Le Conte. Kylie must have thought so, too, because she just stood there for a second, obviously bracing herself, before she squared her shoulders and grabbed the railing. And hauled herself up, one slow step at a time.

I followed, thinking that by the time we got to the top, any booty call would have concluded, and we wouldn't have to worry about interrupting anything.

It took a small eternity, but finally we made it onto the second floor landing. Kylie hung onto the railing for a long time, breathing heavily, before she straightened. "OK."

"OK." I walked to the door and rang the bell. By the time I had stepped back to wait for it to open, Kylie had joined me.

It took a minute, but then the door opened a crack and the waitress's face peered out at us. "Oh," she said. "It's you again."

I smiled sweetly. "We'd like to see Aislynn, please."

The waitress looked from one of us to the other. "What makes you think she's here?"

Many reasons, most of which I have already detailed. And then there was the fact that she didn't come right out and say that Aislynn wasn't there.

My expression must have told her what I thought of the prevarication, because she added, "What if she doesn't want to see you?"

"Then she can tell us so," I said, and raised my voice. "Aislynn! Come out here!"

For a second I thought the waitress would slam the door in my face. I saw the thought flicker through her eyes, and I prepared myself to stick my leather wedge sandal into the gap.

At least the door would squeeze the sole of the shoe, and not my foot. I've had my foot stuck in a door before, and let me tell you, it can hurt.

But then there was a scramble inside, and the next second, Aislynn's face appeared next to the waitress's in the doorway. "Savannah!"

And a second later. "Kylie?"

At least she wasn't handcuffed to the wall.

"We were worried about you," I said mildly, when what I wanted to do was grab her by the shoulders and shake her until her teeth rattled. "You didn't come to the hospital yesterday. And you didn't answer our calls or texts."

She hung her head. "I didn't want to. I was afraid he'd follow me."

"He?"

"The creepy guy writing the letters," Aislynn said. "I got another one."

I nodded. "I know. I saw it. The one you left in the mailbox, right? The police have it."

Her friend jumped like she'd been stung by a bee, but she didn't say anything. When I looked at her, her pale face flushed.

"So how are you involved in this?" I wanted to know.

She shook her head. "I'm not."

"What's Aislynn doing here?"

"She called me," Aislynn said. "It seems I was supposed to work the dinner shift on Saturday, and with everything that happened," she glanced at Kylie, then away again, "I guess I forgot. Until Terry called."

"You told Detective Mendoza you were going to spent the night with your parents."

"I was," Aislynn nodded. "But then Terry called, and I had to go to work. And it got late, and I didn't want to go home to an empty house, and besides, I was afraid that whoever hit Kylie would be back, because he said I was next, so Terry said I could stay with her."

Nobody said anything. Terry looked uncomfortable.

"Kylie said you'd spent a couple of weeks living with a

friend last summer, too. Is this that same friend?"

They both nodded.

"Kylie's on her way home," I said, with a glance at her. She looked awful. "The house won't be empty anymore, if you want to come with us."

Aislynn hesitated. She glanced at Kylie, maybe hoping that Kylie would say something to her. So far, this conversation had been mostly on me.

"The police have the last letter," I added, repeating myself to drive home the point. "They're checking it for fingerprints and anything else they can find. And I'm sure Detective Mendoza wouldn't be opposed to having the local patrol cars drive by from time to time tonight to make sure everything's OK. Although by tonight they may already know who the culprit is, and have arrested him."

Terry twitched, and I added, "Are you sure you didn't have anything to do with this?"

"Positive." She nodded. "I'd never write creepy letters to Aislynn."

"How do you know they're creepy?" I wanted to know.

"She told me," Terry said. I glanced at Aislynn, who nodded.

"I'll just get my stuff."

She bounced back inside the apartment.

We stood in awkward silence until she came back out, with her oversized satchel flung over her shoulder. On her way out the door, she stopped to kiss Terry on the cheek. "Thanks for letting me stay."

She flitted past her, and probably didn't see the look on Terry's face. Kylie didn't, either; she was looking at Aislynn.

I did. But of course I wouldn't be so uncouth as to say anything about it. Although it did explain why they were always scheduled to work together. Terry probably made the schedule. Or switched shifts with anyone else who was scheduled to work with Aislynn, so she could work with her instead.

Aislynn and Kylie headed down the stairs, slowly and carefully. I lingered a moment, to ask Terry a question. "Do you know Stacy Kelleher?"

She tore his gaze from them. "Who?"

"One of your neighbors," I said. "He lives in a building over there." I pointed. "Guy about your age. Drives a Jeep. Works at South Street as a bartender."

"Oh." Terry's eyes cleared. "Sure. I know Stacy."

"Seen him around lately?"

She gave me a look. "I see him every couple of days, coming and going. When our schedules work out that way."

"What about last Wednesday?" The night Virgil was killed.

"No," Terry said, without even thinking about it.

"Did you work?"

She shook her head. "He did."

"What about Friday?" The night Kylie was attacked.

"I worked," Terry said. "I didn't see him then, either."

"Aislynn wasn't on the schedule?"

"Not on Friday night. She doesn't like to work nights." She shot a betraying glance down the stairs. Aislynn and Kylie were on their way across the parking lot to the car. Aislynn had her arm around Kylie, and Kylie's head was on Aislynn's shoulder.

"They're in love," I said.

She looked at me, a look of defiant, deliberate disbelief.

Not much I could do about that. "Thanks for taking care of her," I said.

The look I got this time was full of dislike. Nothing I could do about that, either. So I just nodded politely and turned to go down the stairs. The back of my neck crawled, and I grasped the handrail and turned around again quickly, but it must have been my imagination, because Terry was still standing in the doorway, making absolutely no move to push me down the stairs. Nonetheless, I did move a little faster than usual as I scrambled down a story to what felt like the safety of solid

222 | JENNA BENNETT

ground.

Aislynn was very apologetic about not coming to the hospital yesterday. "I was scared," she told us from the backseat. "And Terry said it was probably safer if I didn't go out. That if someone was following me, I didn't want to lead him back to Kylie."

"But Kylie had already been attacked," I pointed out. "What made Terry think she was in danger again?"

"I don't know." Aislynn sounded surprised, like that thought hadn't crossed her mind before. "Maybe she really just didn't want me to go anywhere?"

Maybe so. "What did the two of you do all day yesterday?"

"Watched movies," Aislynn said. "Played video games."

"Sounds nice and relaxing."

She shrugged. "I'd rather be home."

"I'm taking you there now," I told her. "There's a little bit of work to do when you get there, I'm afraid. The cops left a mess of fingerprint powder everywhere, and the office is still in chaos."

"That's all right. I'll clean it up." She sounded perky and not bothered in the least.

We drove in silence a few minutes.

"Are you going to be all right by yourselves?" I asked.

They glanced at one another. "We'll be fine," Kylie said.

Aislynn nodded. "We'll just hole up and have a movie marathon, or something."

"Didn't you see enough movies at Terry's place yesterday?"

"She doesn't like the same kinds of movies I like," Aislynn said.

"What kinds of movies do you like?"

Aislynn admitted she liked British costume dramas, which was the last thing I would have expected.

"What kinds of movies does Terry like?"

"She's usually into Star Wars and stuff like that," Aislynn said. "Nerdy action stuff. But yesterday she made me sit through a marathon of old CSI episodes."

Crime scene investigations? "That's interesting. Did she say anything about it? Why she wanted to watch something different?"

She shook her head. "I guess she just got tired of the usual stuff. Or maybe she thought I'd like it better."

"Any comments about the episodes?"

"She asked me if I thought some of what they were doing was possible," Aislynn said. "Like, there was an episode about handwriting analysis, and Terry asked me if I thought it was possible to match somebody's handwriting to them."

Even more interesting. Although she'd sounded very adamant about not having written the anonymous letters. Not that I'm always adept at picking up on a lie, but she hadn't sounded like she was lying.

Maybe she knew who'd been sending the letters, and was worried about their handwriting instead?

Aislynn's? Or someone else's?

"There was another one about DNA evidence," Aislynn added. "How it doesn't take saliva or semen," she scrunched up her nose, "to get DNA. Sometimes, all it takes is a skin cell or two left behind."

I nodded. I had heard that, too. "And Terry thought that was interesting?"

"She seemed worried," Aislynn said, which was the most interesting information of all.

Nineteen

I took the two of them home and made sure they got safely into the house. "Where does Damian work?" I asked Kylie on my way back out the door.

She blinked, but told me the name of her bank.

"You work together?" Even after the divorce?

Kylie shook her head. "I'm in downtown, in lending. Damian's a branch manager."

That made it easy. Anybody can just walk into a bank branch and ask to speak to the manager. I made her tell me which branch and where to find it, and then I said my goodbyes and headed out.

As soon as I was in the car, I pulled out my phone and dialed Detective Mendoza. And when he didn't pick up, I tried Tamara Grimaldi instead. "What's wrong with Mendoza?"

"Nice to hear from you, too," Grimaldi said dryly. "A lot of things, I imagine. Why do you ask?"

"He's not taking my phone calls. I tried to call him yesterday—you said he was spending time with his kid—and I tried to call him now, and he didn't pick up."

"He's probably busy," Grimaldi said.

"Has there been a break in the case?"

"Not that I know of. But there might have been a break in another case. The Wright homicide isn't the only case he has."

"It isn't?" I guess I'd never thought about that. Whenever Grimaldi had been working on a case that involved me, I'd always assumed it was the only thing she had to deal with.

"We handle anywhere from two to ten cases at one time," Grimaldi told me. "Some are on the back burner, some are hot and needing immediate attention. But there are too many murders in Nashville for us just to deal with one each. Unfortunately."

Wow.

"So is Virgil's case hot? Or not?"

Grimaldi hesitated. "At this point, I'd say it's probably a little less than hot. We like to solve cases within forty-eight hours or so. If we don't, it usually takes a while. Other cases pile on, and we end up working them while they're hot, so something like the Wright homicide gets pushed to the back."

"That's too bad."

She didn't respond to that, just said, "In some instances, the solution is easy. A man is found clubbed to death in the parking lot outside his work, and you find out he has just accused his partner of embezzling. Chances are pretty good the partner is the killer."

"Did Virgil accuse anyone of embezzling?"

"Not that I know of," Grimaldi said. "It was an example. In Mr. Wright's case, it's not quite as simple. Someone killed him, likely on purpose. But we don't know who, and we don't know why. He hadn't argued with anyone, he hadn't reported anyone to the police, he hadn't cheated on his boyfriend..."

"Are you sure about that? At the funeral, Stacy said Virgil had told him he was tired of Kenny. And if Stacy and Virgil were together, they may have reverted to old times and decided to go for some sex."

"Mr. Grimes says no," Grimaldi said.

"Well, of course he does! If Virgil cheated, and was leaving him to go back to Stacy, Kenny is the killer!"

"Mr. Grimes might be the killer," Grimaldi said, "but we have only Mr. Kelleher's word for it that Mr. Wright was tired of Mr. Grimes. And given the circumstances, it isn't unlikely that Mr. Kelleher was lying."

I guess it wasn't. Stacy could have just seen an opportunity to jab at Kenny, and taken it. With Virgil dead, there was no way to know whether he was telling the truth or lying through his teeth.

"The reason I called Mendoza," I said, as I turned the car onto Interstate 65 and headed for Goodlettsville, where Kylie had said that Damian worked, "is that I just discovered something."

"What's that?"

"It might be nothing. It just struck me as weird."

I told the whole story of following Terry and finding Aislynn and how Terry had insisted on watching CSI reruns instead of nerdy Star Wars movies, and what she'd said about the fingerprinting and handwriting analysis. "I have no idea how any of this hangs together. I didn't get the impression that she was lying when she said she wouldn't want to scare Aislynn. But I thought it was interesting."

"So does she know who wrote the letters and is she worried about their handwriting? And what about the fingerprints? Is she afraid her own fingerprints are on a weapon, or someone else's?"

They sounded like rhetorical questions, but I answered anyway. "Terry didn't bash Kylie over the head with the paperweight." Much as she might have wanted to, to get Kylie out of the way and free up Aislynn for herself. "She has an alibi. She was working on Friday night."

"Convenient," Grimaldi said.

"But irrefutable. A restaurant full of people saw her. Just like Stacy on Wednesday night, when Virgil was killed. He was working too, and a restaurant full of people saw him."

Grimaldi didn't say anything. I waited a minute, and then I told her, "I'm on my way to Goodlettsville. Kylie said her ex-husband works at a bank up there. I want to know whether he came to see her in the hospital on Saturday night, or whether that was someone else."

"You couldn't just call and ask?"

"I want to see his face," I said. "To see if he's lying." As if I had any idea how to spot a liar. And anyway, I wanted to see whether he might have been the guy in plaid shirt I'd seen on Friday afternoon.

"Be careful," Grimaldi said.

"He's a branch manager in a bank. Even if he doesn't like me showing up and asking questions, he isn't going to cause a scene. Not in front of his customers. And if he doesn't have anything to hide, why would he mind talking to me?"

"Just don't let him shut you in the vault," Grimaldi said, and hung up.

The bank was just off the Goodlettsville Town Square, which isn't square at all, but an intersection between Dickerson Road and Long Hollow Pike. I pulled into the lot and found a parking space, and then I nodded politely to the armed security guard and went inside.

There was a counter with a couple of tellers against the back wall, with a drive-through going past outside. A small seating area with four leather chairs and a table stood in the middle of the room, and along the other walls were offices. I dismissed the two that had women in them—Damian definitely wasn't female—and the bearded gentleman in the third had to be close to sixty. I zeroed in on the youngish, reasonably handsome, brown-haired man in a suit in the last room on the right.

I stopped in the doorway. "Knock, knock."

He looked up with a practiced smile. "Come on in. How can I help you today?"

I walked in and closed the door behind me. A tiny wrinkle appeared between his eyes as he looked from it to me and back, but he didn't comment.

I took a seat in one of the chairs in front of his desk and put my purse on my lap. "This won't take long. I just have a couple of questions."

The name plate on the desk said 'Damian Mitchell,' so at least I had the right guy. There were diplomas and awards of various sorts on the walls. Apparently, Damian had graduated from the University of Tennessee Knoxville with a degree in economics a few years ago, and he had won awards for being branch manager of the year more than once since then. There was a low credenza behind his desk, and on it—in addition to file folders and a fake green plant—was a photograph of Damian and a woman with blond hair in what looked like a ski lift somewhere. It wasn't Kylie.

He leaned back and twirled his fountain pen between his fingers. "What can I help you with?"

"Your whereabouts on Saturday night," I said.

There was a moment of silence, then his brows arched. "Could I see some identification, please?"

"Sure." I pulled out my driver's license and showed it to him. Not like I had anything to hide, after all. And anyway, it didn't have my current address on it, so it wasn't like he'd be able to track me down that way. I had changed my address with the DMV when I moved from my apartment to Rafe's grandmother's house in the spring, but I hadn't gotten a new driver's license to go with it.

Now that my last name had changed, I'd probably have to do something about that.

Damian made a note of my (old) name but not my (old) address before handing it back. "Are you with the police?"

I said I wasn't. "I'm a friend of Kylie's. Your ex-wife."

"I know who Kylie is." He almost growled it.

"Do you also know that she was hit over the head by a burglar this weekend, and ended up in the hospital?"

His jaw tensed. "No. I didn't know that. Is she all right?"

He sounded concerned, but not overly so.

I told him that she was back home. "She has a concussion, but otherwise she's going to be fine."

"And why are you here, asking about my whereabouts? You think I hit her?"

"Not necessarily," I said. "The burglary was on Friday night. I'm more interested in Saturday."

"What happened on Saturday?"

"A man came to the hospital to see her. He said his name was Damian Mitchell."

Damian flushed. "Someone pretended to be me? Why?"

"I have no idea. I thought maybe it was you. That'd you'd found out what happened and wanted to see her. And if it was you, I wanted to know how you'd found out about the burglary and where she was."

He shook his head. "It wasn't me. I had dinner with a friend on Saturday night."

"New girlfriend?" My eyes strayed to the photograph behind him.

"Not that it's any of your business," Damian said, "but yes. Kylie and I have been divorced for almost two years. She's found someone else. I have, too."

"Nothing wrong with that." I smiled sweetly. "I just got married last month. For the second time. A lot of us have previous relationships these days."

There was a moment's pause, then Damian leaned forward. "I would never hurt Kylie. We aren't married anymore, but that doesn't mean I want her harmed."

He sounded sincere. He looked sincere, too.

"Any idea who would?"

He sat back. "You said it was a burglar."

"Whoever did it, ransacked Kylie's home office. When she came home, we think he hit her. Maybe to stop her from recognizing him."

"I wouldn't hurt Kylie," Damian repeated. "And if I wanted something from her office, I'd ask her for it. And expect her to give it to me. We get along."

They probably did. Two civilized people whose marriage had ended because one of them discovered she was gay.

"I wasn't accusing you," I said. "She and Aislynn have been getting anonymous letters. We think the burglar might have been looking for them."

Damian looked like he suspected me of pulling his leg. "Anonymous letters?"

"It doesn't matter. Or only insofar as we think the poison pen is the one who broke into the house and hit Kylie."

"You keep saying 'we,'" Damian said.

"The police. I'm talking to the detective in charge of the case."

He nodded. "Well, you can tell him I have an alibi for Saturday night—and for Friday night, as well, if it comes to that. I didn't hit my ex-wife over the head, and I didn't go to the hospital on Saturday. This is the first I've heard of any of it."

"I appreciate your time," I told him and got to my feet. "I assume you can't think of anyone who would want to hurt or scare Aislynn or Kylie?"

He shook his head. "I haven't seen Kylie in more than a year. I've never met her girlfriend. Sorry I can't help."

He pushed his chair back and stood, too. And walked me to the door and out. I got the impression it was more because he wanted me out of his bank before I could decide to ask anyone else any awkward questions, but I couldn't really blame him for that. So I just said goodbye and got in my car. As I drove away, I saw him talking to the security guard. Probably telling him to shoot first and ask questions later if I tried to come back.

Once I was in the car, I called Grimaldi again, to give her my impressions. "I don't think he had anything to do with it. He seemed sincere. And he has a new girlfriend. I think he's over the fact that Kylie left him. And even if his new girlfriend is weird and possessive—which I have no idea if she is—it's not like Kylie would worry her. Kylie's gay."

"Good to know," Grimaldi said. "I spoke to Jaime."

"Did you give him the information about Terry?"

Grimaldi said she had. "And then he gave me some information. About why he didn't answer his phone when you called earlier."

"Why was that?"

"Mr. Kelleher filed a claim with his life insurance company this morning, to cash in on a million dollar policy on Mr. Wright's life."

My foot slipped off the brake and the car jumped forward. So did a pedestrian in the crosswalk, giving me a dirty look when he got to the other side. I waved an apology. "I'm sorry," I told Grimaldi, "would you say that again? I got distracted."

She said it again. It sounded the same this time.

The light changed and I inched forward and onto Dickerson Pike in the direction of home. "You're saying that Stacy had a million dollar life insurance policy on Virgil's life? Even though they weren't together anymore?"

"That's correct," Grimaldi said.

"Maybe it was left over from when they were together? Maybe Virgil had one on Stacy, too?"

"Possible," Grimaldi said. "Although if he did, it was through a different company."

Interesting. "And Stacy has been paying on this policy for the past six months?"

Grimaldi said he had. "Jaime wants to talk to you."

"Me?" I didn't know anything about Stacy's insurance policies, or for that matter about insurance in general. I doubted any company in their right mind would insure Rafe. He's much too high risk.

"Can you stop by on your way home?"

It wasn't exactly on my way home, but what the hell—heck— I was curious now. "Sure," I said. "I'll be there in twenty minutes."

Today was a much busier day at police headquarters. Lots more people coming and going, and no Grimaldi waiting for me in the lobby. No Mendoza waiting, either. I announced myself to the cop on duty, and settled in to wait for one or the other of them to come downstairs to fetch me.

Mendoza must have pulled the short straw, or maybe it was just his case and Grimaldi was busy with her own. At any rate, it was he, not she, who came out of the elevator and across the lobby toward me. "Mrs. Collier."

"Detective." I got to my feet.

He gestured me back toward the elevator bank. "This won't take long. I just want to hear for myself about your conversation with Teresa Dixon and the questions she asked your friend Aislynn."

It would make a lot more sense for him to call Aislynn and ask her what Terry had said—my information was second-hand, after all—but since it wasn't exactly a hardship to look at Mendoza for a few minutes, I just said "Sure," and preceded him into the elevator.

His office was down the hall from Grimaldi's, and had the same compact size and configuration. Like in Grimaldi's domain, there was paperwork everywhere, and filing cabinets along the back wall. Mendoza must clear his share of cases to have amassed so many cabinets.

Unlike Grimaldi, who keeps nothing personal sitting around, there was a photograph in a frame on Mendoza's desk. A small boy, maybe three years old, with big, brown eyes and a shock of black hair grinned out from behind glass.

"Your son?" I nodded to it as I made myself comfortable in one of the chairs in front of the desk.

Mendoza nodded. "Elias. He's three. Lives with my wife, but I spend as much time with him as I can."

"He's cute. Looks like you."

"I've always thought he looks more like Lola," Mendoza

said, with a glance at the image, "but thanks."

He steepled his fingers and became all business. "Tamara told me you tracked down Aislynn Turner at Teresa Dixon's apartment. That she'd been there since Saturday, not against her will."

I nodded.

"Tell me about it."

I told him about it, in excruciating detail. Waiting in the parking lot, following Terry home, knocking on the door, and talking to Aislynn.

"And this is the same apartment complex where Stacy Kelleher lives."

It didn't sound like a question, but he was waiting for confirmation, so I said it was. "I asked Terry about that. She said she knew Stacy, but it didn't sound like they knew one another well." Although she'd been awfully prompt with her answers when I'd asked her about Wednesday and Friday nights.

I added, "Grimaldi told me that Stacy tried to cash in a life insurance policy he had on Virgil."

Mendoza looked unhappy—maybe because Grimaldi had been discussing his case with someone else, and a civilian to boot—but he admitted it.

"He has an alibi for the murder, though," I said. "Doesn't he? Terry said he was working Wednesday night."

"In a restaurant full of guests," Mendoza confirmed, "at least twenty minutes from the crime scene. He might have been able to duck out for ten minutes without being missed, but not for close to an hour."

"So he didn't kill Virgil. Even if he is trying to cash in on Virgil's death."

Mendoza nodded. "About Terry."

"Just a second. How long has Stacy had that life insurance policy?"

"Not long," Mendoza said.

"Well, did he buy it while they were still together, or later? The house went on the market in early December last year, so he and Virgil were already on the outs by then."

Virgil had probably moved out of the house and in with Kenny as soon as he notified Stacy that their relationship was over. Stacy must have been staying in the house until it sold. Or at least until he made other arrangements.

"He purchased the policy in November," Mendoza said.

So right on the border between knowing and maybe not knowing that his boyfriend was cheating. Maybe suspecting, maybe not.

"If he knew that Virgil had taken up with Kenny and was planning to dump him, that could mean he bought the policy because he knew he wanted to kill Virgil."

Mendoza nodded.

"But it doesn't change the fact that he has an alibi for the murder. I don't suppose he has the money to hire a hitman?"

I'd have to ask Rafe how much a hitman costs. He'd been posing as one for a while. He'd know.

"Not without the payout from the insurance," Mendoza said. "The house they sold was Virgil's. He bought it before getting involved with Stacy. So when it was sold, all Stacy got was a small percentage. Virgil got the rest."

"And who inherits Virgil's money?"

"His next of kin," Mendoza said. "A mother in Virginia."

So not Stacy. "I suppose you've checked Stacy's bank account for any big withdrawals?"

Mendoza didn't seem to take the question personally. Grimaldi would have reminded me that she did, in fact, know how to do her job. "Nothing stuck out. He doesn't have much."

So he hadn't hired anyone to kill Virgil. Bummer.

"And that's why I want to talk about Terry," Mendoza said. "You said she insisted on watching reruns of CSI on Sunday."

I nodded. "That's what Aislynn told me."

"And this happened when she usually doesn't like to watch crime shows."

"So Aislynn said."

"And she asked questions about fingerprinting and handwriting analysis."

I nodded. "Aislynn said she did. But you should probably ask her about it. Aislynn, I mean. She was there, I wasn't."

"I intend to," Mendoza said. "I just wanted to hear what you remembered first. Your friend is a bit of an airhead, and I'd like to have some idea of what happened before I try to talk to either of them."

That made sense. Nothing against Aislynn, but she's on a plane all her own. One of those 'different drummer' people.

So I told him, as verbatim as I could remember, exactly what Aislynn had said, while he took notes on a legal pad. I also told him about my trip to see Damian in his lair, and how I didn't think Kylie's ex-husband had anything to do with anything, including visiting her in the hospital. "He said he had an alibi. And he's smart enough that, if he did break into the house and he was the one who hit her, he wouldn't show up at the hospital without a good explanation for how he knew what had happened. Nobody contacted him to tell him. Although Doctor Ramsey saw the guy. Just show him a picture of Damian and see if Doctor Ramsey recognizes him."

Mendoza nodded politely, just as if he hadn't thought about doing that himself. He was a lot nicer to me than Grimaldi used to be.

"And he wasn't the guy I saw outside Aislynn and Kylie's house," I added. "Too big in the shoulders. Also, he's a bank manager. I can't see him wearing a plaid shirt."

"Not even as a disguise?" Mendoza asked. He kept a straight face, but I think he was laughing at me. Very quietly.

"No, not even that. Besides, I'm sure he was at work in the middle of the afternoon on Friday. The bank would have been open. And somebody would have noticed if he left. Although I guess you could ask around and find out whether he took a late, long lunch on Friday."

Mendoza nodded solemnly.

I was just about to ask him whether there was anything else I could help him with, when there was a knock on the door.

"Come in," Mendoza called.

A blond head showed around the door jamb. "Excuse me, Detective."

Mendoza nodded.

"I have Teresa Dixon downstairs in a room when you're ready."

Mendoza smiled. "Thank you. I'll be right there."

The head withdrew, and Mendoza turned to me. "Anything else you remember that might help?"

"About Terry?" I thought about it. "She has a crush on Aislynn. And I think maybe she was lying about Saturday night."

He tilted his head. "What happened Saturday night?"

"Aislynn told you she was going to spend the night with her family in Bowling Green."

Mendoza nodded.

"But then Terry called and told her she was supposed to work. So she went to Sara Beth's instead and ended up spending the night with Terry because she didn't want to go home to an empty house."

Mendoza nodded.

"But what if she wasn't really supposed to work? I mean... I know she's a little scatter-brained. And she had a lot on her mind, what with Kylie and the break-in. But I don't think it's like her to forget she's scheduled to work. She isn't irresponsible."

Mendoza didn't say anything, just watched me.

"So what if Terry called and told her that because she knew what had happened? And because she hoped that if she played her cards right, Aislynn would spend the night—and the next day—with her?"

"How would she know what had happened?" Mendoza asked.

"I'm not sure. Not because she was the one who broke in. She swore she didn't write the letters, and if she didn't, then she had no reason to worry about getting them back. And anyway, she was at work until after nine. Sara Beth's stays open until then, and I'm sure they have to clean things up afterward."

Mendoza nodded. "Would you mind sticking around for a bit longer? I have to go talk to Terry Dixon."

"How long is that going to take?" Because I didn't want to have to sit up here for several hours while he interrogated a suspect. He wouldn't want me messing around on his computer, and there was nothing else to do.

"I'd like to have you observe the interview," Mendoza said. "Through the two-way mirror. Just in case Ms. Dixon says something that doesn't jive with what your friend told you. And then tell me about it later."

A chance to sit in—on the other side of the mirror—from a real, honest-to-goodness interrogation?

"I'd be delighted," I said.

Twenty

The first time I met Tamara Grimaldi—almost a year ago now, the morning Brenda Puckett was killed—she put me in an interrogation room and interrogated me.

To hear her tell it, it was more like an interview. She didn't actually suspect me of having had anything to do with the murder; she was more interested in Rafe for that role. But from my perspective, it was an interrogation. I was in shock, scared out of my wits, and nauseous from the sight of Brenda with her throat slit from ear to ear, and Grimaldi's very pointed questions about Rafe, and about my (non-existent) relationship with him, only made me feel worse.

It was much nicer to take in the interrogation from the other side of the two-way mirror. And even better, Grimaldi was right next to me, instead of on the other side of the mirror, asking difficult questions.

Mendoza was the one inside the room, talking to Terry.

She was leaned back in her chair, as far away from the table as she could get without physically moving her chair back, peering furtively at him through long strands of hair.

At the restaurant, both times I'd seen her, she'd had a scarf on her head, to keep her hair out of the way. Aislynn did too, when she was working. I assumed it was part of the uniform. But now the scarf was gone, and I got my fill of Terry's hair-do. As short as Rafe's in the back and on the sides—shorter than Mendoza's sleek, black cap by at least an inch—and with long bangs flopping over her forehead. Above one ear, from the front all the way back, was a shaved stripe of scalp an inch thick.

She was nibbling on a fingernail, or maybe her cuticles as she listened to him talk.

"Nervous," I said. "I wonder why."

Grimaldi glanced at me. "You were nervous the first time you were here, too. And you hadn't done anything wrong."

"You intimidated me," I told her. "And I'd just found a dead body. I was a little shook up."

Not to mention that I'd just run into Rafe again, for the first time in twelve years, and had gotten a load of that sex-appeal straight between the eyes. I was torn between being attracted to him, and being horrified by that same attraction, in addition to the—quite natural—concern that he might be a murderer.

"I'm sure Jaime's intimidating her, too." Grimaldi glanced through the glass. "And just being here would shake some people up."

Also true. Although Terry wasn't just shook up. She was shaking like a leaf, and looked ready to pass out.

"Let's talk about Aislynn Turner," Mendoza said.

Terry gulped. "What about her?"

"You work together. For how long?"

"Since she came to town," Terry said. "More than a year ago."

"You knew her before she became involved with Kylie Mitchell."

Terry said she had.

"Were you ever more than friends?"

Terry shook her head.

"Did you want to be?"

Terry bristled. "If I did, that's not a crime."

"Of course not," Mendoza said. "It must have upset you when she became involved with someone else."

Terry shrugged.

"Enough to take drastic measures?"

Terry's face darkened. "I didn't go to her house and hit her girlfriend over the head on Friday night, if that's what you're thinking. I was working! I have an alibi!"

Mendoza nodded. "Duly noted. And we'll check, but I can't imagine you'd be telling me that if it wasn't true. What time did the café close?"

"Nine," Terry said. "But there were guests there until at least a quarter after, and then we had to clean up. I didn't get out of there until close to ten. And I wasn't alone. There were two of us, plus the cook."

I had no idea when Kylie had come back from Lauren's house and had been hit over the head. I hadn't asked Kylie. Mendoza might have. And if he had, he must have decided that Terry's alibi stood, because he didn't pursue it.

"You know Stacy Kelleher," he asked instead. "Is that correct?"

Terry hesitated. "Who?"

"Stalling," Grimaldi murmured.

I nodded. "I asked her the same thing this morning. And reminded her who Stacy is. There's no chance she wouldn't remember." Although of course she didn't know that Mendoza knew that.

And he didn't let on. Instead he was patient, or pretended to be. "One of your neighbors. A bartender at South Street Bar."

"Oh," Terry said, and even I could hear how fake it sounded. "Him. Sure. I know him. A little."

Mendoza leaned back. Visually backing off. "Do you recall what kind of vehicle he drives?"

Terry blinked. "A Jeep. The kind with a cloth top."

"Do you remember seeing the Jeep in the parking lot when you came home from work on Friday night?"

Terry hesitated.

"Calculating the odds," Grimaldi murmured.

"Unless she just can't remember."

Grimaldi slanted a look my way. "What are the chances of that?"

"Probably pretty good. I don't remember what the car next to ours in the parking lot at the FinBar looked like on Friday. Or for that matter on Saturday."

"A red Prius," Grimaldi said. "But there's no reason why you should remember who you parked next to at a restaurant. Home's different. If there had been a car in your driveway Friday night, you'd remember. Or a car parked down the street."

Maybe. "Rafe would probably remember the car at the FinBar, too." The way Grimaldi did. "But he's been trained to be observant." Or had trained himself to be. When missing something small can be the difference between life and death, you do whatever you have to do to remember everything.

On the other side of the glass, Mendoza was prodding Terry, who seemed to have a hard time making up her mind whether she wanted to admit to seeing Stacy's car or not. Or maybe she was wondering whether she should throw Stacy under the bus—metaphorically speaking—or give him what might amount to a sort of alibi.

"Let's move on," Mendoza said, "and talk about Wednesday night."

It might have been the lighting, but Terry looked like she turned a shade paler. "Wednesday?"

"Did you know your friend Stacy used to own the house your friend Aislynn lives in now?"

Terry hesitated again. "No?" she said, although it sounded like she wasn't certain that was the right answer.

"Are you sure?"

"I don't know. I might have heard something about it."

"So you did know."

"I'm not sure," Terry said. "I think maybe someone mentioned it once. Maybe not."

Mendoza scribbled a note on his yellow pad. Terry watched the pen slide across the paper, but I had no idea how good she was at reading upside down, and whether Mendoza's handwriting was even legible.

Hell—heck—I don't know whether he wrote down anything at all, or just scribbled something illegible to rattle her.

"Did Stacy and Aislynn ever meet?"

"No," Terry said. "Not that I know of."

"Did Stacy ever mention the house he lived in before? Or the man he lived with?"

Terry blinked. "I'm not sure...?"

"His name was Virgil Wright," Mendoza said. "He was killed Wednesday night."

"Stacy was at work Wednesday night."

Mendoza nodded. "What about you?"

There was another pause while Terry tried to decide what to do. Or at least I assume that's what she was doing. Trying to figure out how much to admit. "No," she said eventually. "I wasn't working. Not on Wednesday."

"Can you account for your whereabouts between six and eight?"

Terry opened her mouth, and then closed it again. "I was having a drink," she said. "At South Street."

"The place where Stacy works? That's quite a coincidence. Especially since, two minutes ago, you weren't even sure you knew who he was."

Mendoza waited. When Terry didn't have anything to say to that, he added, "So if I ask Stacy to confirm that, he will?"

Terry hesitated. "That might have been a different day," she said. "Maybe Tuesday or Thursday. I think I was home on Wednesday night. Alone."

"So no one can confirm your whereabouts." Mendoza made another notation on his legal pad. Terry looked like she wanted to say something, but she wasn't sure what. Mendoza added, "Let's talk about Sunday."

By now, Terry was starting to look overwhelmed. "What happened on Sunday?"

"Nothing," Mendoza said, and had the nerve to sound

surprised. I couldn't see his face, but he probably looked surprised, too. "You spent the day with Ms. Turner, is that correct?"

Terry relaxed. "Yes."

"You worked together on Saturday night, and when she expressed a desire not to spend the night alone in an empty house, you offered her the use of your second bedroom."

Terry nodded.

"Hoping to get lucky?"

The question slipped out so smoothly that it took Terry a few seconds to take offense. Then she flushed. "No!"

"Just happy to be spending time with her?"

"We're friends," Terry said. "I was happy to help."

"What did the two of you do to pass the time?"

"Talked," Terry said. "Played video games. Watched TV."

"What did you talk about?"

"Nothing in particular. This and that. Work. What was going on with her."

"What about the TV? What did you watch?"

"Just stuff," Terry said. "Reruns. You know."

"I don't," Mendoza told her. "That's why I'm asking." He shook his head. "It's not a difficult question. And no reason why you can't tell me. I'm not gonna bust you for watching porn. Not unless there were minors involved."

"We weren't watching porn," Terry said, offended. "And there were no minors. What do you think I am? Some kind of pervert?"

"Of course not." Mendoza's voice was soothing, while next to me, Grimaldi snorted. "We're just getting some background information on what went on during the day. You played games. You watched reruns. You talked. About the shows you were watching?"

There was a beat. "Probably," Terry said.

"Can you remember what you talked about?"

Terry shook her head.

"Did you watch CSI and talk about fingerprints? And about whether it was possible to match someone's handwriting in an anonymous letter?"

"I don't remember," Terry said. Her lips barely moved, as if they were stiff. The rest of her looked a bit stiff, too. Brittle, as if one good knock could shatter her into pieces.

"Would you have a particular reason for speculating about those things?" Mendoza wanted to know.

Terry shook her head.

"Did you write the anonymous letters to Ms. Turner?"

"No," Terry said.

"Did you break into Ms. Turner's and Ms. Mitchell's house on Friday night? Will we find your fingerprints on the snow globe that was used to hit Ms. Mitchell?"

Terry shook her head.

"Anything else you'd like to share with me?"

Terry hesitated, but eventually she replied in the negative.

"Then that's all for now." Mendoza got to his feet.

Terry didn't. "Am I under arrest?" she asked, peering up at Mendoza.

Mendoza sounded surprised. "Of course not. We don't arrest people for watching CSI. You're free to go."

For a second, it didn't look like Terry believed him. Then she flushed and got to her feet.

I turned to Grimaldi. "You're not arresting her?"

"For what? Not for asking questions about fingerprinting during a rerun of CSI. If we arrested everyone who did that, there'd be no more room left at the jail."

Well, yes. When she put it like that.

"She didn't break into your friends' house," Grimaldi added. "She didn't hit Ms. Mitchell with the snow globe. She didn't keep Ms. Turner against her will. And I don't think she wrote the anonymous letters. What are we supposed to arrest her for?"

I had no idea; I just knew I didn't like this. "What about Virgil's murder?"

Grimaldi shook her head. "If you have any evidence at all that she had something to do with it, I'm sure Jaime would be happy to arrest her. So would I. But there's no proof."

"She knows Stacy. And she doesn't have an alibi."

"That's not enough," Grimaldi said. "We have to put her at the scene of the crime during the time the crime was committed. If you can do that, then we'll talk."

Inside the interrogation room, Terry was moving toward the door. Slowly, as if she couldn't quite believe that Mendoza was going to let her walk out.

Grimaldi smiled. "It'll be interesting to see what she does when she leaves here."

Yes, it would. "I guess someone will be following her, to see?"

By now, Terry had made it to the door. She reached for the handle, just as Mendoza said, "Ms. Dixon?"

Terry hunched like a turtle, pulling her head in. She probably wished she could just yank the door open and make a run for it, but she turned around. "Uh?"

"Don't go anywhere. In case we need to talk to you again."

"Home?" Terry managed.

Mendoza smiled whitely. Now that he'd turned around to face Terry—and the mirror, and us—I could see his face, and the smile was positively wolfish. *What big teeth you have, Detective.*

"Of course you may go home," he said genially. "And to work. And anywhere else you usually go. Enjoy your life. Eat, drink, and be merry. Just don't leave town. I don't have the time to hunt you down and drag you back, and if I have to, it'll make me cranky. So just do me a favor and stick around where I can find you."

"Urk," Terry said. Or that's what it sounded like.

Grimaldi smothered a chuckle. "I'm surprised she hasn't

peed her pants."

"It's not too late."

She smiled. "There she goes. What do you want to bet she'll be running by the time she hits the sidewalk outside?"

I shook my head. "No bet." She probably would be. Or if not precisely running, at least moving fast enough to leave skid marks on the ground. "Someone will be following her, right?"

"We'll keep an eye on her," Grimaldi nodded. "And if she remembers to stop and pick up her phone on her way out, we'll also be able to track her that way."

"So if she goes anywhere near Aislynn and Kylie's house, you'll know about it?"

By now, Terry had to have guessed that Aislynn had told the police about the day they had spent together yesterday. Of course, what had happened was that Aislynn had told me and I had told the police, although Terry might not be reasoning that far. She'd probably blame Aislynn. And if Terry was trying to hide something, and feeling vindictive, she might decide to get back at Aislynn.

Grimaldi nodded. "I've also got Spicer and Truman going by on their rounds. They're working the late shift tonight, so they'll keep an eye on the house."

Officers Lyle Spicer and George Truman were old friends of mine. They had been the first to respond to my 911 call a year ago, when we'd found Brenda Puckett murdered, and they had come upon me in compromising situations more than once since then. We went back a long way, and I trusted them. The fact that they'd keep an eye on Aislynn and Kylie made me feel better.

"Thank you," I said.

"We try not to lose any potential witnesses, Ms. Martin." She headed for the door. "C'mon. We can go."

I followed. In the hallway, she took a right, I assumed to join Mendoza in the interrogation room to discuss the interview. I glanced left, in time to catch sight of Terry on her way out. I guess it must have taken her a moment to orient herself once she got out of the interrogation room, and to figure out which way to go.

Or maybe she'd just needed a moment to gather herself after the ordeal.

Either way, there she was, on her way down the hallway. Just before she turned the corner, she glanced over her shoulder. I took a step back, so she wouldn't see me. Then she disappeared around the corner, and I headed down the hallway in the other direction, after Grimaldi.

"That's her," I announced as I swung through the door to the interrogation room. "That's who I saw sneaking around Aislynn and Kylie's yard on Friday afternoon, wearing a plaid shirt."

"I thought you said she worked on Friday afternoon," Mendoza said, looking up from his notes.

"She did. I had lunch at Sara Beth's, and Terry and Aislynn were both there. But after lunch I left and went to talk to Stacy. Terry would have had time to clean up and get to East Nashville before me. She had to come back and work the dinner shift, so she probably got a break in the middle of the day. And chances are Aislynn had to stay, since she wasn't working the dinner shift. So Terry would know the house would be empty. And she looks different without the scarf on her head."

"Scarf?"

"They wear them to work," I said. "To keep their hair out of their faces. And I guess out of the food. Every other time I've seen her, she's had a bandana covering the back of her head. If I'd seen her haircut before, I would have recognized her sooner. But that's definitely her."

"Wish I would have known that earlier."

"Sorry," I said, although there was nothing I could have done about it. "You'll be talking to her again, though, right?"

"Oh," Mendoza said, "most assuredly. I suspect her of killing Virgil Wright. I just have to figure out why she'd agree to do that. Whether Stacy Kelleher was holding something over her—blackmailing her, essentially—or whether something else is going on."

It sounded like he was grinding his teeth, or at least clenching his jaw. Angry, I assumed, that someone was getting away with murder.

Then he relaxed. "Did you hear anything contrary to what your friend told you?"

I shook my head. "She didn't admit much."

"No, she didn't. Which leads me to believe she has something to hide. Innocent people don't mind telling the truth."

"She could just be hiding something mildly illegal. And disgusting. Like being obsessed with Aislynn and breaking into her house to sniff her underwear."

They both arched their brows.

"I told you," I said. "I saw her. On Friday afternoon. She went into the backyard. When I got there, I didn't see anyone. Terry could have taken the key out of the thermometer and let herself into the house. Aislynn might have told her there was a hide-a-key in the thermometer next to the door. They were friends. But even if she didn't, Kylie told me the thermometer was there when they bought the place. The previous owners would have known about it. That means Stacy. He could have told Terry where to find the key."

Mendoza and Grimaldi exchanged a glance.

"So maybe she's just hiding that. Not that she committed murder."

"But if Terry didn't kill Mr. Wright," Mendoza said, "who did?"

I shook my head. "No idea. That's your job."

"It is. And I'm going to do it. And nail Ms. Dixon. Because she picked up that rock and bashed Mr. Wright's head in, and she's going to pay for it."

He snatched up his legal pad and stalked out of the room. I

glanced at Grimaldi.

"He takes his job seriously," she said.

"As he should." I headed for the door, too. "I'm going home. Rafe should be there soon. Let me know if there's anything else I can do for you. Either of you."

Grimaldi said she would, and I made my way out of the police station and to my car, and onto the bridge across the Cumberland River to East Nashville.

Twenty-One

I know I'd said I was going home, but I couldn't go there without first stopping by Aislynn and Kylie's house to tell them what I'd found out, not just about Terry, but about Damian, too. He and Kylie had been married a while; I felt I owed her the knowledge that her ex-husband had had nothing to do with what had happened to her. And I definitely wanted them to know that Terry might be a whole lot more dangerous than we'd imagined, and to not open the door for her if she came knocking.

By now, rush hour had started, and I made my slow way across the bridge, bumper to bumper with a lot of other cars, three lanes deep all the way across. At the light on the other side, the right lane disappeared, as the cars there headed for the interstate. Halfway up the next block, there was an entrance for Ellington Parkway on the right, and a steady stream of cars drove that way. By the time I reached the stop light on Main Street and Fifth, traffic was a lot more manageable.

I drove another few blocks, up to the corner of Tenth, and took a right at Brew-ha-ha, the coffee shop, and from there disappeared into the residential districts. A couple of minutes later I was parked outside Aislynn and Kylie's house.

It took a minute or two for Aislynn to come to the door. She peered out before she unlocked the door. I didn't mind; I was glad she was careful.

"It's just me," I told her through the glass. "Can I come in for a few minutes? I have some news."

She opened the door and let me in, but not without peering up and down the street before she shut and locked the door behind us. "Kylie's resting." She kept her voice low. "I've been cleaning up."

I glanced into the office. Yes, she had. Most of the papers were up off the floor and in piles on the desk. Somehow, I didn't think that Kylie would be all that appreciative of the 'help.' Not unless Aislynn had actually taken the time to sort and organize the paperwork, instead of just scooping it up into piles.

None of my business, though. "I just came from the police station," I said. "They pulled Terry in for questioning and asked me to sit in, to see if she told the same story about yesterday that you told me."

Aislynn blinked. "They arrested Terry?"

I shook my head. "They let her go after they spoke to her. I wanted to let you know, so you could be careful."

"Of Terry?" Aislynn said incredulously. Not surprising, since she'd felt safe enough with the other woman to spend two nights and a day on Terry's futon.

"She has a thing for you. She could have known where you keep your hide-a-key. And she's who I saw sneaking around the yard on Friday afternoon. When I was standing in the backyard, she was probably upstairs pawing through your drawers."

Aislynn's face twisted. "That's sick."

Yes, it was. "And that's why you don't want anything to do with her."

"So did she write the letters after all? To get me to leave Kylie, or something? Or just so I'd be scared and spend the night with her? Did she hit Kylie, too?"

"I don't think she did," I said, "and I don't think the police think so, either. She was working at Sara Beth's Friday night. She couldn't have been here."

"So why do I have to be careful? She didn't hurt me this weekend. And if she didn't hurt Kylie..."

"The police think she may have killed Virgil Wright," I said.

Aislynn stared at me. She opened her mouth, but nothing came out. Then she closed it again. And tried one more time.

"Why? Did she know him?"

I shook my head. "But she knew Stacy. Virgil's ex. They live in the same apartment complex. And while Stacy was working Wednesday night, Terry wasn't."

While Stacy had been free Friday night, when Terry was at work. Maybe the two of them had engaged in a game of you-scratch-my-back-and-I'll scratch-yours?

Maybe Terry had whined to her good buddy Stacy about this girl who wouldn't pay her any attention, and Stacy had realized that Aislynn was the same girl who was now living in the house he'd shared with Virgil. Maybe he had suggested the anonymous letter campaign as a means of scaring Aislynn into leaving Kylie, but also as a way to muddy the waters once he was ready to kill Virgil. He had told Terry where to find the spare key to the house—inside the hide-a-key thermometer on the back porch—so Terry could come and go in Aislynn's house as she pleased.

And in exchange for all this, Stacy had requested—or required—Terry's help in getting rid of his former lover, so he could cash in on the insurance policy he had on Virgil's life. He might have sweetened the pot by telling her he'd give her some of the money after he got his million.

And who knew, he might be planning to use the rest of the money to buy back the house Aislynn and Kylie lived in. If the letters caused Aislynn and Kylie to break up, Terry would be standing ready to offer Aislynn the futon and the second bedroom for as long as Aislynn needed it, and Stacy would be ready to swoop in and take the house off Kylie's hands.

It all made sense. In a weird, twisted, obsessive sort of way that was extremely disturbing.

And I wasn't even sure whether I was more freaked out by Stacy thinking of it, or Stacy using Terry to execute it—and Virgil—or by Terry going along with the twisty plan. I mean, what kind of person agrees to something like this? And for love—or whatever you'd call what Terry felt for Aislynn.

"Please be careful," I told her. Someone who'd kill for her, was likely to do pretty much anything else, as well. Including killing again.

She nodded. "I won't open the door for anyone. I promise."

"Take the extra key out of the thermometer so no one can come in. She knows it's there."

"Already done," Aislynn said.

"A couple of the local cops are supposed to drive by from time to time and make sure everything is all right. Although maybe it would be better if you put Kylie in the car and went somewhere else. In fact, now would be a great time to make that visit to your parents." Only an hour's drive, but safely away from Nashville.

Aislynn hesitated. "My folks really aren't that crazy about Kyle..."

"My mother hated my boyfriend," I said. ""But last month, he got himself hurt. And it changed everything. Now my mother dotes on him."

There had been a little bit more to it than that, of course, but since there was no way Aislynn or Kylie could possibly match Rafe's encounter with the serial killer from his past, there was no sense in even mentioning it. I added, "I bet, if you take Kylie there and explain that she got hurt because some nut job is after you, your mother will do the same thing."

Aislynn looked unconvinced.

"I'm sure they just want you to be happy," I said. "And once they get to know Kylie, they'll see that she loves you, and that she makes you happy. You just have to give them a chance. If my mother could change, there's hope for anyone's mother."

"I don't know..."

"You'll be safer if you leave. And so will Kylie. She can't go back to work for a day or two anyway. And I'm sure you don't want to go back to Sara Beth's while Terry is there. Do you?"

She hesitated.

254 | JENNA BENNETT

"And this way, you won't get any surprise visits from Lauren, to check on the invalid."

That did it.

"I'll just throw some things in a bag," Aislynn said, already making for the stairs, "and then we'll be gone."

She took the steps two at a time, with those long, skinny legs. I turned my attention to the desk.

As I had expected, she had just haphazardly thrown things together in piles. Kylie would have a hell—heck—of a time trying to straighten it out when she recovered enough for the task.

The piece of paper on top of one of the piles was a copy of Kylie's dissolution of marriage from Damian Mitchell. So that was one mystery solved: namely how the fake Damian who had come to the hospital had known Kylie's ex-husband's name. He must have seen it while he was here on Friday night.

And that proved pretty conclusively—if you asked me—that the guy at the hospital and the burglar were one and the same.

It also proved that Terry hadn't been the burglar, since surely Dr. Ramsey was able to tell that she was female, and not Kylie's ex-husband.

Upstairs, I heard drawers and closet doors opening and shutting. Aislynn packing bags, I guess. And I heard soft voices, probably Aislynn explaining to Kylie what was going on.

I headed down the hallway to the backdoor, to make sure it was locked and that the key was, indeed, not in the thermometer. That done, I went back to the front of the house, in time to see Aislynn steadying Kylie down the stairs to the first floor, an overnight bag in her other hand.

Kylie looked marginally better, so resting must have been good for her. She still looked pale and wan, though, and was moving slowly. I took a step forward to grab her other arm when she came off the staircase. "How are you feeling?"

"Better." Her voice was weak, and she cleared her throat.

"It's nice to be back home."

"And now we're taking you away again." I grimaced. "I really do think you'll be safer somewhere else, though. Just for a day or two. If we're right, this woman has already committed one murder. She might find it easier to commit another."

Yet another reason to believe it hadn't been Terry in the house Friday night. After bashing Virgil's head in on Wednesday, I'm not sure she could have resisted doing the same to Kylie when she had the chance.

"It's all right," Kylie said. "All I need is a bed and I'm good. It doesn't matter where it is." She smiled. That, too, was weak. "I just want to survive this."

"Let's get you in the car," I said, turning toward the door. "I checked the back door. It's locked."

We stopped on the porch so Aislynn could lock the front door too, and then I got them both settled in Kylie's Volvo. I stood on the sidewalk and waved until they'd driven away, and then I got into my own car and went home, feeling a lot better about the fact that they were out of harm's way.

The house was empty when I got there. So was the yard. Rafe was not outside mowing the grass today. I let myself in and set about preparing dinner.

The phone rang twenty minutes later, just as I was getting ready to put the food on the table. (Chicken fajitas with black beans, green peppers, and onions, in case you were wondering. I was planning to take extra Tums again afterward.)

"Sorry, darlin'," my husband told me, "I'm gonna be late."

I looked at the two plates, the two glasses, the heated tortillas, and the pan full of sautéed vegetables and chicken, and sighed. "How late?"

I could imagine him shaking his head. "Dunno, darlin'. This thing with Jamal's going down tonight. I gotta be there to make sure he don't get himself in too much trouble."

Of course he did. I turned off the heat under the fajita mixture. "That's too bad. I just finished making black bean fajitas."

"Well, damn," Rafe said, since he's quite fond of my black bean fajitas, and since he also knows that there's a lot of chopping involved. "Sorry, darlin'."

"It's all right. You can't help it. And Jamal's more important than coming home for dinner."

For the record, I did mean that. It wasn't like this happened all the time. Or like I felt he put too many other things above me. He loved me. I knew that. But he had an important job where lives sometimes hung in the balance—sometimes the life in the balance was his—and when it came down to a question between being home for dinner or making sure Jamal was safe, the answer really was a no-brainer.

"I'll just eat on my own," I said, "and put the leftovers in the fridge for later. You can heat it up in the microwave when you get home."

"I don't imagine I'll be home until pretty late, darlin'. Too late to heat anything up."

"That's too bad."

I could hear the smile in his voice. "I could wake you."

"I don't mind if you do. Although you might be too tired."

"I ain't never too tired for that," Rafe said. There were voices behind him, and he was silent for a moment, I guess to hear what they were saying. Then he asked, "So how're you gonna spend the rest of the night?"

"I figure I'll probably eat while the food is warm. I can't skip meals these days. The baby gets cranky."

"I don't blame him," Rafe told me. "I get cranky, too. I just can't do nothing about it right now."

"Maybe you can stop for a burger or something on the way."

He chuckled. "Sure. I'll just keep the burger in one hand and the gun in the other."

"Gun?"

His voice was easy. "Just business as usual, darlin'. Don't worry."

Sure. I wanted to pursue it, but figured I'd probably be happier not knowing the details. "Just make sure you come home in one piece."

He smiled. I could hear it in his voice. "Always."

"And try to keep Jamal in one piece, too."

"That's the plan."

Well, if anyone could do it, he could. "I'll probably just crawl into bed," I said, "and watch a movie or read a book or something while I wait for you to get here."

Nice and normal. Something that had been sadly lacking in his life so far.

"Don't wait up," he told me. "I have a feeling it's gonna be late. Just take care of yourself and the baby. I'll take care of this."

"I know you will. Stay safe. I love you."

"Love you too, darlin'." He hung up. I did the same, and settled in with my lonely fajitas and a romance novel.

In my former life, before Rafe, I used to be a fan of steamy historical romance. My favorite author was Barbara Botticelli, who wrote such masterpieces as *Tartan Tryst, Apache Amour,* and *Stand and Deliver.* All of her heroines were innocent, blond, and well-bred, while all her heroes were tall, dark, and dangerous, with more than a passing resemblance to Rafe. I stopped reading the books when I realized that in real life, Barbara was none other than Elspeth Caulfield from Damascus, Tennessee, who'd had a one-night-stand with Rafe in high school and never gotten over him. The fact that she'd imagined him naked every time the hero unbuttoned his buff britches, turned me off.

And since I now had Rafe in my bed every night, and was living my very own romance with Mr. Tall, Dark, and Dangerous, I had switched to reading mysteries. Cozy mysteries, the kind with cats and gimmicks and very little blood.

I was halfway through a holiday mystery—the Fourth of July, not Christmas—and after dinner, I crawled into bed with it. There was nothing else to do, I was tired, and anyway, bed was where Mr. Tall, Dark, and Dangerous would want to find me when he got home.

It took a couple of hours to finish the book, and by then my eyelids were drooping. It was almost ten, and Rafe wasn't home yet. He probably wouldn't be here for a few hours, judging from what he'd said on the phone. I turned out the light and crawled under the covers, while I tried not to worry about what might be going on, and the danger he might be putting himself in.

It had been a while since I'd worried like this. Except for the twenty-four hours last month when he'd gotten himself kidnapped and tortured, of course, and we didn't know where he was or what had happened to him. But that hadn't really been an occupational hazard, or only indirectly. A blast from the past that none of us could have predicted. This was putting his life and safety on the line in the line of duty, and he hadn't had to do that for a while. He'd gotten out of undercover work last December, and had taken what amounted to a desk job in February. At that point, I'd stopped worrying so much, since he wouldn't put himself in danger all the time.

And now here he was, putting himself in danger again. Strapping on a gun and walking into a war between rival gangs to protect his protégé.

It took me a while to fall asleep, and when I did, I was plagued by bad dreams. It could have been the beans and onions, although it was more likely to be worry. And as usual, my nightmares were a strange mixture of things that didn't necessarily belong together. Rafe was going to the mailbox outside our house at 101 Potsdam to see if we'd gotten any more poison pen letters, but he was carrying a gun and looking left and right for gang members while he did it—like we were under siege or something—and when he got there, a car came rolling down the street with the subwoofer blasting, and as it came closer, the tinted windows rolled down, and I knew it was the poison pen... except the points of semi-automatic weapons stuck out of the windows, and they started spitting bullets, and Rafe returned fire as he zigzagged through the yard toward the front door, and I called to him to hurry, but then he stumbled and fell... and I woke up with the sheets twisted around my legs so I couldn't move, and a scream caught in my throat.

It took at least a minute before my heart settled into a normal rhythm and I could unwind myself from the sheet and kick my feet free.

The lighted numbers on the digital clock said 12:43. I was still alone in bed. I didn't even have to look to know that. Rafe is a light sleeper, and if I'd had a nightmare, he would have woken up before I did, and would have been soothing me now. Or distracting me; whichever he thought would do the trick. Since he's pretty much always happy to get laid, he might have opted for distraction.

But since nothing like that was going on, I was definitely alone. His side of the bed was cold and untouched, the comforter still smooth.

I settled back against the pillows and concentrated on breathing. In and out, slowly and carefully. Everything was all right. Rafe was safe. Nobody had gunned him down in the front yard. I would have heard the shots.

And I knew it, logically, but even so, I pushed the comforter back and padded over to the window. The old floorboards were cold against the soles of my feet, and the air conditioning vent sent a blast of icy air at my ankles as I moved past.

The bedroom window overlooks the front yard: the circular driveway, a lot of old oak and hackberry trees, and beyond the yard, Potsdam Street. At this time of night, there was very little to see. Most of the neighboring houses were dark, with the occasional porch light above or beside a front door, and here or there the blue flicker of a TV where someone had gotten caught up in a late movie. Straight below me, I could see the roof of my Volvo, parked in the driveway, and I could also see that Rafe's Harley wasn't parked there with it. Whatever he'd been doing with Jamal, he was still doing it.

Down the street, there was a flash of light. As the vehicle came closer, I saw a pair of matching headlights approaching slowly. Not Rafe coming home, then.

I squinted, but couldn't make out the car itself. Maybe it was Spicer and Truman, driving by to make sure everything was all right. Or just a neighbor, coming home from a late night on the town. Malcolm, the nineteen-year-old who lived two houses up, worked at the gas station on the corner of Dickerson Road and Dresden. His shift ended at eleven, but maybe he'd put in an extra hour and a half, or something.

But no. The car passed Malcolm's place and kept going until the red taillights winked out up the street.

I stayed where I was. My feet were cold and I was flagging, but the baby was wide awake, doing what felt like cartwheels inside my belly. Maybe it was excited that I was up and about, since that was rather unusual for this time of night.

Practice for after it was born, when I would have to get up for nightly feedings.

I was about to go back to bed when something moved outside. And instead of heading back to curl my cold toes into the covers, I leaned closer to the window and squinted.

A dark shadow moved down the street from the direction of Malcolm's house.

Now, that's not anything unusual. People do walk around the neighborhood sometimes, coming and going. I wouldn't choose to do it, but that doesn't mean other people don't, either because they want to, or they have to. People go to or get off work at any hour of the day or night these days. Cars run out of gas and people have to walk home. We have a few homeless in the area, who get rousted from one place and have to move to another in the middle of the night, for one reason or another. And we live in a fairly high crime area, so we have our share of drug dealers, hookers, and other undesirables wandering our streets. Including some of the gang members Rafe was hunting tonight. They tend to avoid the area right around our house, though, since word has gotten out that Rafe works for the TBI. The law-abiding neighbors love him, since crime has gone down since he moved in, while the not-so-law-abiding take the long way around.

This person did not take the long way around. He—or she; it was impossible to tell in the dark—hesitated at the bottom of the driveway. I expected him (or her) to flit across, and continue down the sidewalk, but instead, he—she—ducked inside the yard and vanished among the shadows of the trees.

A second later, another shadow followed.

Two of them. In our yard, on their way toward the house.

And I was alone, without Rafe—or his gun—to protect me.

Twenty-Two

My phone was on the bedside table, charging. I ran to it, yanked it out of the charger, and ran back to the window, terrified I'd miss something. Only to realize when I got there that the glow from the screen was probably visible outside, and might show them—whoever they were—that I was standing there watching them. So I ran back to the bed and crawled under the covers for long enough to dial the number I wanted.

"There are two people in my yard," I told Grimaldi when her sleepy voice picked up on the other end of the line, "and Rafe isn't here."

"Shit." She was wide awake immediately. "I'm on my way. Did you call 911?"

"I called you first. I'm in bed, under the blankets. I was afraid they'd see the light from the phone and realize I was awake."

"Get out from under there," Grimaldi said, "and get dressed." I could hear scuffling from the other end of the line as she was already doing what she was telling me to do. "Don't worry about making any more calls. I'll get the nearest black-and-white on its way to you. Put on some clothes and find a weapon. I don't care what kind. Knife, gun, fireplace poker."

The knives and fireplace pokers were downstairs. So was my lipstick-canister pepper spray, along with my lipstick-canister serrated blade. And there was no gun in the house. Not without Rafe.

"Shit," Grimaldi said again when I told her so. "Can you get downstairs and out the back door?"

"Probably not. They were on their way toward the house a minute ago. Besides, I don't know who's back there. The two in the front might have split up. Or there might be more than two.

Someone could be outside the back door already."

Grimaldi muttered something. I don't think it was critical. Or at least not critical of me. "I don't suppose you have any secret rooms or staircases in the house?"

We didn't. "There's a third floor with a big ballroom. But other than that it's just the usual bedrooms and bathrooms and common rooms and closets."

"Just do your best to stay alive," Grimaldi said. "I'm on my way." She hung up.

OK, then. I slithered from under the blankets—slithering was becoming more difficult as my pregnancy progressed—and padded back over to the window. I know Grimaldi's instructions had been to get dressed—and I would, since I didn't want to face burglars (or whoever I was dealing with) in my nightgown—but first I wanted to see how far they'd gotten, and whether they were actually on their way into the house. Maybe they were just cutting through the yard or playing war games or something.

Maybe they weren't after me at all. Or after Rafe, which was much more likely.

It took a few seconds for my eyes to focus outside the house again. At first everything looked quiet, but then I saw movement among the trees in the yard. They were taking their time, gliding smoothly toward the house, sticking to the shadows under the leafy branches.

There were still just two of them, or at least I didn't see any more. And it was too dark for me to make any kind of identification. They were dressed in dark clothes, and they either had dark hair or dark caps or hoods covering their heads. It was impossible to see faces, or anything other than just moving patches of darkness. I watched as one of them made it out from under the cover of the trees and scurried around the front end of the Volvo. Three seconds later, the other one followed.

They disappeared from sight as they approached the stairs to the porch.

Time to move.

My hands were shaking so badly that it was hard to dress. I choose a pair of black yoga pants, thinking they'd be easy to pull on, but it was like fitting my legs into a pair of control-top pantyhose: slow and agonizing. All the while I struggled with my uncooperative hands and the uncooperative fabric, I kept my ears peeled for sounds from downstairs.

For the first few seconds there was nothing. Then a small sound, followed by the tinkling of glass.

A very small sound. Much smaller than I'd expected.

Once upon a time, last fall, someone had shot out one of the front windows of the house, trying to kill me. The sound had been deafening. Both the shot itself, and the sound of the pane of glass shattering onto the floor. By comparison, this was so small it was almost comforting.

At least until I heard the front door open and footsteps on the floor downstairs.

I pulled one of Rafe's black T-shirts over my head and tiptoed out into the hallway.

They were both inside now. I heard murmurs, but no words. Certainly not voices I could recognize.

Then I heard the scuff of a foot on the bottom step of the stairs, and it was the kick in the pants I needed to get going.

As I'd told Tamara Grimaldi on the phone, we have a ballroom on the third floor of the house. Not that we ever have balls, but in the days when this house was built, during the Victorian era, wealthy families did just that. Invited friends over, had dinner, and waltzed the night away. Many of the big Victorian houses in East Nashville and Germantown have ballrooms.

If we ended up having more children, I figured the big room on the top floor, from which you could see the downtown skyline, would make a good playroom.

At the moment there was nothing much up there. Just a

cavernous room full of shadows and boxes, with a dusty floor and a bit of starlight floating in above the treetops.

I scurried across the expanse of floor and crouched behind a stack of boxes, trying to regulate my breathing.

The door had shut behind me—thankfully without squeaking. I made a mental note to thank Rafe for keeping the hinges oiled, if I got out of this alive.

And then I hunkered down and waited to see what would happen.

Time dragged on. I keep my ears peeled for noises from downstairs, and for the sound of sirens outside. Grimaldi had said she'd call 911; surely someone was on their way? She lived on the other side of town, at least twenty minutes away, and while time felt like it was dragging, I knew it hadn't been that long. She wasn't anywhere close. But surely there was a squad car within a few minutes of me? And the East Precinct was just up on Trinity Lane, no more than five minutes away.

Why wasn't anyone coming?

A brush of a foot on the stairs brought my head up, and suddenly the idea of cowering here, behind my stack of boxes, seemed like a bad idea. I was a sitting duck, just waiting for my burglar—whoever he was—to come and find me.

Maybe I should be proactive instead.

Praying that the closed door between us would mask the sound of my movements, I slid out from behind the boxes and along the wall. My bare feet didn't make a sound, and I held my breath, hoping the old floorboards wouldn't squeak and alert him to my location. If he'd been through the second floor, he would know I wasn't there, and that it was likely I was up here somewhere, but I didn't want him to know my exact position.

The doorknob turned.

I started moving faster.

By the time the door opened, I was five feet away.

And by the time a dark shadow stepped up into the

doorway, and starlight glinted on the barrel of the gun in his gloved hand, I threw myself forward and propelled him back.

I'm almost five-eight, and I've always carried a few pounds extra. Not that I'm fat, but I've always been a bit broader in the beam than I'd like to be. I'd gained a few more pounds since getting pregnant, too.

In other words, I'm not a small person. And I was terrified, on my own behalf and for the baby. Terror, combined with rage—how dared these people come into my house in the middle of the night and threaten me?—combined with my physical attributes, might not have been enough to take on someone like Rafe. He's a lot bigger than me, and he fights dirty. He's also prepared for any eventuality, and it isn't easy to take him off guard.

That was not the case with the burglar. This guy—whoever he was—wasn't any bigger than me. And he obviously wasn't prepared for a hundred and forty-five pounds of terrified female.

My palms slammed into his chest—which was a lot squishier than I had expected.

A woman?

By the time that thought registered, it was much too late for it to do any good. And honestly, I don't know if it would have made any difference anyway. A person with a gun is a person with a gun, no matter the gender. And anyway, that first push had taken her back a step, and then it was too late. Her heel came down beyond the edge of the step outside the door, and when her weight landed on it, she tipped over backwards and tumbled down the stairs.

A shrill scream rang in my ears. Simultaneously, the gun went off with a deafening bang. The bullet whizzed past me and buried itself in the wall above my head. A trickle of plaster dust floated down.

I clapped my hands over my ears, so I didn't hear the sound

of her body hitting the steps and sliding the last few feet onto the second story floor, but I did hear the silence when her scream was cut off. My ears were still ringing, but not so loudly that I didn't hear the wild scramble from the first floor. Running footsteps in the hallway downstairs, the sound of the front door being yanked open, and then the slamming of said door again as burglar number two took to his heels down the porch steps and through the yard.

I let him go. No way was I going to jump over the body—dead or alive—at the foot of the third floor stairs to give chase. I didn't want to catch anyone. I wouldn't know what to do with him—or her—if I did. I just wanted to be safe.

It took at least a minute before I had calmed myself down enough that I was able to make it down the stairs, clinging to the banister the whole way.

At the bottom of the stairs, I clicked the light switch. Bright light seared my eyeballs for a moment. My pupils protested, but then adjusted. The body didn't twitch. She was either out cold, or dead.

I had to force myself to creep over to her, to check whether she was still alive. And before I did it, I looked around for the gun, to make sure she wasn't going to suddenly rise, like a phoenix from the ashes, and shoot me.

The gun had fallen from her hand and landed several feet away. She would have to scramble to get to it, and to be honest, she didn't look like she was in any condition to scramble. Just to be sure, though, I moved in the direction of the gun and nudged it a little farther away with my foot before I turned back to the body.

She was lying on her back, with her neck at a very uncomfortable angle.

Broken, my mind supplied, and I swallowed.

It was just a month since I'd killed someone. He would have killed me—and my mother, and David—if I hadn't, and he'd also killed a few other people and been well on his way to killing Rafe, so I couldn't regret it too much, but it still bothered me, deep inside. I had taken someone's life. I—Margaret Anne Martin's perfect little girl, who had been brought up to be a gracious hostess, devoted wife, and elegant Southern Belle—had killed a man.

And now I might have done it again.

She wasn't moving. Not so much as a finger twitched. And I couldn't see her chest moving. It had been long enough that it wasn't likely she was holding her breath to fake me out, either. Not without turning blue.

I crept closer and knelt next to the body.

She was dressed in black. Black sneakers, black jeans, black hooded sweatshirt. And under the hood...

"Shit," I said. "I mean... shoot. I mean..."

It was Terry Dixon. She looked different now—more dead—but there was no mistaking her.

She didn't stir when I spoke. I reached out and gingerly put two fingers against her throat. And moved them around when I didn't feel anything. I don't know anything about where to find someone's pulse, after all. This isn't something I do every day.

I had found Kylie's pulse without a problem Saturday morning. So why couldn't I do it now?

I fumbled up the black sleeve of the sweatshirt instead, and stuffed my fingertips under the top of the rubber glove she was wearing.

Still nothing.

Downstairs, the front door slammed against the wall, and I froze. But only for a second. "Savannah!"

"Rafe!"

I scrambled to my feet, away from the corpse, and headed for the stairs. He was faster, taking the steps two or three at a time. I'd only reached the top of the stairs when he burst into the second floor hallway.

I'm not sure he even took the time to look around, although I imagine he must have. It wouldn't be like him not to make sure we were safe. But he took in the scene in a fraction of a second, and then he wrapped his arms around me and pulled me in. I could feel his body shake, and his voice, when he spoke into my hair, was rough. "Can't leave you alone for a minute, can I?"

"I couldn't help it," I protested, my voice muffled against the front of his shirt. "I was just minding my own business, being asleep. It wasn't my fault that someone tried to break in."

He didn't answer. He didn't have time, because now there were more footsteps downstairs. His body stiffened for a second, and then relaxed again when he heard a voice call out. "Savannah!"

This time it was Grimaldi's voice.

I lifted my head from Rafe's chest. "Up here."

She took the stairs almost as fast as he had, but rather than grabbing me—not that I'd expected her to—she stopped at the top of the stairs and took in the scene a lot more slowly.

She only gave the two of us a glance in passing. Just to make sure I wasn't bleeding or anything, I guess. I'm sure she figured that if Rafe was just standing there, holding me, I was all right. If something had been wrong with me, he would have been hustling me down the stairs.

So she brushed past and headed for the end of the hallway, where the body lay. We both watched as she crouched and put her fingers against its throat.

"Dead?" Rafe asked softly.

"I think so. I couldn't find a pulse."

"What happened? Did he fall down the stairs?"

"I pushed him," I said, with a shudder. "I was going to hide upstairs, but then I decided I didn't want to cower like a scared rabbit, so when the door opened, I pushed him. And he's a she."

His brow arched. I nodded. "Terry Dixon. She works with Aislynn as Sara Beth's. Mendoza thinks she killed Virgil."

"Why?"

"She knows Stacy," I said. "He was here, too. Or at least she wasn't alone. There were two of them. But when she fell... when I pushed her, he ran. Or whoever was downstairs, ran."

"Damn." He raised his voice. "D'you hear that?"

Grimaldi shook her head. "She's gone."

"So's her buddy," Rafe said. "Savannah says he ran when she fell."

Grimaldi straightened and came toward us. "Did you see him?"

Rafe dropped his arms from around me, but kept a hand on the small of my back to steady me.

I shook my head. "He—or she, whoever the other person was—stayed downstairs. I heard them come in, and heard them whisper. Then one of them came up the stairs, so I headed to the third floor. And when the door opened, I pushed her."

I shuddered, at the thought of the body tumbling backwards down the steep stairs, and Rafe's hand moved in a soothing circle.

"She had a gun," Grimaldi remarked.

I nodded. "It discharged when she fell. There's a bullet buried in the wall up there. She screamed, but then she stopped when she hit the hallway floor."

"Her neck's broken," Grimaldi said. "I'm sure she was dead on impact. It could have gone a lot worse. If she had survived the fall, she might have become a paraplegic."

Rafe muttered something. I didn't ask him what it was, since I could guess.

"I didn't mean to kill her," I said. "Maybe I should have waited until she came into the room. Maybe I could have done something different. Hit her with a box, or something. I just didn't want to hide, and wait for her to find me."

Rafe shook his head. "You didn't do nothing wrong. You were defending yourself."

"I killed her."

"The fall killed her," Grimaldi said. "And she had a gun. She probably planned to kill you."

She put a hand on my arm. For Grimaldi, that's pretty much the equivalent of a warm hug. "Don't worry. There isn't a judge in the world who'd find you guilty of anything other than self-defense."

Maybe not. But that wasn't my concern. "This is the second time I've killed someone. I'm not sure what that says about me."

"That you're strong enough to do what's necessary," Rafe said. "She threatened you."

"She didn't have time to threaten me. I pushed her as soon as she opened the door."

"She came into your house with a gun," Grimaldi said. "In the middle of the night, when you could be expected to be sleeping. That's a threat, whether she told you she was going to shoot you or not. You didn't do anything wrong."

She fumbled for her phone. "I better call for transport." She went past us and down the stairs. A few seconds later, we could hear her in the downstairs hallway, identifying herself and explaining that she needed a van from the medical examiner's office to come by and load up a body.

I glanced down the hallway and shivered.

"C'mon." Rafe pulled me in the direction of the stairs. "Let's go downstairs. We can't do nothing for her, and I don't wanna have to keep looking at her."

I didn't, either. So I let him lead me to the top of the stairs and steady me down.

Grimaldi was standing in the foyer, nudging the pieces of broken glass on the floor with her toe and examining the jagged hole in the front door window. When we reached the bottom, she looked at us over her shoulder. "Somebody knew what he was doing. Or she."

Rafe nodded. "Have Mendoza run some background on the

two of'em. And check for juvie records. This whole letter writing thing sounds like a high school prank to me."

"It wasn't a prank," I said, and he nodded.

"I know, darlin'. Somebody coming into my house with a loaded gun had better not try to tell me he was just trying to be funny. But it's the kind of thing high school kids do to get attention."

It was. At least up until the point when people started dying and bullets started flying.

Rafe turned to Grimaldi. "Did you send somebody after Stacy?"

"Not yet. It isn't my case, for one thing, and for another, I don't have anyone to send. I don't know why someone didn't get here before the two of us. There should be cars in the area. Spicer and Truman are working tonight."

And Spicer and Truman always jump when Grimaldi calls.

"I'll go get Stacy," Rafe said, and Grimaldi shook her head.

"No, you won't. It isn't your case, either, and if I send you after him, I'd be afraid he wouldn't make it to interrogation."

"I wasn't gonna kill him. Just rough him up a little."

"No. The last thing we need is for him to cry police brutality and then get all the gay rights organizations involved."

"I ain't stupid," Rafe told her. "I wasn't gonna hit him for no reason. I woulda made sure he resisted arrest first."

"And how were you going to make sure of that?" She rolled her eyes. "Don't answer that. No. You may not go and pick up Mr. Kelleher. What you may do, is stay here with your wife until we've got him into a box in downtown. And then you may come and observe the interview."

"That won't be as much fun."

"No," Grimaldi agreed. "But we've already killed one suspect tonight. I don't want us to kill another. At least one of them should survive to answer questions, don't you think? And go to prison."

"I told you I wasn't gonna kill him," Rafe said. "Maybe put him in the hospital for a few days. He can go to prison later."

"No. I'm not going to tell you again. And if you don't start listening, I'll recant my invitation."

"Fine." But he sounded like a petulant five-year-old who's been told he can't stay up to watch another episode of Scooby-Doo. "Just go get him. Before he goes in the wind and you lose him."

"He won't," Grimaldi said. "He thinks he's got us all snowed. Besides, he's got an alibi for Virgil Wright's murder. There's no way we can pin it on him."

"You can't?"

This was from me, of course. I'm sure Rafe knew better than to ask.

Grimaldi shook her head. "He didn't kill Mr. Wright. He was pouring drinks in front of multiple witnesses when the murder took place. And as far as we can tell, he didn't pay Ms. Dixon to do it, either. That makes it not a murder for hire."

"Conspiracy to commit?" Rafe ventured.

"Sure. But how do you prove it? She's dead."

"I'm sorry," I said.

Rafe's arm tightened around my shoulder, but it was Grimaldi who spoke. "Don't be. You did what you had to do. And we'll get him for something. Somehow."

There was a moment while no one said anything. Then Rafe told her, "Let me know when you get him in the box. I'll come down and watch. And if you can't get what you need from him, I'll get it for you. I ain't leaving the bastard free to come back here one more time."

"I don't think he will," Grimaldi said, "but we'll get him and make sure of it."

She turned toward the door and the yard beyond as the van from the medical examiner's office—right down the road from the TBI—pulled into the driveway.

Twenty-Three

It ended up being the next morning before the police managed to corral Stacy Kelleher and drag him downtown for an interview. Rafe didn't sleep for the rest of the night, of course. First we had to wait for the medical examiner to determine cause of death—not a difficult task in this situation—and then the morgue attendants had to take the body away. While all of that was going on, Rafe found a piece of cardboard and tape, and boarded up the broken window until we could get it fixed.

Grimaldi had stuck around for all of this, and in the middle of it, a black-and-white squad car pulled into the driveway and to a stop behind the van from the morgue.

As an aside, we had quite the array of vehicles in our driveway at that point. My Volvo, Rafe's Harley, and Grimaldi's sedan, followed by the M.E.'s SUV, the morgue van, and now Spicer and Truman's patrol car.

It was a good thing it was the middle of the night, or we'd have had all the neighbors hanging over the wall to see what was going on.

Spicer parked the car and they both got out. Grimaldi and I were standing on the porch, while Rafe was doing his thing with the cardboard and tape, and the M.E. and morgue attendants were upstairs dealing with the body.

"What the hell happened to you two?" Grimaldi wanted to know. "We had a situation here, and I counted on you for support. Where the hell were you?"

Truman hung his head and looked ashamed. He's in his early twenties, with a tendency to blush if you look at him too hard, and he was clearly bothered by being chastised. Spicer, meanwhile—in his forties, and with twenty additional years on the job—was made of sterner stuff. "Sorry, Detective. We had our own situation."

Grimaldi wrinkled her nose. "You reek."

They did. And while it wasn't a very nice thing to say, in this case it was true.

Truman brushed futilely at his uniform—as if he could brush away the smell of smoke—while Spicer shrugged. "You told us to keep an eye on the house where Mrs. Collier's friends live. So when we saw the flames, we didn't wanna leave until we knew everyone was OK."

My breath caught. "Aislynn and Kylie's house caught fire?"

Spicer nodded, while Truman continued to brush at himself. "It wasn't bad. The fire department's just a couple blocks away. They were there in a minute. And it turned out to be a bucket of rags someone had left on the back porch. There's a bit of water damage at the back of the house, but nothing too bad. And the house was empty, so nobody was hurt."

"Wow."

And then what he'd said registered, and I added, "A bucket of rags?"

He nodded. "Someone musta left it on the porch."

"Aislynn and Kylie drove to Bowling Green this afternoon," I said. "I checked that the back door was locked before they left. There was no bucket of rags anywhere in sight then."

Spicer shook his head. "The fire chief said it looked like a prank. Some kids put a bucket of oily rags on the porch and lit it on fire."

Sure. A prank. Like the anonymous letters saying, *I'M WATCHING YOU.*

"Three guesses who the prankster was," I told Grimaldi.

She shook her head. "No deal. They must have meant it as a distraction. They probably figured we had the house under some sort of surveillance, and they wanted to keep us busy while they came over here."

276 | JENNA BENNETT

"Everything all right here?" Spicer wanted to know.

I nodded. "One of the burglars is inside with the M.E. The other got away."

I remembered the car I had seen drive slowly up the street just before I'd noticed the shadows, and added, "If you want something to do, you can check up the street a block or two for a car with a lot of bumper stickers about food and farms and bicycles."

Spicer and Truman exchanged glance, and then glanced at Grimaldi.

"What makes you think the car is still here?" she asked me. "Wouldn't Stacy have left in it?

"Not if he wanted us to think that Terry was acting alone. He probably doesn't realize that I was awake when they arrived, and that I know there were two of them. If it were me, I would have taken off down the street and left the car. It would be hard to explain how she got here otherwise."

Grimaldi nodded.

"Of course, they might have come in Stacy's car. A black Jeep Wrangler. But if they did, he probably left in it, too." And if he had any sense at all, he'd have talked Terry into using her car. He wouldn't have wanted his Jeep anywhere near the scene of the crime, in case anyone noticed it.

"Take a look," Grimaldi told Spicer and Truman. "Let me know what you find."

They returned to their squad car, and reversed out of the driveway since they couldn't make it past all the vehicles parked there. They kept their windows down even as the air conditioning was blasting icy air. Guess they didn't enjoy the smell of themselves, either.

"You all right?" Grimaldi asked me.

I glanced at her. "Sure. You asked me that earlier, didn't you?"

"I meant about the fire."

"Oh." I hadn't really thought about it, other than to feel a bit wobbly when I first heard. "Of course. Aislynn and Kylie weren't there. They don't have any pets. And it's just a house. I'm sorry it got damaged, but they're both all right. I guess I'll have to call and tell them."

"Wait until morning," Grimaldi advised. "There's no need to wake them up in the middle of the night to tell them that they'll have to get a disaster cleanup company in to make their house livable again."

She had a point.

"Stacy loves that house," I said. "I'm surprised he was willing to risk damaging it."

"At this point, he's probably more worried about saving his skin," Grimaldi opined. "And you'll notice the house wasn't damaged. Not other than some water."

But water could make the wood wet, which would then attract termites and carpenter ants, which could do a lot of damage.

Although she had a point: if the bucket of rags had been placed far enough from the wall of the house itself that there hadn't been any actual fire damage, it seemed like Stacy might have done his very best to mitigate the risk.

"I really don't like him," I said. "Terry at least had some sort of obsession with Aislynn. She'd probably call it love." Not that she could call it anything now, since I'd killed her. I winced and continued, "But Stacy just seems obsessed with the house. And the money. And getting revenge on Virgil for dumping him."

"Sociopath," Grimaldi nodded. "It's all about him and what he wants, and he'll remove anyone who stands in his way. He won't shed a tear over Terry. She was useful to him for a while, and then she afforded him the opportunity to escape. Right now he's planning how he can spin the situation to leave all the onus on her."

He probably was. Wherever he was at the moment.

278 | JENNA BENNETT

Rafe finished attaching the cardboard to the window, and the M.E. left, with a nod at Grimaldi and the information that the case seemed open and shut and he'd have the death certificate for her in the morning. The morgue attendants carried the gurney carefully down the stairs from the second floor, across the porch and down the outside stairs over to the van. I tried not to look at it as it went by, but it was hard.

"I should head out, too," Grimaldi told us. "Check in with Jaime and tell him that Mr. Kelleher might be on foot."

"Hang on a minute," Rafe said. "Wait for your minions to come back. See what they have to say. Then you don't have to go crawling to Mendoza to tell him you were wrong if it turns out Kelleher isn't on foot after all."

"I don't crawl," Grimaldi informed him, but she did come inside with us to wait for Spicer and Truman to return. We made some coffee—the other two drank that; I stuck to milk—and sat around the kitchen table and waited. We didn't talk much. We were all tired, and there wasn't much to say that hadn't already been said.

It didn't take long. Ten minutes, and then Spicer knocked on the door. "Two blocks up," he said, with a gesture with his thumb over his shoulder. "Small gray car." He pulled out his phone and showed us where he'd taken a picture.

I nodded. It was obviously the same car Kylie and I had followed earlier today. Or yesterday, since we were well into the dark hours after midnight by now.

"The plate comes back as Teresa Dixon," Spicer said. "I called a truck to have it towed to the impound lot."

"Good job," Grimaldi told him. "Thank you. Stay with the car until the tow truck comes, and then go clean up."

"We can last until the end of shift," Spicer said, although Truman did look wistful at the thought of soap and water.

"C'mon, kid." Spicer slapped him on the shoulder. "Let's get to work."

The two of them took their smelly selves out of the house and into the squad car.

"I'm going to go, too," Grimaldi told us when they'd left. "Places to go, people to see." She got to her feet. "Try to get some rest. I'll let you know when we find Stacy."

She headed out. Rafe locked the door after her, before coming back for me. He took me upstairs to bed, and we made love. I think we both needed it. Him to reassure himself that I was OK and that he hadn't screwed anything up by not being here—as if I'd blame him for being at work and trying to keep Jamal safe—and me for the comfort. I knew Grimaldi was right. I hadn't had a choice. But it was still difficult to process the fact that Teresa was dead, because I'd pushed her down the stairs.

I was able to fall asleep for a bit after that. Or at least doze. Rafe wasn't. He spent the rest of the night prowling the house. Making sure nobody else got in, and probably beating himself up for not being here when I needed him.

Grimaldi called at seven-thirty to say that Stacy had made it home and into Mendoza's waiting arms. He was cooling his heels in an interrogation room in downtown—Stacy, not Mendoza; although Mendoza was probably twiddling his thumbs, waiting for things to get underway, too. If Rafe wanted in on the interview, he had to move.

"Wait for me!" I pushed at the blankets. I was still in bed when he told me, while he was sitting on the edge with another cup of coffee. That was probably what had gotten him through the night.

"You don't have to come, darlin'." Although he moved out of the way so I could scramble out of bed.

"I want to," I said. "He was in my house last night. He left Terry behind and ran. And one of them scared the crap out of Aislynn and hit Kylie. Not to mention that one of them—probably Terry—killed Virgil. I want to know how it all hangs together."

He shrugged. "Better hurry, then."

"I'm hurrying." I disappeared into the bathroom to pee and splash cold water on my face.

We got to downtown before eight, something of a record with what we had to do before getting out of the house, plus the beginning of rush hour traffic.

Only to find, when we got there, that Mendoza had gotten impatient and started the interview without us.

Like yesterday, Grimaldi was observing through the two-way mirror. She gathered us from the lobby and took us back there. "They just started," she said as she opened the door. "Jaime figured the more time he gave Mr. Kelleher, the more composed he'd be, so instead he jumped right in."

"Wouldn't sitting around and waiting make Stacy more rattled?"

"Depends," Grimaldi said, shutting the door behind us. "Some people use the time to calm down and come up with their stories. For them, it's better not to give them time to think."

We walked up to the window separating us from the interrogation room.

Like yesterday, Mendoza had his back to us. He was wearing the same shirt, so he probably hadn't had time to go home and change yet.

Stacy sat opposite him, dressed in dark jeans and a dark gray sweatshirt with a zipper over a gray T-shirt. It didn't look sinister now, but in the middle of the night, zipped up and with the hood covering his head, he would have looked just like one of the shadows slipping through my yard.

If he was nervous, it didn't show at all. He was chatting with Mendoza as if they were old friends, sipping from a Starbucks cup and gesturing with his other hand.

And Mendoza was playing right along, talking back as if nothing was wrong.

"Bastard," Rafe muttered.

Grimaldi glanced at him. "Give him time. He'll get there."

Rafe grinned. "I wasn't talking about Mendoza. I've done my own share of building rapport and sweet-talking suspects. I know how it works."

"And here I thought you just waded in and let your fists do the talking," Grimaldi said dryly. "Just watch."

We watched, as they talked about the coffee, the weather, Mendoza's tie—Stacy liked it; he even attempted to flirt a little, although surely he could tell that Mendoza wasn't batting for his team.

Eventually he must have gotten tired of it, or just wanted to get the show on the road, because he put down his cup. "What am I doing here?"

"We're talking," Mendoza said.

"We've already talked. You know I didn't kill Virgil. I was at work. With at least thirty witnesses around."

Mendoza nodded. "I know that."

"I'm not really sorry he's dead. He cheated on me. He left me. But I didn't kill him."

"I know you didn't."

"And I know you think that life insurance policy is suspicious. But I got it when we were still together. And I've been paying on it. I have the right to cash it in."

Mendoza nodded. "This isn't about that."

"What's it about, then?"

"The death of Teresa Dixon," Mendoza said.

There was a beat. Then— "She's dead?" Stacy said. And I could be imagining things, but I swear I heard a note of jubilation in his voice. Maybe he'd been afraid that Terry was still alive and could implicate him.

"You know who she is? Or was?"

"Of course," Stacy said. "One of my neighbors."

"You grew up together, too. Didn't you?"

I glanced at Grimaldi. "Did they?"

She nodded. "We took your husband's advice and looked for juvenile records. Neither of them had one, but we did discover that they grew up in the same small town in Mississippi. And went to the same schools."

Inside the interrogation room, Stacy was explaining the same thing, and explaining it away as no big deal.

"One of your friends died when you were in high school, didn't he?"

"I wouldn't call him a friend," Stacy said, "but yeah. One of our classmates died."

Mendoza checked the file in front of him. "Beaten to death with a rock."

"Like Virgil," I said. Grimaldi nodded.

"I was at work," Stacy said.

"In middle school?"

He giggled. "Of course not in middle school. I was at home. Grounded, if you have to know. For getting into a fight with that same kid. So I couldn't have killed him."

"The police talked to you?"

He tossed his head. "Of course they did. But I was home. My mom saw me. She told them. And I'm not a killer. I've never killed anybody. Give me a lie detector test if you want to."

"That won't be necessary," Mendoza said. "It's all here." He tapped the folder. "The police cleared you. You were at home."

Stacy nodded.

"What about Teresa?"

Stacy blinked.

"Where was she the night Virgil Wright was killed? Or the afternoon Marcus Jefferson was beaten to death?"

"That's a long time ago," Stacy said. "I have no idea where Terry was that day. Or last week, for that matter. I was at work. I didn't see her."

"Do you know where she was last night?"

Stacy shook his head. "What happened? You said she's dead."

"She fell down a staircase," Mendoza said, "and broke her neck." I winced. "Death was almost instantaneous."

"Almost?"

I turned to Grimaldi. "What does he mean, 'almost?' She died instantly. You said so."

"He don't know that," Rafe said, nodding to Stacy. "Watch."

I turned back to the interrogation room.

"She had time to say a few words," Mendoza said. "Specifically, about you."

Stacy was quiet for a moment. "I don't believe you," he said.

"She said you were there together. That you set a fire at Aislynn Turner's and Kylie Mitchell's house—your old house, the one you shared with Mr. Wright—and then you drove to Mr. and Mrs. Collier's house."

He waited to see if Stacy wanted to say anything, but when he didn't, Mendoza continued.

"You might remember her better as Ms. Martin. Savannah Martin. The real estate agent who helped Ms. Turner and Ms. Mitchell buy your house. The house you wanted to keep, but that you couldn't afford when Mr. Wright was no longer paying the bills."

He paused, but Stacy still didn't have anything to contribute.

"The same Ms. Martin who knocked on your door on Friday and asked you about anonymous letters someone had been sending to her clients."

"I remember her," Stacy said. "Why would Terry go to her house in the middle of the night?"

"She had a gun with her, so we assume it was with the purpose of doing harm to Ms. Martin."

"Why?"

"We were hoping you'd be able to tell us that," Mendoza said; Stacy shook his head, "but we assume because Ms. Martin works for Ms. Turner and Ms. Mitchell, and was instrumental in bringing them back together after the attack on Ms. Mitchell and the last letter you sent Ms. Turner."

For a second I wasn't sure he was going to pick up on it, but then Stacy said, "The last letter *I* sent Ms. Turner? Why would I do that?"

"Something else we were hoping you'd explain," Mendoza said genially. "We assume it was something of a game of tit for tat. You wanted the house back, and you wanted Mr. Wright out of the way so you could cash in on the life insurance policy. But you knew you couldn't kill him yourself. You had to be far away, with an unbreakable alibi, in order to get that money. So you recruited Terry."

"Why would Terry kill Virgil for me?"

Stacy tried to sound insouciant, but it didn't quite come off. His voice had an ever-so-slight edge.

"You knew she was the one who killed Marcus Jefferson all those years ago? You threatened to turn her in? There's no statute of limitations on murder."

He waited a second, but when Stacy didn't take the bait, he added, "Or maybe you simply convinced her that the letters would make Ms. Turner and Ms. Mitchell break up, and Teresa would have her chance to woo Ms. Turner back. They were involved, weren't they?"

"They lived together for a few weeks last year," Stacy said, distractedly, "but I don't think it was serious. Not on the girl's part. Terry was crazy about her, though." He giggled. "Crazy. Get it?"

We got it. I'm sure Mendoza did, too, but he didn't comment.

"So maybe that was enough. Just the promise that she'd get Ms. Turner back if she went along with your plan. She'd kill Mr. Wright while you were provably somewhere else, with a solid alibi, and in return, she got a second chance with Ms. Turner. Maybe you offered her money on the back end, after you got the payout from the insurance. And if everything went well, and Ms. Turner and Ms. Mitchell broke up and put the house on the market, you'd have the money to buy it back. Mr. Wright's house, that he took away from you."

Stacy smiled and shook his head. "You can't prove any of that, Detective. And anyway, Terry's dead."

"But she didn't break into Ms. Turner's and Ms. Mitchell's house on Friday night," Mendoza said. "She didn't hit Ms. Mitchell over the head and leave with the anonymous letters. Teresa worked that night. And she certainly didn't show up at the hospital the next day in an effort to try to finish the job. Were you afraid that Ms. Mitchell had seen you? That she'd recognized you from last year, when she bought your house?"

"I don't know what you're talking about," Stacy said.

"I'm sure you don't. We'll see if the doctor you spoke to at the hospital recognizes your face when we show him your mug shot."

Stacy pushed his chair back and shot to his feet. "What mug shot? You can't arrest me. You have no proof. And I didn't break into the house and take the letters. Terry did. I told her where the key was, OK? In the thermometer on the back porch. Virgil and I kept a spare key there. She could come and go when nobody was home, and dig through the girl's underwear or do whatever she wanted. But she's the one who wrote the letters. Not me. And she's the one who went there on Friday night to get them back. I told her that what's-her-name came to talk to me about the letters, and that made Terry nervous. So she went there that night after work to get them back. The restaurant is only open until nine. Not like South Street. When I work, I'm there until two in the morning. Terry could close up early and leave. She's the one who hit the other girl. Not me. And she's the one who set the fire. And she probably killed Virgil, and Marcus too. But it has nothing to do with me."

"You were with her last night," Mendoza said. "Ms. Martin

saw you."

Stacy shook his head. "That's not possible."

"Can you prove where you were?"

"No. But you can't prove I was there, either."

Rafe and Grimaldi both looked at me. I shook my head. I had no idea whether it was Stacy who had been with Terry at the house last night. I hadn't seen his face. I hadn't seen him well enough to recognize him in any way. He'd just been a shadow outside, and inside the house, he'd stayed on the first floor. Terry's partner in crime could have been anyone. I was sure it was Stacy, as I'm sure we all were, but could I prove it?

No.

Twenty-Four

"Get him out here," Rafe said.

Grimaldi turned to him. I did, too, but she was the one who spoke. "Who?"

"Mendoza. Get him out of there."

Grimaldi arched her brows, but pulled out her phone and sent a text. Inside the interrogation room, Mendoza's phone buzzed. He glanced at the display and pushed back his chair.

"Excuse me. I'll be right back."

Stacy nodded. "I'll be here."

He sat back down in his chair. Mendoza let himself out. A few seconds later, the door to our little room opened and he came in. "Bastard," he growled, his face dark and his brows lowered. "Sitting in there smirking at me. He's behind this whole thing. I know he is. Probably was back in Mississippi, too."

"He might be right about Teresa Dixon being the one who hit Ms. Mitchell," Grimaldi said. "Hitting people with rocks seems to have been her M.O. And we can't be sure when the attack happened. Ms. Mitchell doesn't remember, and Ms. Dixon isn't around to tell us. It could have been after she got off work."

Mendoza directed a fulminating glare through the two-way mirror, to where Stacy was sitting calmly, one leg folded over the other, sipping his probably lukewarm coffee and waiting for Mendoza to come back. He looked calm and confident, although I think there was an ever so faint tremor in the hand that held the cup.

"Maybe," Mendoza admitted. "But even if she did, it's been all about him. Everything comes back to him. He wanted Virgil dead. He wanted the money. And the house. He probably wanted that kid in Mississippi dead, too. Killing him might not

288 | JENNA BENNETT

have been his idea, but if he knew about it, I'm sure he didn't do anything to talk Teresa Dixon out of the idea."

He fisted his hands. "I want him behind bars. I want him to pay."

"You really can't prove any of it?" I asked. "I know he didn't kill Virgil. He has an alibi. And he might not have hit Kylie or written the letters. Or killed the Marcus Jefferson kid in Mississippi all those years ago. But he was at my house last night. Wasn't he?"

"Of course he was," Mendoza growled. "But unless you saw him well enough to make a positive identification, we can't prove it. We know he wasn't at home. I sat outside his apartment for hours, waiting for him to get there. But we can't prove where he was. And he isn't telling us."

"What about the money? The insurance?"

"Circumstantial," Grimaldi said. "Suggestive, but not illegal. And he can prove that he didn't kill Mr. Wright."

"So he could get away with it?"

They both shrugged. "We can charge him with conspiracy," Mendoza said. "But any halfway decent defense attorney could get him off. There just isn't any proof. He's covered his tracks very well. And now that Terry Dixon's dead, he'll dump it all on her. And probably get away with it, since she isn't alive to tell a different story."

We'd all been so busy talking that none of us had been paying attention to Rafe. Or maybe Grimaldi had been. She'd been less involved in the conversation than Mendoza or I. She might have realized what he wanted. Mendoza didn't. When the door shut, Mendoza turned to it, and it took a second for him to put the pieces together.

"What the hell—!"

But by then it was too late. The door into the interrogation room had opened. Instead of going after Rafe, Mendoza turned to the mirror, just as Grimaldi and I did.

Rafe stepped into the room behind the mirror and closed the door quietly behind him. Stacy watched him a little warily—he could obviously tell it wasn't Mendoza coming back, and he could also see that the newcomer was both bigger and more muscular—but it wasn't until Rafe turned around that he recognized him. I was pleased to see his throat move when he swallowed, and I don't think it was the coffee.

"Morning," Rafe said.

It should have sounded friendly, but didn't.

Stacy opened his mouth, but nothing came out. Instead, he watched as Rafe came closer. And closer.

Instead of sitting on the other side of the table, the way Mendoza had done, Rafe scooted his hip up on the table on Stacy's side, so close that they were almost touching. Crowding Stacy. And then he folded his arms over his chest.

He had his back to us, but he was wearing a short sleeved T-shirt, and I know what his arms look like. Muscles moved, a lot of them. The sleeves of the shirt strained across his biceps, and the snake tattoo curling around one arm probably stretched and winked.

Stacy watched, fascinated and more than a little wary. "You must work out a lot," he said. And although he was probably going for nonchalant and flirtatious, it came out choked instead.

Grimaldi made a sort of choking noise, too. Even Mendoza snorted.

Rafe didn't dignify the remark with a response. "You know who I am?" he asked instead, his voice sort of scary bland.

Stacy hesitated. I'm sure he remembered meeting Rafe before—my husband isn't the kind of guy you forget—but it sounded like something of a rhetorical question, so Stacy may have thought it safer not to respond.

"I'm the guy whose house you broke into last night."

Stacy swallowed. Audibly.

"The house where my wife lives. My pregnant wife."

One thing about Rafe: he's a scary guy. You can tell he's been places and seen things most of us haven't. That he's done things most of us haven't, too. And the quieter he gets, the more scary he is.

He was very quiet now. So quiet that those of us in the other room had to strain to hear him. Although I'm sure Stacy had no such problem. Just as I was sure he was ready to pee his pants at any moment.

He moistened his lips. "What are you doing here? You're not a cop. Are you?"

Rafe shook his head. "The detective had to step out. I thought I'd step in. So we could have a talk."

"I don't have anything to say to you," Stacy said.

Rafe nodded. "That's good. 'Cause I don't wanna hear about how you wasn't there and I musta made a mistake."

Stacy opened his mouth and closed it again.

"You brought a gun into my house. Where my wife was sleeping. Alone, 'cause I was out trying to keep two gangs from killing each other."

Stacy didn't even attempt to speak this time.

"Your friend's dead," Rafe told him. "My wife pushed her down the stairs and broke her neck."

I winced. He made it sound like I'd done it on purpose, and I hadn't.

"You're damn lucky I wasn't there, 'cause I woulda done a lot worse. And if I ever meet you outside this place," he glance around took in the interrogation room, and beyond it, police headquarters and all the cops who would stand ready to save Stacy from him, "I will."

Somehow, Stacy managed to find his voice again. "You can't do that! You'll go to prison!"

"Prison don't scare me," Rafe told him. "I've already done time. I damn near killed the bastard who hurt my mama when I was eighteen."

And much more recently, he'd killed someone who tried to hurt me, although he hadn't gone to prison for it. I wondered if it would help or hurt to tell Stacy that.

Or maybe it wouldn't make a difference. Stacy made a noise that sounded like, "Urk."

"You might should consider it," Rafe told him, "since, if you walk outta here, I'll be waiting for you."

"I think that's probably my cue," Mendoza said with a nod to Grimaldi and me. "Excuse me."

He headed back into the hallway. A second later, he opened the door into the interrogation room and stepped through the opening. "Sorry about that—"

He stopped when he saw Rafe, as if he hadn't expected to see him. "You're not supposed to be here."

Rafe uncoiled himself from the top of the table, smoothly and unhurriedly. "Just talking to your suspect here."

Mendoza looked from him to Stacy and back, as if to make sure that Stacy was unharmed by the exchange. "Are you all right, Mr. Kelleher?"

Stacy nodded, although he looked a little green.

"Did he touch you?"

Stacy hesitated, and I could see him weighing the possibility of claiming police brutality. Or brutality while in police custody. But Rafe really hadn't touched him, and in the end he must have decided not to take the chance. "No."

Mendoza nodded. "Get out of here," he told Rafe, who sauntered toward the door.

"Don't forget what we talked about," he told Stacy over his shoulder.

Stacy gulped.

A few seconds later he was back with Grimaldi and me again.

"Nicely done," she told him. "I think you made him wet himself."

I added, "That was scary. You sounded like you were ready to kill him."

A little of that black rage lingered in his eyes still, but it was fading. He didn't smile, though. "If I ever meet that guy in a place where there are no witnesses, he ain't walking away." He clenched his hands into fists. "He came into my house with a gun. *My* house. Where my wife was. With a *gun!*"

"He deserves to pay for that," Grimaldi nodded. "Now let's see what happens."

She turned toward the two-way mirror. I put my hand on Rafe's arm, and felt hard-as-granite muscles against my fingers. It took several moments before he relaxed, but eventually he let his breath out in a sigh, and wrapped his arms around me.

"I was scared outta my mind," he murmured into my hair. "When Tammy called and told me you'd called her, and that somebody was in the house with you, I was scared shitless. Now I want him dead."

"You can't kill him," I answered. "I appreciate the thought, but I want him to go to prison. For a long time. Not just for breaking into our house and scaring you," and me, "but for what he did to Aislynn and Kylie, and for Virgil Wright, and for Marcus Jefferson, even though I'd never even heard of the guy until today. Terry is dead. You'll have to be satisfied with that. Stacy needs to pay another way."

He didn't answer, but he turned us both toward the mirror so we could watch what went on in the interrogation room. He kept his arms around me, though, his hands protectively covering the baby inside my belly.

Mendoza was still insincerely apologizing for Rafe, and twisting the knife a little with each word. "Sorry about that. He wasn't supposed to come in here. But he tends to go where he wants."

"He's crazy!" Stacy said with a shiver. "He said he'd kill me!"

Mendoza took his seat on the other side of the table again,

with his back to us. "Nice of him to give you advance warning."

Stacy stared at him. "Are you kidding? You're the police, aren't you? Are you just going to sit there and let him threaten me like that?"

"There's nothing much I can do about it," Mendoza said, "is there? It's your word against his. Of course, if he lays a hand on you, I can arrest him for assault."

"Fat lot of good that will do," Stacy said bitterly. "I'll be dead. Or at least in the hospital with a lot of broken bones."

"I wouldn't worry too much about it," Mendoza soothed him. "If you weren't at his house last night, you have nothing to worry about. I'm sure he won't kill you without proof."

There was a pause.

"OK," Stacy said. "I was there, all right? But I swear it wasn't my idea. Terry wanted to go. She had a gun, and she was talking crazy. I went with her to make sure nothing happened."

Rafe muttered something. Grimaldi nodded.

"What?" I asked.

She glanced at me. "It almost sounds reasonable. He's good at spin."

Which was another way of saying that Stacy was a good liar, I assumed.

"It's too bad you couldn't keep her from getting killed," Mendoza said inside the interrogation room. "It would have helped to have her version of events, too."

Stacy bristled. "You don't believe me? I'm confessing! I was there. I broke in. And I helped Terry set the fire at the other woman's house. I tried to make sure that it didn't burn anything down, but I helped her. I'm guilty."

"You want to go to jail?"

"If you can get me transferred out of state," Stacy said. "Somewhere like California. Away from here, where that... that... *man* can't find me."

"Sure." Mendoza's voice was calm. "We can arrange that."

294 | JENNA BENNETT

"Montana," Grimaldi told me. "Or maybe Alaska."

"Or Mississippi. Where maybe they can find some proof that he and Terry killed Marcus Jefferson."

"After all this time, I don't think that'll be easy to do," Grimaldi told me, "but we'll let them know what we've learned. Maybe they can close their cold case, if nothing else."

"Confessing to breaking into my house and setting a bucket of rags on fire on Aislynn and Kylie's porch won't keep him locked up for long, will it?"

Not like murder. If he'd confessed to murder, or even conspiracy to commit murder, they could really lock him up and throw away the key.

"You'd be surprised," Rafe told me. "Home invasion's a felony. Carrying a gun during a burglary is a big deal. He just admitted he knew that Terry had one, so he can't come back and say that he didn't know about it. And since you're two people, it's twice the crime."

"I'm two people?"

"You and the baby," Grimaldi said. "The law is particular when it comes to violence against expectant mothers."

Ah. "Of course."

"He'll be going away for a long time, just for this. We'll keep digging, and see if we can make a case for conspiracy on any of the murders, but it may be that this is the best we can do." She was watching through the mirror as she talked, instead of looking at me. "Sorry."

"It's fine," I said, turning my attention to what was going on in the interrogation room, as well. "Aislynn and Kylie are still together, and have their house, that they love. There'll be no more anonymous letters. If Terry was the one who committed the murders, she's paid for what she did. And he'll be in prison, a state or more away. It's all good."

Rafe grumbled something—probably along the lines of it not being good until Stacy was six feet under, where he'd put the victims we wouldn't prove he'd planned to murder—but he didn't say it out loud. I put my hand in his.

"It's enough."

He glanced down at me, but didn't say anything. His hand tightened around mine, though, and the corners of his mouth turned up.

Inside the interrogation room, Mendoza told Stacy to get to his feet and put his hands behind his back. We watched as Mendoza snapped a pair of handcuffs around Stacy's wrists and led him toward the door.

I yawned. It had been a long night, with not much sleep.

"Tired?" Rafe asked.

I nodded. "I could go back to bed."

"Funny you should say that. So could I."

Grimaldi rolled her eyes. "Get out of here," she said. "Get a room."

Rafe grinned and pulled me toward the door. "You heard the detective. Let's go home and to bed."

"Don't mind if I do," I said, and followed him through the door and out.

# # #

About the Author

New York Times and *USA Today* bestselling author Jenna Bennett (Jennie Bentley) writes the Do It Yourself home renovation mysteries for Berkley Prime Crime and the Savannah Martin real estate mysteries for her own gratification. She also writes a variety of romance for a change of pace. Originally from Norway, she has spent more than twenty five years in the US, and still hasn't been able to kick her native accent.

For more information, please visit Jenna's website:
www.JennaBennett.com